"A powerful, touching, and fascinating memoir that takes us into a magical, mysterious world known to but a few. Not just for the professional—the anthropologist, the ethnographer, the historian, the scholar of religion or Native American studies. Armchair explorers will be riveted as they learn about the old Lakota ways, rituals, and teachings."

—**Dale C. Allison Jr.**, author of *Encountering Mystery: Religious Experience in a Secular Age*

"As a Lakota medicine person with access to power, some might call what Richard Moves Camp does 'magic,' but it goes deeper than that. The teachings and ceremonies that he describes in *My Grandfather's Altar* have changed literally thousands of lives—from curing impossible medical illnesses to relieving substance abuse to reconnecting broken families. When we first met more than three decades ago these teachings and practices were well-guarded secrets. And no wonder— Native peoples' ways of life were systematically destroyed, erased, or stolen. Ceremonial ways that could heal, transform, and give hope were outlawed and performed in secret. Now, when so many of us are searching for meaning and direction, here they are, available for all to take in and contemplate."

—**Peter Bratt**, Peabody Award winner, Emmy-nominated film producer, and writer and director

"Richard Moves Camp's book is a fulfillment of Crazy Horse's vision: 'the Red nation shall rise and be a blessing for a sick world.' As organized religions began to fade because of lack of Spirit, Richard gives us the meaning of God as spirit in motion and alive in all that is. His words are truly medicine for all humanity as we gather under the Sacred Tree as the Earth becomes one circle of many colors again. A must-read for spiritual seekers as these ancestors in the story are alive and their prayers flow with God's power in our epigenetic landscape."

—**Eduardo Duran**, coauthor of *Native American Postcolonial Psychology*

T0341406

"An epic story centered on the generations of medicine men in Richard Moves Camp's family's lineage. His story demonstrates the power of an oral tradition that is deeply rooted in family, tribal culture, spiritual practice, and Indigenous resilience and survival."

—**Lupe Avila** (Mexica), retired social worker

"Richard Moves Camp generously shares oral histories and personal reflections. Readers will discover generations of Lakota family stories and how the holy man Wóptuȟ'a and his descendants developed and maintained the Lakota Yuwípi ceremony."

—**Akim Reinhardt**, author of *Welcome to the Oglala Nation: A Documentary Reader in Oglala Lakota Political History*

"Richard Moves Camp serves as a rare spiritual paleontologist who unearths and shares enduring elements in Lakota history and spirituality. . . . His book invites you on a journey with him, a journey few have taken before. If you are interested in Lakota history and spirituality, you won't find a more honest and experienced guide."

—**Jim Green**, co-director of the Institute for Indigenous Teaching, Sinte Gleska University

"Not since *Black Elk Speaks* have we been gifted such a heartfelt account of the lives and work of Lakota holy men during times of great change to sustain a culture for future generations."

—**Suzanne Owen**, author of *The Appropriation of Native American Spirituality*

"The intimacy of this personal family account brings us into relationship with Richard Moves Camp's ancestors and his family. . . . *My Grandfather's Altar* is a 'can't put it down' story of survival, strength, and beauty."

—**Paul Haible**, executive director of Peace Development Fund

"An excellent contribution to the literature on Lakota spirituality and worldview. Moves Camp tells his family's story of well-regarded spiritual leaders from a grounded and insightful perspective. Most beautifully, he provides a compelling teaching about the importance of spirituality being linked to a way of life, an insight that provides us a healthy pathway for the future. . . . The whole volume resonates with truth and wisdom."

—**Waziyatawin**, author of *Remember This! Dakota Decolonization and the Eli Taylor Narratives*

"If you want to know more about American Indians, read this book. It presents us with a deeply authentic voice of a traditional Lakota elder and spiritual leader; it is a narrative that displays the American Indian worldview in all its depth and complexity. . . . Richard Moves Camp's story will be read for generations to come as a wonderful tool for holding onto important cultural truths."

—**Tink Tinker** (Osage Nation [wazhazhe]), professor emeritus of American Indian cultures and religious traditions at Iliff School of Theology

"Not since Luther Standing Bear has Lakota spirituality been portrayed with such sincerity. . . . Richard Moves Camp's *My Grandfather's Altar* evokes the everyday relevance of Lakota beliefs and values with true-to-life detail. In recounting his grandfather's story and legacy through family history, Moves Camp shows the reader a Lakota way of doing things, a *wouncage*, that is as meaningful today as it was during the time of Crazy Horse."

—**David Martínez**, author of *Life of the Indigenous Mind: Vine Deloria Jr. and the Birth of the Red Power Movement*

"*My Grandfather's Altar* is a revelation of intergenerational Indigenous survival in the face of omnicide. . . . More than an autobiography, this is the story of the *olówaŋ wičháša*, or spiritual code, of generations of Lakota people immersed in lifeway knowledge who transmitted that knowledge even when it was outlawed by the U.S. government. . . . This book has the power to resonate and linger with you just like that."

—**Christopher J. Pexa** (Mní Wakháŋ Oyáte, Spirit Lake Dakota Nation), author of *Translated Nation: Rewriting the Dakhóta Oyáte*

"Richard Moves Camp's story is unique, significant, and moving. It is an important contribution to both the living oral tradition of the Lakota people and the scholarly canon. *My Grandfather's Altar* is an engrossing read. . . . I highly recommend this book to anyone interested in Lakota culture, history, and ceremonial traditions."

—**David C. Posthumus**, author of *All My Relatives: Exploring Lakota Ontology, Belief, and Ritual* and coauthor of *Lakȟóta: An Indigenous History*

"Richard Moves Camp provides a rich, powerful narrative based on his family's experiences. This book gives us an intimate window into Lakȟóta spirituality and way of life. This is a Lakȟóta story told in a uniquely Lakȟóta way by those who experienced it firsthand. This book is a must-read for anyone interested in Lakȟóta past and present."

—**Rani-Henrik Andersson**, author of *The Lakota Ghost Dance of 1890* and coauthor of *Lakȟóta: An Indigenous History*

"This is a remarkable, honest, and heart-centered book. In everyday language, Richard Moves Camp narrates the oral traditions of the distinguished Chips family, a history of suffering, spiritual accomplishments, miraculous events, and successful healings. The context is colonialism, and the consequence is a multigenerational struggle to maintain sacred authenticity and living connections to the spirit worlds. It is an honor to read such a book, a rare treasure, revealing the deep truths of Lakota spirituality."

—**Lee Irwin**, author of *The Dream Seekers: Native American Visionary Traditions of the Great Plains*

"This eye-opening memoir is essential reading not just for anyone interested in Native American spiritual traditions but also for understanding forms of religious consciousness more broadly defined. In more senses than one, the book is a revelation."

—**Philip Jenkins**, author of *Dream Catchers: How Mainstream America Discovered Native Spirituality*

MY GRANDFATHER'S ALTAR

American Indian Lives

SERIES EDITORS

Kimberly Blaeser
University of Wisconsin, Milwaukee

Brenda J. Child
University of Minnesota

R. David Edmunds
University of Texas at Dallas

K. Tsianina Lomawaima
Arizona State University

MY GRANDFATHER'S ALTAR

Five Generations of Lakota Holy Men

RICHARD MOVES CAMP

Edited by Simon J. Joseph

University of Nebraska Press *Lincoln*

The University of Nebraska Press is part of a land-grant institution with campuses and programs on the past, present, and future homelands of the Pawnee, Ponca, Otoe-Missouria, Omaha, Dakota, Lakota, Kaw, Cheyenne, and Arapaho Peoples, as well as those of the relocated Ho-Chunk, Sac and Fox, and Iowa Peoples.

Library of Congress Cataloging-in-Publication Data
Names: Moves Camp, Richard, 1956– author. |
Joseph, Simon J., 1966– editor.
Title: My grandfather's altar : five generations
of Lakota holy men / Richard Moves
Camp ; edited by Simon J. Joseph.
Other titles: American Indian lives.
Description: Lincoln : University of Nebraska Press,
[2024] | Series: American Indian lives |
Includes bibliographical references.
Identifiers: LCCN 2023040073
ISBN 9781496236913 (paperback)
ISBN 9781496238702 (epub)
ISBN 9781496238719 (pdf)
Subjects: LCSH: Moves Camp, Richard, 1956– |
Wóptuȟ'a, 1836–1916. | Lakota Indians—Social life and
customs. | BISAC: SOCIAL SCIENCE / Ethnic Studies /
American / Native American Studies |
LCGFT: Autobiographies. | Biographies.
Classification: LCC E99.T34 M68 2024 | DDC
909/.04975244080092 [B]—dc23/eng/20231002
LC record available at https://lccn.loc.gov/2023040073

Designed and set in Adobe Text Pro by L. Welch.

Genealogical charts courtesy of Karli
Ledkins, Family ChartMasters LLC.

Contents

List of Illustrations   vii

Acknowledgments   ix

Editor's Note   xi

Prologue   1

Introduction   7

1. My Grandfather's Altar   11

2. Wóptuȟ'a   37

3. Moves Camp and Horn Chips   71

4. Grandpa Sam   99

5. Present Times   125

Epilogue   175

Appendix: The Wóptuȟ'a *Thióšpaye,*
a Family History   179

Glossary   199

Notes   203

Illustrations

1. Wóptuȟ'a-Chips and wife in
   Kyle, South Dakota, circa 1911   68
2. Richard Moves Camp, Wóptuȟ'a
   grave site, Hisle cemetery,
   Hisle, South Dakota   69
3. Tȟahúŋska, son of Wóptuȟ'a,
   circa 1890   69
4. Samuel Chips Moves Camp, 1910   70

Acknowledgments

From the Editor

I would like to thank Richard Moves Camp for the invitation to collaborate on this project. It has been an honor to help him share his story. Wóphila!

This book would not have been possible without Jennifer Jessum. Jennifer was present at every meeting and every visit to the Pine Ridge Reservation and contributed significantly to the editorial work and production of this book. Jennifer is the founder of the Mitakuye Foundation, a 501c3 dedicated to empowering Native youth on the Pine Ridge Reservation. It was within the context of facilitating the foundation's programming that this book came into being.

It has been a pleasure working with the University of Nebraska Press. Thanks to Matt Bokovoy, senior acquisitions editor, and Heather Stauffer, former associate acquisitions editor, for seeing this book through from conception to completion. Thanks also to Haley Mendlik, project editor; Rosemary Sekora, publicity manager; and copyeditor Wayne Larsen for their work. I would like to extend my gratitude to the editorial board of the American Indian Lives series for supporting this project. Thanks also to the two reviewers of the manuscript for their helpful and constructive suggestions for improvement. A heartfelt thank you to all those who generously provided prepublication promotional endorsements for the book. Thanks as well to Matthew Zatkoff, the graphic arts designer who touched up the photographs of Sam Chips Moves Camp and James Tȟahúŋska Moves Camp; Karli Ledkins of Family ChartMasters LLC for the family tree files; and History Nebraska for allowing the use of the Chips image.

The author's and editor's proceeds from this book will be going to the Wičháhpi Khoyáka Thióšpaye Foundation in Wanblee, a 501c3 founded by Richard Moves Camp.

—Simon J. Joseph

From the Author

I would like to thank Wičháhpi Khoyáka Thióšpaye, Rural America Initiatives and the Bruce Long Fox family, the Chips and Moves Camp family, the Tom and Laura Lablanc family, the Fred and Evelyn Sitting Up family, and the Bay Area relatives: David Magahee and Lupe Avila, Pete and Maya Bratt, Georgia Bratt, the Nadia Bratt family, the Marlyn St. Germaine family, Paul Haible, the Ben Eiland family, the Martin and Helen Waukazoo family, Oscar Osorio and Barbra Daniels, the Nigha and Amy Tran family, the Wahpepah brothers, and the Dallas and Sandino families. I would also like to thank the community of Wanblee Lip's Camp relatives, the Russell Eagle Bear family, Mike Burbank and Vickie Eagle Bear, the Chief Duane Hollow Horn Bear family, Fred Little Bald Eagle, the Spotted Tail relatives, the Sičháŋǧu relatives, the Waln sisters, the Steven and Hattie Horse Looking family, the Lionel Bourdeaux family, the White Hat family, the Ryan White Feather family, the Yellow Elk family, the Between Lodges family, the Bad Cob family, the Full Knife family, the Randall family, Rick and Ethleen Two Dogs, the Roy Stone Sr. family, Gene Thin Elk, and the Wasé Wakpá Thióšpaye.

I thank the people listed here for their support. Any relative not mentioned here is not intentional. All are in my heart full of gratitude. Wóphila.

I am most thankful to my family, my wife, Arvella; my children, Tina, Dawn, Sylvia, Faith, Loretta, and my son, Bernard; their families; and my grandchildren, for being there for me always. Wóphila Tháŋka.

This book is dedicated to my grandchildren and all my relatives for the future generations.

—Richard Moves Camp

Editor's Note

I first met Richard Moves Camp—the great-great-grandson of Wóp-tuȟ'a (Chips),[1] the holy man remembered for providing Crazy Horse with war medicines of power and protection—in the summer of 2017. I had been visiting the Pine Ridge Reservation regularly since 1992, but had never had the opportunity of meeting him in person until then. I initially contacted Richard a year earlier regarding an article I was writing about the Lakota Yuwípi ceremony for the *Journal of the American Academy of Religion*.[2] I knew that Richard was a descendant of Wóptuȟ'a, and I had hoped that he could help me better understand the role his family had played in preserving traditional Lakota life during the early days of the reservation.[3] I was especially interested in the official prohibition period (1883–1934), when the United States Indian Religious Crimes Code outlawed Indian ceremonies.[4] I was working under the assumption, still shared by many, that the origins of Yuwípi were somehow connected to Wóptuȟ'a.

My wife, Jennifer, and I met Richard and his wife, Arvella, at their home in Wanblee, South Dakota. We visited for several hours, our conversation ranging over a number of topics, including the historical origins of Yuwípi.[5] Richard suggested that it would be good to tell the story of the origins of Yuwípi from his family's perspective, so we made plans to begin working together. My article was already in production, so I simply thanked him in a footnote for "our preliminary discussions toward a collaborative oral history project on the origins and history of Yuwípi," adding that "the historical origin(s)" of Yuwípi "remains a mystery preserved most faithfully within Lakota community oral-memory traditions" and that "more work needs to be done . . . in remembering the lives and careers of those who kept this tradition alive throughout the early reservation period."[6]

Over the next two years, Richard, Jennifer, and I met a number of times to discuss various projects. At one point during a visit to us in Los Angeles, Richard began to share his spiritual experiences as a young boy. It was then that he revealed the title of this book, *My Grandfather's Altar*. At his suggestion, we then began a series of meetings and started working together on this book.[7] Each evening, Richard would initiate the main topic or topics of discussion. These meetings were not "interviews," nor was Richard an "informant" or "participant." Our job was to record—and occasionally to ask questions—but never to direct, let alone to "reexpress" Richard's thoughts in English.[8] Despite the particular social context of our collaboration—and the fact that Richard was speaking English to non-Natives about Lakota history and culture—we were always aware that his *intended* audience was, first and foremost, his own people.

There were many things Richard was forbidden to tell.[9] There were also many things that would inevitably get lost in transcription. Traditional Lakota storytelling is a multidimensional, visual, aural, intellectual, and emotional experience that utilizes body language, intonation, inflection, emphasis, pause, and an ever-present, mischievous sense of humor that regularly relieves narrative tension by shifting tones from the dramatic to the comical and then back again. There is no easy way, therefore, to fully capture the many subtle verbal, physical, and emotional cues and codes that occur during a live conversation nor the fluid nature and dynamic qualities of oral narration and tradition.[10]

Richard is a fluent Lakota speaker. As an authority on Lakota history, culture, and spirituality based on five generations of ancestral family memory and a living oral tradition dating back to before the reservation period, Richard could easily have told this story in Lakota. His decision, therefore, to compose and publish this book in English signifies not only a desire to communicate to both Native and non-Native readers, but an intention to preserve traditional

Lakota knowledge in a medium accessible to both Lakota speakers and nonspeakers.[11] A glossary of Lakota terms is included to facilitate readers' comprehension.

Every effort has been made here to retain the stylistic conventions and formulaic expressions of Lakota oral narration ("he/she says") as well as the many occasional Lakota terms and phrases used throughout for semantic clarity and cultural context, reflecting Richard's bilingual dexterity between English and Lakota. Editorial work involved a number of minor stylistic modifications in punctuation and grammar. This work also involved rearranging narratively linked stories,[12] transforming the initial transcript of informal, fluid meetings into a thematically coherent set of chapters with subsections. It was necessary to redact some information for stylistic clarity to avoid interpersonal, familial, or tribal conflict and to withhold sacred knowledge not intended for public disclosure. What I did *not* do, however, is alter Richard's vocabulary, sentence structures, or worldview. After I assembled an initial rough draft, Richard and I then went over the entire manuscript together making additional modifications.

Richard's interest in telling these stories was to preserve his family's history. Since Richard's personal family (*thiwáhe*) is part of an extended family (*thióšpaye*) and a complex family tree of ancestors and descendants, there was never any doubt that this book was not going to be yet another "as-told-to" (auto)biography for non-Native commercial consumption.[13] Rather, it would represent an oral-literary narrative account of a Lakota family history and tradition: the authentic voice, agency, and authority of an Indigenous perspective intent on preserving the past and present for future generations.

MY GRANDFATHER'S ALTAR

Prologue

I remember the taste of wild chokecherries. They bring me back to my childhood days and memories of my grandparents, Winnie and Sam. It was August 1967. The day was clear skies, light breeze, midafternoon. My grandma was sitting on the ground in front of the *thí ská* (white house). She rolled out a canvas on the ground and began mashing chokecherries with two round stones, making patties out of them to dry. I was sitting next to her and helping lay out the patties. When she looked the other way, I would sneak a piece and put it in my mouth, thinking she doesn't know. But she knew. Finally, she made me stand in front of her, put a dry patty in my pocket, and said, "Take a small piece of this patty and soak it and enjoy the sweet taste. It will last you a long time." She dried a lot of chokecherries that day. It was for the winter so the family could eat *wóžapi* (sort of like dessert pudding). Sometimes they were made into *wasná* for ceremonies. Grandma would tell stories while she worked, and I would listen and enjoy her stories. Sometimes she would pause and drink some coffee or tea. She would talk about Grandpa, or my father, or my uncle Richard, the one I'm named after, and his horses and livestock. She would say, "A family has to all work together hard, and the Creator will bless the family."

As she was talking, suddenly a man appeared from the north side of the house from the plum bushes. I looked and said, "*Uŋčí*, there is a man coming." She paused and looked and said, "*Ohhh he ye.*" She yelled at Grandpa Sam, "Sammy, get up. He's here." My grandpa was taking a nap close by. The man was fairly tall, kind of an older person. He had white hair in braids tied with yellow cloth to hold them together. He was wearing a gray shirt and brown pants. His hat was brown and flat-brimmed, like an Indian hat. The shadow from the hat made it impossible to make out his face. Grandfather woke up, looked, and said with surprise, "*Hey heyeee*," acknowledging his visitor. He got up and walked toward the man. They met each other a short way from us. They were having a conversation. Both looked north while talking. It didn't seem very long until they parted from each other. Then the man walked back into the bushes and disappeared. Grandpa came back over and sat down to roll his Bull Durham tobacco, sighed, and said something like "*Hown Hown heyyy*," a slang word my grandpa used all the time. I got up and ran to look where the man went, but there was nothing in sight, not even a car or a wagon or a horse in sight. My grandma and I sat next to Grandpa Sam as he explained why he had a sudden visitor. I'm sure he told the story to Grandma many times before, but I believe this occasion was meant for me to hear. Grandpa indicated that the man was his friend.

It was June 22, 1911, when he first met this man. Grandpa Sam was seventeen years old, and Grandma Winnie was seventeen years old as well. Grandma was pregnant with my father, Bernard. My father was born at midday, the same day my grandpa went on top of Eagle Nest Butte for *haŋbléčheya* (vision quest) for *wóphila* (thanksgiving). Back in those days, it was a cultural practice and tradition that when the first child is born, the father goes up on the hill as *wóphila*. Grandpa Sam's grandfather, Wóptuȟ'a ("Chips"), put him on the hill. At that time, the man that came to see Grandpa was a little boy. He became friends with my grandpa and took him on a journey to other worlds. That little boy grew up along with my grandpa, and they journeyed through life together. On that day in August 1967, he came to visit Grandpa as an old man. Grandpa told us that day that his time was very near. He had to prepare for his journey to be with them. The man told Grandpa that he had chosen me to continue my grandfather's altar and work. Grandpa told me, "Keep this to yourself until the time comes. If not, your relatives and friends will despise you and jealousy will come towards you and discourage you." I went home and told my father privately about what happened. He said, "Better help your grandpa from here on after. There's not much time that he has left."

I was born in 1956. I grew up around the present-day Moves Camp village. As a young child I grew up around my relatives, my aunts, uncles, and cousins. Some relatives would come to check in with us from the village in Wanblee. My relatives lived in log cabins, and my grandparents lived in the *thí ská*. In my early childhood I remember other people also lived around us down below, with hundreds of tents, tipis, and people as far as a person could see. But they never come up to our place, which was only less than a couple hundred yards. They lived along the creek. I assumed they were relatives of ours and never questioned or said anything to anyone, I figured my relatives also saw them and ignored them out of respect. Over the years I met a friend from down there, a boy my age. He'd come by when I was alone, and we'd visit and talk and hang out together. I remember that he'd never come inside our home, and I was forbidden to go to his camp. So we have an understanding.

*

It was around June 1968. My grandfather and I were playing cards. I asked him about our neighbors down below the creek. I said, "*Kaká* (Grandpa), how come those relatives never go anywhere, but they always have food and seem to be happy?" He paused and looked at me and said, "What people? Who are you talking about?" I said, "Those people down there at the creek." So we both went outside and walked toward the east part of the house. I pointed at them. He took my wrist and held it and then he saw them, too. He kind of looked surprised and said, "How long have you seen these people?" I said, "All my life, since I can remember. I even have a friend from there." I called out to my friend, who was nearby. He came running up and said, "*Tókȟa hwo*?," which means "What's up?" in Lakota. I said, "I'd like for you to meet my grandpa." They shook hands, and my grandpa smiled. The more he looked in that direction, the more he began to recognize a few people from long ago. We both went back inside and continued to play cards. He said, "Did you tell anyone about those people?" I said, "Only my father." We both agreed that someday soon I must go on the hill.

My father and I visited Grandpa Joe Ashley to talk about the rituals of Wóptuȟ'a and Sam's way to *haŋbléčheya*. Grandpa Joe took the time to explain the meaning of *haŋbléčheya*, including the stones, the prayer sticks, and the pipe. *Haŋbléčheya* can be dangerous. If one makes a mistake, a person may not come back from this journey. But if done right, one can receive power. It was August 1968. I overheard Grandpa Sam talking to my father. My grandfather was saying that we need to put up his grandfather's altar and help his *thakóža* (grandson, meaning me) because I had been around people from another world. My schooling began that night in August.

In June 1970 the time had come for me to go up on the hill. I prepared myself for a year or so to get ready. The most important thing that I remembered from Grandpa Joe was to prepare *wóȟeyaka*, a gift of honor to compensate the medicine man. That way no mistake would fall back on him. My grandpa filled my pipe, and my father and uncle put me back among the trees.

It was midafternoon. The sun was very hot. As they left, I kept hearing people's voices—men, women, children—all over. It didn't take long until I realized that the voices were coming from the trees. The tree nations are like people, too. They have feelings, voices. They're people like us. It was evening time when my friend showed up. Suddenly, the wind stopped and the voices stopped as well. My friend said, "*Kȟolá*, it is time for you to tell Wakȟáŋ Tȟáŋka why you're here." I stood up and, for the first time in my life, I felt the presence of God and all other beings looking at me and listening. I asked that my grandpa could stay with us a little longer and that when he leaves us that his friends will not leave us, for we will have a very difficult time in our life. The dark cloud will come over us, and there will be hard life for all of us. I remembered what those old men had said. There will be substance abuse, incest, violence, and loss of honor among our people. My emotions got the best of me. I dropped my pipe and started crying. I cried so hard I felt my breath almost stopped. I fell to the ground. I begged for my relatives' lives to be saved and that my grandpa's friends would not forsake us. It didn't matter who'd take care of his altar. I saw lights on the ground. I didn't realize that it was raining hard. Suddenly my friend put his hand on my shoulder and said, "*Kȟolá*, do not cry anymore. We will never leave you."

I finally stood up and picked up my pipe. My blanket was soaked with water. I hung my blanket on a tree branch and went back into the pit, using a second blanket to keep warm. Suddenly there was a tap on my canvas door. It was my friend. He said, "*Kȟolá*, these beings, the trees, have decided to give you a gift to take with you. It is *wówačhiŋtȟaŋka*—the power of patience and tolerance. From now on, for every year you *haŋbléčheya*, you will receive a virtue, a spiritual law. Then you will qualify to pursue the healing power." My friend said, "*Kȟolá*, sing me a song. I will dance for *wóphila* and happiness for you." The only song I knew was my grandfather's personal song. I sang the song, and my friend started dancing like a traditional dancer, giving war hoops and smiling. As he was dancing, he started to become smaller and then vanished in thin air. His voice hollered from far away, saying, "They are coming after you now."

Suddenly I heard a vehicle pulling up. It was my dad and uncle. I didn't realize that I'd been out there for two days. The whole thing seemed like an hour. My grandpa was happy that I had made it. My grandmother, mother, and aunt cooked breakfast. My family did a *wóphila* ceremony that night. I was very honored to give my grandpa the *wóȟeyaka* that I had saved for a year or so. The *wóȟeyaka* is a gift to the healer for his services. I had collected a thousand dollars for him. From thereon after, I kept a very low-key profile and did not pursue anything any further. I did not realize that I was the last person Grandpa put on the hill.

Introduction

I remember in the 1960s nobody ever called my grandpa a "medicine man." The only way to identify a medicine person—they'll say Olówaŋ Wičháša. It's a secret code. A code of honor. There's a fine line underneath that language. I didn't know that until I figured it out. Nobody ever in my lifetime ever called him a medicine man. It's a secret. It was a hidden way.

We were invisible people in the last century. Nobody talks about medicine men. Nobody wants to. It's dangerous. It's kind of like gang life. You're going into a dangerous zone. For many years, Wóptuȟ'a was a mystery. They knew he was a powerful medicine man, but nobody really knew the details. It was a mystery. Wóptuȟ'a was targeted because he did the ceremonies. The government outlawed the ceremonies. That's why the Chips family kept it quiet until the proper story of their family could come out. If we had tried to write this book about Wóptuȟ'a when his sons were alive, we probably wouldn't survive. We'd get a lot of opposition. Back in the 1940s and '50s, you'd be kicked off the reservation, because that was one area where Tȟahúŋska and Horn Chips and that generation, they don't want to expose it. They don't want to expose the concept of them spirits coming in. They protect them people. It's okay now, but back in the old days when those guys were alive, they wouldn't go for that. The only reason why we're able to tell about it is because we are limiting some information.

We're setting the record straight about Wóptuȟ'a's life. It really had nothing to do with buffalo chips. There's so many stories that people just made up. They say he was born in Canada, that he was a Canadian Indian that came down. All kinds of untruthful stories. But until somebody comes up and speaks out, it's going to always remain that way. So that's what our journey is, to correct those things. We're gonna tell people there's another version.

I will speak for my grandpas. I won't speak for all Lakotas.

These are some of the teachings that Wóptuȟ'a shared with my grandpa Sam. It's just an overview summary of his life and what he was about. But it educates people what it is like to live as a descendant of a medicine person like Wóptuȟ'a. I won't be able to tell all the stories, or all the spirits and where they come from. Because that's unacceptable to our ancestors.

Some of the information about Wóptuȟ'a cannot be heard because it's very sacred. Some of the stuff about Wóptuȟ'a is forbidden to be told. You can't tell too many of those stories. Because it's deep, deeper meanings and a reader probably won't get it. But those ones that could be told, I'm writing them down. We won't go into detail. Because it's not necessary to go into detail. It's like we have to have his permission to carefully select certain parts of what we're doing today, sharing his life a little bit, but it's impossible to share all of it. He probably wouldn't like that. Wóptuȟ'a never talked about how he received his power. He only talked about his life. Wóptuȟ'a's story starts with a sad beginning and a very powerful ending.

This book mainly describes Wóptuȟ'a's life with ceremony and how it was able to be saved and handed down to his grandchildren. It touches on the precolonial ceremonies and how we practice our ceremonies today. There's a big difference. Wóptuȟ'a, the old man Chips, the messages he sent through his grandson Sam, that's one part. The second part is my grandpa Sam's father and uncle, Tȟahúŋska and Horn Chips. Their work was not associated with my grandpa Wóptuȟ'a. There's two different worlds there. When I'm talking about my grandpa Sam, we're talking about his teachings from his grandpa Wóptuȟ'a, and Wóptuȟ'a's father and grandfather. When I talk about Tȟahúŋska and Horn Chips, those are different spiritual teachings.

The problem in the past with other scholars is that they'd get my grandfathers mixed together and the people get confused. There's a real big confusion about my grandparents. When they talk about

Wóptuȟ'a-Chips, they sometimes write about him as Buffalo Horn Chips and they get him mixed up with his son, Ptehé, Charles Horn Chips. So people get confused about the whole thing. It gets people confused because in the literature, Wóptuȟ'a is also known as Horn Chips. They mistake him with his son, Charles Horn Chips. There's also a lot of information out there on Google about Wóptuȟ'a being friends with Crazy Horse, but a lot of it's mistaken.

So part of the purpose of this book is so the younger generations will know where they came from. I figured that this has to be done, because if I don't, if I left, the generation after me will have no idea. They'll never know. We want to make sure that the children know who they came from. And so I think this is the time for it to be written from the closest source of information for the people, especially the grandchildren, and the future generations.

My Grandfather's Altar   **1**

I remember growing up in a log cabin. The roof is all sod dirt. It keeps the heat out and the cool air in during the summer, and it's warm in winter. Our home was pretty warm. You don't need much firewood to keep a stove going, even when it's below zero like the way it is out here. You can't even tell. People really have a cozy time. We don't have TV or nothing, so in the evening time my father would crank up the stove and tell bedtime stories, old stories from a long time ago. You'd hear a lot of them. Sometimes early in the evening hours, uncles or aunts would come and tell their stories or they'd just have conversations with each other and we'd get to listen in. A lot of interesting stories. That's how a lot of my kids, my generation, grew up with a lot of history, knowing probably just about every angle of our culture.

We had food but no money. We were never out of food. My grandpa had my dad and my uncles work really hard when they were young. They built a root cellar with chicken wire and some kind of claylike cement. The floor was solid. The roof was really well made. Inside there's like a barn with stalls full of carrots, potatoes, onions, and squash. And then on top of the roof there's poles with dried meat hanging there. So it's like a Safeway. It's like a warehouse with a lot of food. So there was no need for money. We had an outhouse, kerosene lamps, and a lot of firewood. Later on, in the late 1960s, we upgraded a little. Somebody bought my grandma a propane stove. So we were all standing outside looking at that propane tank, going, "Wow, what's in there?" He turns it on, and that blue light comes on. So we thought that was really modern. A whole bunch of us were all standing around looking at that propane stove.

When I went to school, it was like going to a foreign country. And even though it was on the reservation, you have that feeling of loneliness because they don't talk about your people at all in there. Just some little bitty pieces, like the Mayflower story, the Boston Tea Party story. They make the Indian way look like we're savages, like we're not so nice people. And then to top it all off, you're forced to go to school and study all of that.

So a lot of my people in my generation got turned off by school. They like going to school because of the food, and because you're able to socialize with other students and visit, but you also have to try your hardest to get through the day by trying to study what they're showing you and pass the grade. The concept of school is real different for Native people. You have to take your Indian ways and leave them outside for a while, trying your hardest to learn those colonial teachings, until school's out and you pick up your Indian ways and go back home again. Well, I found out that most of my classmates didn't have an Indian home to go home to. They had a colonialized way of life living in Wanblee. There's not much to do. They go out on dates, spend time chasing each other, trying to be happy and have fun, but it's not a good ending.

I was lucky. I came back to a village. When I'd be coming back on the bus, I could already see the fire going, my uncles building up a sweat fire. That was something good to come home to, you know, a home-cooked meal and watching the door at the sweat lodge. Just being around the old people. It felt good. That went on for a while, up until toward my high school days. A lot of my classmates fell into substance abuse, and the drop-out rate really went up. They just didn't want to go to school. Many dropped out after one year, got married early, had kids. They were my age, but they're already walking around with a baby. That's a big responsibility.

I grew up a few yards south of the white house in a one-room cabin. There were several log houses around where my grandpa Sam lived. My aunts and uncles all lived around there. It was kind of like a little village. Every few yards there's another little cabin. We had a barn with corrals and chicken coops, all kinds of different stuff. It was kind of like a little farm. We had a root cellar and a sweat lodge area. Today they're all gone. That village kind of came to an end around the seventies. Everybody started moving away. That ceremony house, we still use it. When my grandpa died, it sat there for a while and nobody used it. Finally, my dad and uncles and aunts, they gave me the title or the deed to that house. We started fixing it up. We put new drywall in there, and a new roof, but we only use it for ceremonies. Nobody lives in it.

Growing up, I used to get together with my neighbor—he's a white boy—who lived over the hill. We'd get together, get on our ponies, and ride all over the Badlands. We'd go looking for wild fruit, the strawberries that grow wild out there, the wild plums, and chokecherries. Somehow he managed to steal some kneepads from the school that he was going to, so we'd park our horses down by the creek and spend most of the day crawling on our knees and picking strawberries. They were really tiny strawberries but they're really sweet, so we had these baskets and we'd fill them up and then we'd eat them up in five minutes.

For the longest time, I used to go to the store or to my neighbors around here, and when we'd sit around talking, they'll say, "Well, Richard, maybe you can do the rain dance." I'd have no idea what they were talking about, but I knew what they were trying to say. He's saying, "You're an Indian." They're reminding me that I'm an Indian. Indians are supposed to have connections to the thunder. I'm like an animal, you know, I can talk to the horses. That kind of stuff. But I just played along with it, because I didn't see anything offensive in that comment. They don't even know why they say that. They thought they were saying something about us, but when they found out that it wasn't fazing us, then they quit saying that.

*

I've worked since I was about twelve. I worked for ranchers. I started working in 1968. My first job was with a farmer over the hill. He knew me all my life, so he liked me. Of course I was one of the local people around here, so when I was looking for a job,

I didn't need an introduction, I didn't need a résumé. I just went on my own character, and I said, "I'm looking for work." He said, "Well, what can you do?" I said, "Well, you know me, I can do just about anything." He knew I was lying. But he took me in. He said, "Okay, well, let's put you to work today." Back in those days it was ten dollars a day. That was a lot of money to us. You can buy a candy bar and a soda pop and potato chips with a quarter.

So when I earned my money, my mom, she kept my money. So when I go to school, I take two quarters, so one for me, and one for my buddy at school. So I would go to school, but what's funny is that when I take three quarters to school, one is for me, soda pop, candy bar, and a small potato chips. That was my lunch. I wasn't supposed to drink soda, but I snuck. And then my buddy from Wanblee, I'd give him a quarter and he'll get the same thing. Then, before I came home, I'd use the last one to buy the same thing for my little friend. I'd give it to him. I don't know what happened to that stuff, because I knew he wasn't human, but he took it. He'd say, "Oh, good, thank you." I told him, "I never forgot about you, you know." I went to school, but he never went to school. He's just a little guy. He took it pretty well. I don't know what he did with it. I still think about that today. Because he's not human, he didn't drink them, he didn't eat them. Where did he put that stuff? I looked everywhere. I didn't see it anymore. I often wondered where my little friend's home was at, but I never asked him, you know. But I only have one friend. A lot of people think I have many friends, but I only have one.

When I was a child growing up, my grandfather said, "Don't drink sodas." I don't know why I was prohibited, but I was forbidden to drink sodas. I knew that came from my grandfather—that I can't drink sodas. That was a tough one growing up, because all my peers drank Coca-Cola on a hot day. I don't know why I couldn't do that. I honored it until I was about eighteen, nineteen years old. I still don't drink too many sodas, but I'll have one once in a while, a diet soda or something. But for the most part, I try and stay away from sodas. I think maybe my grandpa knew that I was going to be diabetic someday and have a hard time with my health. So he never allowed me to drink sodas. I was always a sickly type person when I was a boy. I was always skinny, and I was always fatigued. I could never understand why. I could never gain weight. Something's always wrong with me. He said, "One of the reasons is that your blood level is not good, you're sick all the time." So he told me not to drink sodas. "Don't ever drink sodas." He said that the spirits he works with told him that I wasn't supposed to drink sodas. And that my heart was not good. He kind of diagnosed me with all kinds of stuff when I was little. So I really took care of myself. And somehow it got better on my own. But that was hard growing up around your peers and everybody's drinking Coca-Cola on a hot day and enjoying it.

*

I remember 1969. I was a little guy. I was probably about thirteen years old. I remember sitting outside the house playing with some homemade cars and Grandpa was the only one inside the house. I don't know where Grandma went. I don't know where everybody else went. But sometimes they all go away. So it was just him and I at home. And I was sitting there on the ground just doing something. And an old, old-time car—I'd never seen one like that before, kind like a '49 black, real old car—it drove up to the house and made a circle. And two old men got off. I never saw them before. I just took a glance at them. They were old people. They were wearing round hats and moccasins. One of them had a bundle. He came up and says, "Where's your grandpa?" He said it in Lakota. I said, "Oh, he's inside." And then I just kept on playing. I didn't pay attention to them. But they went inside the house. And then I heard my grandpa talking with them, laughing and talking. It didn't take very long. It only took about ten minutes.

And then they came out, mumbling to each other. They got in the car and drove off. And I watched them head out, thinking to myself, "That's the oldest car I've ever seen in my life." I hadn't seen many cars back then, but that was an old one. It went up to the gate, and then it drove south, and I can see the dust as it went over the hill. My grandpa came out and asked me if I'd seen them. I said, "Yeah, who are those guys?" And then he sat down and he said, "That was my father and my uncle." I didn't catch it right away. I was kind of little. "Oh, well," I thought to myself, "that's one father and uncle I've never seen before." It didn't hit me until years later. Jesus Christ, I even talked to them, and I didn't even know! I had no idea it was them. I was just too little, just visiting with my toys, you know. But they show up like that.

They came in a physical form to talk to him about something. They brought him something, a bundle, and then they drove off. Nowadays I'm thinking—was that in my mind? Was that an illusion? Or did that really happen? It must have really happened, because my grandpa was visiting with them and said, "That was them." And he still had the bundle. Later on he passed that bundle to my father, and to this day I still have that bundle.

I never did ask him why they came like that. They could have come at night, in ceremony, but they didn't do that. They showed up during the day, when other people could see them too, and then they headed out. They showed up like normal people, as they were. Except for me, I didn't know who they were. If I knew them, I would have been shocked. But the only reason that can happen is because in their lifetime they had that connection with their friends. They earned the privilege of going in and out of our world and that world. That's how they showed up. They had that privilege. They got a free pass. That doesn't happen all the time. I could have sat in a ceremony with him, and when the spirits come in, he could have shown me, and I would have believed it, too, but this one I had to figure out myself. If I'd known that that was them, I would have said something, but I had no idea that they were them. But I did see them. They talked to me, and I answered them. But if I knew that that was them, shoot, I would have offered tobacco, the whole nine yards. It's just meant to be that way. That never ever happened again. It probably never will. That was a once-in-a-lifetime thing there.

Hayblečheya

All my life when I was a boy, I saw people go on the hill. I used to think, "Wow, man, I'm never going to do that." I think my grandfather knew I was really a chicken. But that changed, you know, actually doing it. It was kind of like, "Oh, wow." When I went out there, I expected somebody with a bunch of feathers, an Indian coming to me or like some big old ugly ghost. It didn't happen like that. It's not what you expect it to be. That's what I thought too when I was young. I thought it would be somebody with feathers on, riding in the skies and showing me a Hollywood-type vision, but it never happened like that. The reality was way different. There's some privilege involved in there. I mean, I think I was picked for a reason. They could have picked anybody. You know, growing up, I never cared if it happened to me or not as long as they stayed here with us. I was naïve and not so smart. I didn't even know that I had a friend from that world already. It was fate that I was chosen, but I just learned to be humble about it.

Even today, I'm sixty-five years old and I'm still scared to go on the hill. That's just natural. You get a little nervous. Going on the hill gives you the butterflies. You get a butterfly in your stomach. You get scared a little bit. Nervous. That's natural. Coming back, it's the opposite. I learned that every medicine man like my grandpa went through great sacrifices. You would think to yourself, "Wow, man, I ain't never gonna do that," but in that world, it's necessary, they knew they had to do that. I wasn't fearful, but only because I'd already been around a lot of those people all the time. If I knew I was just the only one seeing them, then I would have been really scared. I'd be running the other way. My friend, I grew up with him. We were little, and when I went to *hayblečheya*, he followed me there. That's when I found out that he was one of them. He wasn't human. My friend, he's still about my same age. I haven't seen him very much, but he shows up once in a while. He's gonna probably tell me he's coming after me someday. That's what I expect more and more, that someday it's gonna happen.

I went on the hill around 1970. I was about fourteen years old, somewhere around there. At that time nobody really had it in their mind that our grandpa was gonna leave. They kind of had it thinking that he was always gonna be around.

*

My grandfather was a very humble person. He don't talk about his altar too much. You could have a whole conversation with him, and he'll never tell you that he's a medicine man. You'll have no idea. He's in disguise all the time. He's a normal human being, but if you really pay attention to him, you'll see that there's a lot of special things about him. He was pretty quiet, but when you know him, he'll talk, he'll tell stories and talk. But he's not really an outspoken person. He'll talk to you if you ask him something, if you start a conversation with him, but he can also sit there quietly with you like you don't even exist for a whole day. He just sits there quietly by himself most of the time, with his eyes closed, so you can tell he took off. And he'll tell you when the stories need to be told. You can't pump it out of him.

One day I went to him and he told me I was his student. So I went there and ate breakfast with Grandma. Then I said, "Well, Grandpa, I'm right here, what are you gonna tell me today?" So he just looked at me and says, "Did you eat breakfast?" I says, "Yeah." He says, "Go wash your bowl then." So he told me to wash my bowl, but then he never taught me anything that day. He just went on with his business. So I told my uncles, "He didn't teach me today. I asked him and he asked me if I ate and I said 'yes,' he told me to wash my bowl." And then one of my uncles thought about it and says, "Yeah, he taught you today. He taught you a deeper meaning than sitting there talking to you. In a few words, he taught you a big lesson today."

So I went home and I thought about it. I thought about it for several days, and he was right, you know, when you eat you have to be all there, and then you have to wash your bowl, wash your dishes. That's a habit that we all have to make. We eat and we wash our utensils. That's an important thing, it's part of life. Simple things like that, he'll just tell you.

Our ancestors, they teach you about balance. Don't overdo it. And don't underdo it, whatever you're doing. Everything you're doing, you have to be there, present. Everything you do, you have to be there. You can't be somewhere else. They teach you not to be ahead of yourself. When you eat breakfast, you have to be there to eat breakfast. You cut off the world, and you just enjoy that breakfast. It's a sacred virtue, being there. And then when you're done, you clean your bowl, and you move on. But in the modern world, a lot of people don't do that. They're already talking to somebody while they're eating breakfast, moving way ahead of themselves. And that nourishment, the spiritual energy that comes from the food, it died. Because you weren't there while you were eating it.

That's what I learned from the old people. We weren't really rich growing up. Sometimes at breakfast we only have rice and raisins, maybe skillet bread, *kabúbu* bread, and coffee, but we all learned to really enjoy it, be there, finish it, and then clean your bowl and go. That's what people are missing today. The Lakota word for that is *thawáčhiŋ oúŋ*, which translates as "mindful living," the "mindfulness of living." If you live this spiritual way, it's an ethical requirement. You have to be that way. You've got to be there. It's old teachings.

Sometimes it's kind of hard to follow him. Sometimes he doesn't have time for you. He'll be talking to somebody else we don't see. But he sees them. He'll talk to them. It was like a fantasy world being around him, because things happen from the other world. Even if it's just a little bird sitting on his lap. How come that happens to him, you know? They don't come around me. They fly away. That's the energy and the power that he acquired. But he always tells me, "You can do that, too." He used to tell every one of us grandkids, "You can do that, too." And he was right. Anybody can obtain power. They just have to go get it. It doesn't come to you on your own. You have to go get it. It takes courage. So that's what I learned. I always tell people that. I say, "You want that power to come to you. You can't just sit here. You got to go get it. It's a hard journey, but you got to go get it." The spirits are like humans, too. I mean, if you don't call them, they're not gonna call you either. Anybody in this world can be a medicine person. All you have to do is have the willpower. You have to go get it. It's floating around out there. You just have to know how to grab it. The power that we look for is flying in front of us every day. You've just got to know how to grab it. Go on the hill. Don't be afraid to go on the hill. He says, "I'm just a human being, but I was taught the right way to go do it." I'd say, "I don't know about me." I'm scared of my own shadow sometimes.

So that was his kind of way of living. He plays a lot of roles. Sometimes we don't have TV, but he'll be the TV. He'll show us magic tricks. That's how we entertain ourselves in the evening after we eat. We have card games. He's really good at poker. He's really good at cards. That's how he passes his enjoyment, but he's really tricky with those cards, though. You can't beat him. Nobody wants to play against him. But he just plays for joy. Me and my grandpa used to play cards. I spent a lot of time with that guy in the ceremony room, sitting at that little round table in his living room.

There was a lot of people hanging around my grandpa all the time. Both bad and good people. He treated everybody equally. He helped anybody regardless if they're bad people or good people. He'd still help anybody. One of the things my grandpa said that I've never shared with anybody was he says, "I don't care what a person does to make a living. It doesn't apply to me." He doesn't judge anybody, which means he's friends with a lot of people. And some of those friends are bootleggers, too, but he doesn't judge them. He just looks for the heart of kindness in everybody that comes to him, and the rest is theirs. It's not for him. It took me a while to catch that, too. It took me a while to really understand that. Every person that comes to you for help has their ups and downs. But you look for the goodness and the kindness in everybody that comes through. And that's where you stay. You don't get involved with the rest of their garbage. You give that back to them.

That's the ethical law that my grandpa has. It's the medicine man's law that you treat everybody good. And it'll always be okay. You become friends with people, but you don't get personal with them. You don't do business with them if there's some shady parts of them. My grandpa would visit and eat supper with bootleggers, but he never gets involved in any of their business. So they don't have anything in common, just friendship and love. That's it. He never gets involved with peoples' personal lives, but he helps them, though. It's the difference between helping them and getting involved in their lives. There's a clear boundary there between the two. You've got to be conscious about that. My grandpa would say, "You can't be careless." Even me, sometimes I make a mistake. I try not to be careless, but I'll slip up somewhere. We're human beings. We're gonna make a mistake once in a while. So it's a struggle. That's why we pray every day to make sure we don't make bad mistakes.

I call it my grandpa's laws. He told me that "if you're going to walk this way," he says, "don't ever turn your eyes away from God. Never. For no reason." That'll be hard for anybody to do nowadays because in between you and God, there might be gold. Your attention might go with the gold, and you'll lose connection with that power. It's either this or that. And a lot of people choose the gold. You have to stay loyal to the Creator. Never turn your eyes away from God. You've got to be 100 percent loyal to him. If you turn your loyalty one bit away from him, all that will disappear. You'll never see it again. Those are God's laws, God's rules. When you make your loyalty to your center of your soul, to Creator, that will never change, no matter what happens in your life. The power is called *wówašake*, the energy, the strength. The sacredness, *wówakȟáŋ*, the sacredness of power. *Maheta wówašake*, the premium power. We all have limits in our power. But it can become premium if we want to. There's a way to do it. It's what people are looking for all over the world, a sign of God. In the Western world, the closest they got was gold.

When the Darkness Becomes Light

My grandpa Sam really didn't have too much ritual stuff. When they asked him to go somewhere to have ceremony, all he took was a pipe. That's all he took. He didn't take anything else with him when he does ceremony at different places. He just has a little dirt that he'll get over there wherever he's at, put the [tobacco] ties around there, and the pipe, and that's it. He doesn't have all these feathers and stuff like that. But when his friends come, when they turn off the lights, they bring their own rattles, their own stuff. So it looks like there's a bunch of stuff in the dark, about five rattles floating all over. But when you turn on the light, he doesn't have anything. He just has his pipe. When he puts up an altar, it's just a board, a few little items, but then when they turn the lights off, it's amazing, like there's a whole city out there! And then when they turn the light on, it's just a little bitty old humble altar. He just puts it away, puts it in his backpack, and it's off he went. It was amazing. I remember there was a woodstove in the ceremony house, but it was empty. There's no wood in there. But when those rattles came in, they hit that stove all over, and here it was burning in there, the stove was red-hot! When it was over, there was no wood in there, it was completely cold.

Most of the medicine people today, they do their ceremonies in the dark, with the lights off. But my grandpa Sam, he has his ceremonies when there's daylight, when there's no need to turn off the lights. That's what makes him special. So he made a believer out of a lot of people. If you go into his ceremony, you will probably leave 100 percent convinced that there's spirit power out there. His power, his *wówakȟáŋ*, is in his body. He doesn't have to take a suitcase or a bunch of stuff with him everywhere. He doesn't have to do that. Just by himself, he'll go somewhere. And then his friends come with all the rattles, all the whistles. They show up.

Sometimes the spirits will say to him, "People in here don't believe you. They think it's you. They don't believe we're the ones that come." They'll tell him that. That's why from time to time Wóptuȟ'a and Tȟahúŋska and Horn Chips and Sam, they'll do what they call a *wówakȟáŋ pazó*. They show their power to the people, just to show that it's not them. When Tȟahúŋska and those guys used to get wrapped up, tied up, and all the spirits come in there, with rattles and stuff, sometimes right in the middle of it, they'll turn on the light, and those old men are still tied up and then they'll sing a song and those rattles will move around all by themselves in the room. Because we're human and we're weak, so sometimes, maybe one out of every ten people will think that it's not real, they'll say, "Oh yeah, he's the one that's doing it." Back in the old days, with Grandpa Sam and them, sometimes they'll show you. They'll show you that there's different beings that come there. You can physically see them. They do that to keep everybody balanced. They normally do their ceremonies at dark, but once in a great while, they'll show them that these people are coming in. It kind of reassures your belief, gives you reassurance that, yeah, there are different beings coming. Once in a while he'll keep his followers in line by showing them a different power. That helps them with their spirituality, helps them stay focused with the Creator. We're human beings, so once in a while our minds wander off.

I think he enjoys it, doing ceremonies. He likes to do things that make people amazed, like "Wow, how'd you do that?" For example, he'll have somebody make a ball of sage in their hand, or he'll have a ball of sage in his hand and he'll talk to them and say, "Now look at that sage," and it'll be a black stone, a rock, in there. He'll do that to several people, and those people say, "Can I keep it? Could I have it, please, Grandpa?" He said, "Go ahead." By the time they got back to their house, though, it's just a ball of sage. They'll come back the next day and say, "Hey, it turned back into sage! You said I could have it!" "Well, that's all that was—sage!" But they wanted to keep that rock, you know. He was really good at that, though.

When people with cancer come to him, he'll do the ceremony with the light on. He'll take the black stone and put it on their neck, and then he'll slowly push it inside their skin until it disappears. He says, "That's gonna be with you for several days, maybe like five days. Come back after five days." And then they'll go away. What they'll tell us later is that they could feel that stone moving around in their body. Sometimes it goes through the intestines. I guess you can feel it. But then when they come back, he will sing a song, and he'll have one of his nephews, or my dad or somebody, rub the back of the person and then pretty soon it'll look like they're gonna throw up, but that stone will fall out of their mouth, with a blood clot and stuff like that. And then they'll clean it, and burn it, and that rock will just turn back into sage. And then he cures whatever's wrong with them. Mostly he cures cancer that way.

So the spirits that my grandpa Sam works with, he interprets their language. The ancestor spirits that come to his altar speak our language, but they have a different meaning. Imagine somebody speaking to you and you can hear it, but you have to know that there's a deeper inside meaning to what was just said to you. You have to learn to read in between the lines. That's what it's like in the old people's language. So when my grandpa doctors a patient and his friends come in there, they'll say, "You know, when all the birds come in the sky, fly, not all of them die at the same time," which means that that person is probably gonna die. He'll be one of the ones who die in their own time. That's a deeper meaning. Or when a patient is doctored and his friends come, they'll say, "This person has two faces." And then you wonder, "What does that mean, two faces?" But when you break it down, he might have a bipolar disorder. Or he might have a habit of gossip, or he's a real good person when he talks to you, but when he's not talking to you he's talking about you. That's what that means. Some people are like that. Some people come to visit me and they act like I'm their elder, or the best person in the world, but when they leave, my ears are ringing. They're talking about me. That's just their habit. They always want something. They don't just come to see me. That's what the spirits tell my grandpa, he says, "He has two faces." That doesn't mean he's a bad person. He just has a disorder.

*

In my grandpa's work, the songs play a major role in the ceremony. Songs have a lot to do with the ritual, calling the energy. The song catches the attention of the inner self, your inner being. It's a language attached to emotion. It catches our attention. It does something to your body. That's the magical thing about it. The magic behind the ceremonies was the songs. In our language, they call it *olówaŋ*. It's another form of language, another way of speaking. It's an inner spiritual language. You translate your voice into a rolling sound to communicate with the Creator. So it's another level of language which attracts your inner being. That's what they call *olówaŋ*. It was kind of like the core of our nations. Every nation has their own songs.

Today nobody knows the songs that Grandpa Sam used. Nobody knows what they are. No one sings them today, anywhere. They're not available. Nobody knows them.

Back when my grandpa was young, I used to watch the door with my grandma. They would sing the sweat songs, but I never heard anybody praying in there. I never once heard anybody pray, except for my grandpa. He would call them or say some words, and they'd all sing four songs a round, so I was used to it. That's how I grew up. But I asked my grandma one time. I said, "What are they saying?" Because I didn't even know that they were praying, that you're supposed to pray in there. I had no idea. I was a little guy. But when they go in there, they sing. And then when they come out, they say, "Oh, that was a good prayer." So I didn't realize that when you go in the sweat and sing specific songs, that is the prayer. It turns the prayer into a voice of rolling sound, and the Creator hears it. They all said it together by singing together. So the *olówaŋ* is the prayer. That's why I didn't hear anybody else verbally praying or speaking. They all sat there quiet. When they opened the door, they smoked the pipe, and when they closed it, my grandma filled the pipe again and then they sang another set of four songs.

So I asked a lot of questions to my grandma while she's sitting outside watching the door. But they're really short rounds. After the fourth song, they open the door and they pass the water out. And then the second dipper goes around. They usually pass the water out twice in there. The first one, you drink. The second dipper, you wash yourself down with that, then pass it back. Those little buckets, sometimes you use two of them. But they're all just drenched wet. And the reason for the second round with the water is that you're washing off all the toxins on your body that you sweated out. And when they close the door they sit in there with the sage and rub themselves all down. So they're really clean when they came out.

The songs are the prayers. It don't matter what kind of voice you have, as long as the song relays the message to them, then they accept what you're saying. You've got to remember that the words in that song is a prayer, so you're asking them something. It doesn't matter if it's in a real beautiful tone. To them they're just getting the message. They don't have any emotions. It's just us humans that get emotionally attached to a song. So guys like Wóptuȟ'a, their ceremony songs, nobody knows them today. Nobody sings them because they don't know them.

In Wóptuȟ'a's days, they never sang sun dance songs in ceremonies. They only sang his songs. The same way with my grandpa Sam. Each ceremony required different songs. There were Ghost Dance songs. Sweat lodge songs. Yuwípi songs. Horse dance songs. There's so many of them, songs for every ceremony. The songs are powerful. In the Yuwípi ceremony, the songs have a lot to do with the family. Grandpa Sam came to the Yuwípi later on in life, in the 1940s or 1950s. He didn't have any specific songs to go with that, because that was not his original altar, so he had to borrow them from his dad, Ťȟahúŋska. He had to earn it, though, and go on the hill overnight, do some things. So what he came up with is that he honored all his generations. The first song represented Wóptuȟ'a's father. The second song represents Wóptuȟ'a. The third song represents Ťȟahúŋska. The fourth song represents his uncle, Horn Chips. So there are four songs that go with his Yuwípi altar. That's how he made it work. But Ťȟahúŋska's songs were all different. They go back to Holy Arrow, and the songs describe the Little People, who they are, how they came here. Horn Chips is the same way. His songs tell his own story.

When they sing the songs for my grandpa's ceremony, it starts you off on a journey. In your mind, you take off. Being in that song, placing yourself in that song, is the real power. You go on a journey. You arrive here. You arrive there. You arrive at a certain state of mind. If you understand those songs and you put yourself in that song, you just go and arrive at the point where you pray and you get answers and then you go in another direction and you come home to reality again. That's how it's supposed to be made. For me, growing up listening to those songs, the fun part was going on a journey. I take a pillow. I sit there. I was little, so I didn't really get them right away, but as I grew older, I had my mom, Grandma, my father, and Grandpa explain to me the words and the meaning of the songs.

Grandpa would say, "Pay attention to these songs. Be in it." He said, "Be in it. Be in that song." I kind of struggled with it at first, but later I figured out what he meant. When they start hitting that drum, my mind goes off and I'm placing myself in the story being told in that song. The magic part of that was now we're taking off, we're going on a journey, where the eagles are our relatives, and have landed, and give you a message. And then after the next song, you go to another door and walk through and it tells you another story. And on and on until they sing about seven songs that first round, and then you stop. And then while you're in that state of mind, the people pray, and you can hear what they're asking for to them guys that come. And they're listening to it, and you're part of them. You become part of them listening to that request. And then they take off again, and these little men will take that request and they'll process it through. Somehow they'll get the answer and translate the answer to my grandpa. They tell him this is what it is. So you're a part of that journey listening to that as well, the answer. After that, you go on to a final journey, closer to home, and then pretty soon you arrive where you left off.

That's what made it really fun for me. It was exciting. I felt like I was going to go on a journey.

Lówáŋpi. They call it Lówáŋpi. The "Singing." So I take a pillow, and I relax my body while my grandpa talks about his dreams. They start drumming, and I felt like I was in his world. I don't know about the rest of the people. I don't know if they were there or not, but for me, that was it. He called his friends, and now they're answering.

They're coming one at a time, not a whole bunch of them either, maybe two or three, and they tell you the story. At the same time, the words that he's singing open up a screen and you're in it, experiencing it. Your own healing starts happening. That's the magic part of it. You might have had a bad day. You let it float away, and then you start going through that process. So even though you're helping and supporting the person who sponsored that ceremony, you've got your own stuff taken care of, too, just by following the songs. It's not just sitting in the dark someplace. You're going on a journey inside. You are in that song. That's why it's really important for those songs to stay alive.

My grandpa used to call it "When the Darkness Becomes Light."

I saw what he meant. It's dark in there, but you have to be in a world of dark to see the light. So when they sing them songs and you really pick up that song, then all of a sudden it feels like a screen opens up, like a theater, the projector hits that screen and you see a picture. The words in the songs are the pictures. You imagine it open up in there, and you see clearly, eagles flying or eagles walking, and the *thuŋkáŋ oyáte*, a lot of people in a crowded place, some going this way, children playing. Some of those songs describe that. So you go on each journey, seven journeys. While you're in that state of mind, while that person prays, you're hearing it from a different perspective. Of course, you're hearing it with your ear, but you're in a different world, so what he's saying makes sense, but deeper. It seems like you can almost interpret it yourself. You get to see it. You get to see that. You understand immediately what it is.

That's the beautiful part about being in ceremony. It's light. And then when he starts singing and you come back, you go, "Whoa, I just went through a trip." And then sometimes people bring food and juice or coffee, and that kind of closes the whole ceremony with good feelings. That's the beautiful ways about the ceremonies, but you've got to know them songs. It touches you deep in the heart. That's what I miss about those days, my grandpa and my father. That's what was beautiful about it. I got it when I was growing up. And that's what made me hang around my grandpa, looking forward to the next one. Who's coming for ceremony? When they come, I jump up right away and do what I can to help out, lay out the rugs, and fix it all up. Smudge the hell out of the house and get it all ready!

My grandpa's songs were all given to him in visions. He composed all of them. He had help, though. He had help from his *kȟolás*. For example, there's one song that says, "All the eagles landed, and they turned into men, walking." That's what it says. But that really did happen. In his vision, that happened. He translated that into a song, so it's power-related songs. It's not made up. That gave it power and energy. What moved me was that "wow, that happened to Grandpa." Grandpa was taken to that world, so he made a song about it. That became part of a song. So we still sing that song today. We acknowledge where we came from.

One night I was part of it. The darkness became light. They turned off the lights, but when they prayed together as one, I saw the whole room light up. Nobody turned on the lamps. But everybody saw each other. We didn't see the *kȟolás* that came there, but we heard the rattles rattling around. They'd go right by you, but you couldn't see it. That was because everybody understood the meaning and the ceremony and had belief. There was not one person doubting in that ceremony. Everybody believed in Creator and what we were there for. That happens once in a while. If one person in the crowd doesn't believe, then that'll never happen. It'll just stay dark. That's a privilege. It's called Darkness Becomes Light. You'd be lucky if you sat in one of those ceremonies one of those times, but everybody has to be on the same page. So that was something I saw that I never saw again in my life. I'll probably never see it again.

*

My grandpa was a very kind man. If you were in distress, confused, and sad, all he had to do is sit with you and visit with you for a while, without even touching you, and you'd be well. I remember when I was about sixteen years old. I worked and earned my paycheck. And I had just got paid. I felt like I earned it, so I cashed it and says, "I'm gonna spend this on myself. I can spend my other money on other people, no problem, but this money, I'm gonna keep it to myself. I'm gonna buy myself a shirt." I forgot what I was gonna buy, but it was gonna all be on me. No one saw it. I rolled it up, with a rubber band, and stuck it in my pocket. I kept saying to myself, "It's gonna be my money today, I'm gonna go to Kadoka and I don't care if I spend it on funny papers or whatever. It doesn't matter. It's mine." So we're all just sitting drinking coffee and tea, and Grandpa Sam walks in. He sits next to me and visiting, just visiting, about this and that, and then all of a sudden, my whole feeling changed—like I love my grandpa, you know—I would do anything for him. He didn't say anything to me. We were just talking, but before he left, I just reached in my pocket and said, "You can have all this, Grandpa. Go ahead." It was the energy, the power. He didn't say, "Could I borrow some money?" He didn't say any of that. He just sat there and visited, but his power touched something in my heart. So I didn't care about the money, so I just gave it to him. If you have good energy, the worst person in the world will still be nice to you. The biggest criminal might let you get by and just say, "I won't rob you today, you can just go." It's the energy, the power that you carry. How you get that energy is being with Creator, being with God, walking his ways, not afraid to stay in continuous prayer, talking to Him, first thing in the morning and the last thing at night, talking to Him. You don't realize that you get your answer, that some energy came to you. You wake up, and without really even thinking about it, you've got some real positive energy around you. That's reality.

But he's human too, my grandpa. He has his ups and downs. I've seen him really sad sometimes. I've seen him in the worst part of his life. I've seen him feel helpless. Sometimes he has his moments where he's really sad. I think one of his biggest disappointments was his children. His children all started drinking, and they all went the opposite way. That was his greatest sadness and disappointment. But they were spoiled by him because he took care of everything. His children felt like they were privileged. They could go get in trouble and dad will fix it, things like that. Except for my father and a couple of my aunts, they all died of alcoholism, all his children. That's the sad thing about it. Many of his grandchildren died of drinking, too. I wish that it wasn't that way, but it was that way.

*

So that was life with my grandpa Sam. It's a privilege and an honor to live with a medicine man like my grandpa Sam. You have to know his world. A lot of people that grew up around him, or lived around him, lacked understanding and didn't take care of him. So he'll get sick a lot. You have to take care of him. You have to know how to live with a medicine person, how to cook for him, when to cook, and when not to cook for him. If you're a woman, if you're in your time, you can't cook for a medicine person. So he doesn't eat at restaurants, only if the cooks are all men. So it's a real hard life. Because he's vulnerable. He wants to be a human being. He wants to be normal, so he tries to live a normal life as much as he can. But he has these strong restrictions. He has to watch what he does.

That's how it was with my grandpa. He doesn't say anything. He'll eat what you give him, but he'll pay the price later. He'll get sick. So you've really got to understand his lifestyle. Like in the morning, my grandma would make grits, oatmeal, or cornmeal. She'd make him fresh bread, water, and coffee. It all has to be fresh. But sometimes he'll wake up one morning and say, "I can't eat today." That energy inside of him required him to fast all day. He gets instructions from somewhere, so it's unpredictable. Sometimes his friend will tell him something ahead of time. He says, "Go away for a while." So then for no reason at all, we'd get up in the car and be driving to Kadoka. No reason why. But sure enough, some people will come to his house looking for him, probably for bad reasons, too. So his friends protect him that way. So every day is not ours. It's really guided and controlled by them, his friends.

You ever seen that movie called *The Milagro Beanfield War*? In that picture, there's an elder. He had a gift. A spirit from another world would come and tell Grandpa Sam what was gonna happen. Other people can't see the spirit, only him. That's what my grandpa Sam's life was like. Sometimes he'll have visitors. He has a friend who shows up once in a while. My grandpa would be sitting outside with somebody, but we don't see him. We'd sit around not too far away waiting for his visit to end so we can visit him too. But he'd be yacking away. One day I said, "Grandpa, why don't you just let us in on this talk, too? You're just having too much fun! We want to see them, too!" Nowadays, when I think about it, I should have never said stuff like that, but we understood that he has friends on that side.

My Grandfather's Altar

My grandpa gave me instructions to watch his altar, but it's not my altar. There's no way I can say it's mine. But I just set it up in his honor to pray and remember him. When I put my grandpa's altar up, I never sit in the middle of it. That's his empty seat. He's not there anymore. I come late, Johnny-come-lately. I'm a generation after my grandfather's, so I'm really just doing my grandfather's work. I don't have an altar myself. I'm just a messenger. I've never called myself a medicine man. Other people assume that. They'll call me that, but I never call myself that. Neither did my grandpa. And neither did their grandpas. We only call ourselves messengers. We don't call ourselves prophets or saints or holy men.

So poor old me, I never had a chance to earn my own altar. I'm almost halfway over my time here, so I probably won't. I'll probably just continue sending that message from my grandfather's work, a caretaker of my grandfather's work. I took care of my grandpa's pipe in ceremonies. I never owned one. I use Grandpa's pipe. My grandfather gave me a lengthy talk about the pipe. We take good care of our pipes, especially my grandpa's pipe, Sam. I still have it and use it like he's still around. But I never claim ownership. I just say it's my grandpa's pipe. My grandpa's altar. And the plants that I take care of are the ones my grandfather used. And a lot of the work that I'm doing is what my grandfather did. I keep up the process. Everything he did, I try to do a little bit of it. So every year, like my grandpa, I get fixed up. I get maintenance. My friends come and doctor me. Everybody sponsors a meal and tobacco ties and stuff.

And then again in the spring around May I get doctored again. My wife, Arvella, makes the ties, and people cook, and we do a four-day ceremony here. So that was a process that we still continue today.

For my grandpa Sam, an altar is like a center between you and the other world. It's a sacred center, a place where you and the other world can meet. It also applies to the human being. You have your own altar, your sacred being. Your altar is your heart. That's what an altar is. *Hóchoka*, a center. When you say "*hó*," it describes something sacred. *Hó* is a voice, a sound. Sounds are important to that altar, the prayer and the songs, the words you say while the altar's being set up. Those sounds go into a world that we can't touch, but we can feel, your voice is sent somewhere. When you send your voice to the Creator, he'll hear it, but it'll first go through a lot of channels. No one in this world has direct authority to send their voice directly to God's ears. You pray, and somebody heard that prayer, and delivered it to someone who delivered it to another one, and then finally he gets it. That's how it works. There's not a human in this world who has the power to directly talk to him. We wish we did. But it has to go through channels. It's just like the stars. They say it takes about three days for the stars' light to show up over here. The speed of light. We think that we can see it in an instant when we go outside and we go, "Wow, it's really beautiful out there." But there's another reality. It took years for that light to show up. By the time it gets here, maybe that star's not there anymore.

Altars have a psychological influence on people. When you see a ritual being laid out, you automatically respect it and behave around it. You honor it because you can see the center being built. So when my grandpa Sam sits with his altar, nobody questions him about what this or what that is. You don't ask him, "Could you tell me what that is right there?" or "Could you tell me why you do that?" That's Anglo-ideology learning. When the ceremony's going, you don't ask him questions. There's a different place for that. All my years I never questioned. I just followed. Until he feels it's okay to tell me what that is. That's how it works. But it's his. He doesn't share with nobody. And he doesn't have to. It's his own. A part of him goes on the altar.

I don't have Wóptuȟ'a's altar. I only have Sam's. That kind of lightens things up for me a little bit. If I were to practice his grandpa's altar, my life would be different. I wouldn't be able to go around anywhere. So I got lucky. I'm satisfied with his altar. His grandpa's would be very hard. It would be very difficult. I don't have a whole bunch of spirits and stuff like that. I just only have one person. I call him a person because sometimes he'll show up like a person. But he has many friends. That's how I've been able to work with a lot of different ones. They all talk to him, and he's the only one that talks to me. My power, the power that I carry, is nowhere near what Wóptuȟ'a had. He had extraordinary power. There's no way I can ever equal myself to somebody like him. He was an extraordinary person. That requires a lot of hard work. I'm too old to go back and try and get any of that power. Not in my lifetime. It'll never happen. A person has to start out really young, and have the proper upbringing; then he can obtain power like that. It took me years and years to create my own altar so that I could say it's mine, my connection with them. But the information I put in there, that's nonshareable. I can't tell you what that means. There's some stuff on Grandpa Sam's altar that I can never understand. But he used it that way, so I put it up that way. I'll never be able to interpret it. The same way with Wóptuȟ'a's. Wóptuȟ'a's got limits on there. What he drew on the altar is what he saw in his heart, in his vision. It has an explanation inside his heart, how he made those friends. It's very sacred. A lot of people don't know that. So he just gave instructions to us. He says, "If you ever get in trouble, or if you ever have despair, a difficult time, set up my altar." Basically, what he's saying is, "Call my name, and my friends will be present." He didn't say they're going to come talk to you. He says, "My friends will come and see you."

It's been that way for a long time. So we set up his altar. Not very often, but once in a while. We call his name, we pray, and we sing his songs, and we see signs of his friends. They don't talk to us. We just see signs, and that's good enough for us. We get done, take it down, and we eat. We don't have the energy to talk to Wóptuȟ'a or any of his friends directly. We can't do that, but what we do is we have our friends ask them, get the message from them. I don't have the energy capacity to sit with him and talk to him. He will never come. If he does, all of us will probably die or pass out or something. That energy is too much. Even when my grandpa was alive, there were some times, once in a while, he would pass out in a ceremony, he would go out cold. And we have to sing songs forever to have him come back alive, come back to us. And he's really tired, but he'll say all he saw was a face appeared and that's the last thing he remembers. That happens once in a while with my grandpa. You have to always keep an eye on him.

I think the majority of what I learned came from the other world. It came through my grandfathers, passed on through the generations. But it still came from the other world. They were just sending messages down. It runs in the DNA. Years from now, it'll be known as my altar. They'll probably say, "Oh, that's Grandpa Richard's altar." They would never know that I got it from my grandpa. And my grandfather Sam took over his grandfather's altar. That's how that one works. But people do ask me that: "How did you end up with this?" But they don't ask me the right way, so I always give them a real crazy answer.

Wóptuȟ'a

Wóptuȟ'a-Chips was born around 1836 in the foothills of the Big Horn Mountains. His father's name was Tašiyótȟaŋka Máza, Iron Whistle. His mother's name was Waŋblí Hupáhu Wíŋ, Eagle Wing Woman. Wóptuȟ'a's grandfather's name was Wanáǧi ób Máni, Walks with the Ghost. He was also known as Ghost Hail (Wanáǧi Wasú). He was a healer who worked with the ancestral world. They say he married a woman from the ghost-spirit world. Her name was Panke Ská Lúta Wíŋ, Red Abalone Shell Woman. More details about Ghost Hail are forbidden to be told.

Before Wóptuȟ'a was born, his grandfather Ghost Hail told Iron Whistle that his first son was coming, but that he will not be an ordinary man. He will be *wakȟáŋ* and have supernatural powers that will change the people's lives and help them to be close to Wakȟáŋ Tȟáŋka. Ghost Hail said that before he came into this world, this child would travel to four worlds and when he arrives in this world, he will visit another four worlds in order to receive his power.

The day Wóptuȟ'a was born, many people came to greet him. Among them were an older couple that no one had ever seen before. The couple brought him gifts, including a blanket and a cradleboard. Then they went away, and no one ever saw them again.

When Wóptuȟ'a was around two or three, he went missing one morning. The whole camp went looking for him, but he was nowhere to be found. He was missing for four days. On the evening of the fourth day, the family and people heard a child's voice. It was Wóptuȟ'a. He was with the old couple that came to visit him when he was born. The old man told Iron Whistle that Wóptuȟ'a was with them the whole time and traveled with them to four worlds to look for blessings from the source of power. Each place they went,

Wóptuȟ'a received a small "chip" of power. And so they named him Óuŋčhaǧe Šaglógaŋ Étan Táku Wakȟáŋ Uŋkúpi. They gave him a "chip" of power from each world. His name was real long. So they just shortened it to Wóptuȟ'a, "Chips." That's the spiritual meaning where he went to different worlds. He received a "chip" of power from each world. As the years went by, his name was shortened to Wóptuȟ'a, "Chips," referring to the "chips" of power he received from each world he visited.

If you look on Google today and look up Wóptuȟ'a-Chips, there's all kinds of stories about Wóptuȟ'a and they describe his name as Wóptuȟ'a-Chips. They say that he earned the name from a buffalo's horn, the chips of a buffalo horn. That's totally false. That's not his real name. That's not true. It has nothing to do with chipping buffalo horns or anything like that. So there's a lot of misinformation out there regarding Chips. But we never really said anything about it. Hopefully this book will correct a lot of that stuff.

Today a lot of people ask me, "What is power?" Well, first of all, every human being has some type of power, the energy that makes us move. That's power. But for some reason, people like Wóptuȟ'a, their power has become a premium power. When you reach out to the Creator and send your voice in prayer, somebody hears it. He gets a reaction from that other world. Things show up. When he sends his voice to the four-legged people, they answer him back. That's power. It's all in your voice, your belief, the way you conduct yourself. When you send your voice to a four-legged and he hears it—just like he has ears, just like he understood your language, and he tries everything he can to answer you back physically or verbally—that's power. Anybody can do that. They just have to have the courage to go get it. It's floating in the air. You just have to know how to grab it. The premium power is in prayer. That's why you dedicate your life. You sort of have to give your soul to Nature, to the natural world. Now, if it accepts it, then you earn yourself a little power and you can use that for healing. So when you pray for a sick person with your supreme power, and you ask that person to get well, he will get well. It don't matter if it's cancer, or life and death. If you're given the privilege to send your voice and somebody hears you, they'll answer your request. That is supreme power, the premium power. And for some reason, Wóptuȟ'a was born with all that. He had that power.

Wóptuȟ'a was born *wakȟáŋ*. He didn't have to go train. He didn't have to get sanctioned by anybody. He was just born sacred, *wakȟáŋ*. He's the only medicine man that got his power without going on the hill. He was born with it. Everybody else had to go on the hill. That's what makes him different from the rest of the medicine people. Generally, the holy men in Lakota country start their journey as holy men and healing by going on the hill and by going to school, but for some reason Wóptuȟ'a inherited power. He didn't have to go on the hill. He was born with power. And that's what catches the attention of Native people. How did he do that? How did he come into this world with so much power?

Wóptuȟ'a's mother and father were told by the ancestors that they were going to have a sacred child. So he had power before he came into this world as a seed in the womb. But he still had to go on a journey. Wóptuȟ'a traveled to eight different worlds, four before he came to this world, and four after he got to this world. To the spirit people, to the *kȟolás*, one year to us means one day to them. They call it *aŋpétu*, a day. And when they come from wherever they come from, they stop at different dimensions, and then they pass over here. My great-great-grandfather went to eight worlds, and when he came to this world, each world represented ten years. So he died when he was eighty years old. This legacy of his teachings stayed with him and all through his future generations, his sons and grandkids, and probably even me. It's fate. We will only live eighty years in this world. If we do things right, if we do things ethically, and follow the path of his teaching, then eighty years is our limit, our guaranteed limit. They all did that, you know, even my father. He was seventy-nine years old and on his eightieth birthday, he passed away. We did everything we could to keep him alive, but in the early morning hours of his eightieth birthday, he just stopped breathing and died. My grandfather could have done that too, but he was given the privilege to live two more years after his eightieth birthday. And then my great-grandfather, Moves Camp, he died when he was eighty years old as well.

My grandfather was supposed to have died when he was eighty, but he waited two extra years because I was coming up slow. I was a Johnny-come-lately. But all my grandfathers died when they were eighty. They weren't really sick. They just reached their limit, and then they died. The same way with Wóptuȟʼa. On his eightieth birthday, he passed away. So eighty years is kind of like a limit. But it only happens to the male side of the lineage. On the female side, his daughters or granddaughters, they can pass eighty years old. They can live a long time.

Wóptuȟʼa and the Wolves

When Wóptuȟʼa was eight years old, his father Iron Whistle passed away. Wóptuȟʼaʼs mother remarried another man, and they had two sons. Wóptuȟʼaʼs half brothers were named Kicking Bear and White Squirrel. The problem was that Wóptuȟʼaʼs stepfather was not so nice to him. His stepfather didn't like him. So one day Wóptuȟʼaʼs mother told her son that she had made arrangements for Wóptuȟʼa to live with his uncle in Canada, among the Húŋkpapȟa people.

One evening Wóptuȟʼa was brokenhearted. He didn't feel like he had a family, so he ran away from home. He couldn't wait any longer. When he turned ten, he decided to make the journey to his uncle. One evening he went outside and just started walking. He ran away from his stepfather, his mother, and siblings. He took off. He journeyed to find a dad in his life, not a biological dad but somebody that he could consider a father figure. The only one that he knew was his uncle, his mother's brother, so he traveled from the Black Hills to Canada. That's a long ways for a little kid to travel by himself. So he had courage, but he's still a human being. He had his feelings hurt. He had his disappointments. He felt abandoned, unwanted. Imagine a ten-year-old or a twelve-year-old. He got the message that he wasn't really wanted. He wasn't really considered part of the family. So he got his feelings hurt. So he made a journey, and he didn't care if he died or not. So Wóptuȟ'a sort of gave his life up by making that journey. He didn't care if he got killed. He didn't care if anything happened to him. He just wanted to disappear. And the further he went away, the less pain he felt. Being out there alone eased his pain. He felt better by thinking positive thoughts and tiring himself out by sleeping and waking up and walking. Soon he learned from his own experience that he had power.

He journeyed from the Black Hills. His journey was to reach Canada. That was on his mind. So he kept going. He ran out of food. He ran out of resources. All he had was a blanket, but he just kept going. Sometimes he'll stop along the creek and get some water, and then he'll keep going. Pretty soon he was really alone. Out in the middle of nowhere, no food, no direction, and really hungry. He thought he was gonna die out there somewhere.

During the day, he would hide and sleep, and then he would walk through the night. The moon was out, so his travel was a bit easier, except he didn't know where he was going. Soon he came to realize that he was not alone. He was being stalked by wolves. And the wolves were closing in on him. At first he thought they were going to eat him. From a distance they were watching him, and they were starting to close in on him. Wolves do that when they see prey. They'll surround him, slowly move in on him, and then they'll attack him, eat him up. That's the way of life for the wolf people. He thought that was happening to him. It's just a matter of time before he gets eaten up. And he knew that they were all closing in on him fast. He couldn't run away. He couldn't defend himself. He didn't have any weapons. So he just gave up.

He just kept walking. He laid down to rest, and here he realized that those wolves lay down around him, protecting him, and that they weren't going to harm him. One of those wolves came up real close to him and talked to him. He says, "We're taking you to your destination. Don't be afraid of us." He says, "We'll take care of you." They were protecting him. They were guiding him. That thought came to him. So he started sending his voice to the wolves. He said, "Thank you for guiding me," and they reacted to him. They answered him back in a way where he understood that they heard him. They understood what he said. So now what he had was an ability to communicate with them, so he felt at home. He felt safe. After a while, the body language of those animals started becoming very vivid. He realized that they were not going to hurt him, that they were his relatives. Now he found another set of relatives. Instead of human beings, he found out that he could talk to the four-legged and they understood what he said. That's a blessing. He even thought about forgiving those people who hurt him.

So along the way, one of them broke through the barrier and communicated with him. The wolf understood what he was saying. He spoke Lakota. And now they had a conversation. And miracles started to happen around him. At first he thought he was having delusional problems. But he wasn't. It was real. Now he talked to them, and they answered him back. Not all of them, just one. And so now he's really happy. Instead of being sad, he turned it all around. The wolves began to communicate with Wóptuȟ'a and make friends with him.

Now he realized he had a purpose in life. As a young man, he found Wakȟáŋ Tȟáŋka, God. He surrendered himself to God, the supreme power. And he thanked him for bringing nature to life around him. And those four-legged people told him, "We pray to the same God your people do, too. We're all the same."

One day the wolves said, "Go to the creek, and we'll help you." So he went to the creek to fetch some water, and a fish peeked out enough for him to grab. The wolves said, "Grab that fish." So he grabbed it. "That's your supper." And he had the stones and things to make fire. So they gave him guidance. So he ate fish to fill himself with energy. The wolves with their ability were able to grab fish, too. And they ate. He says, "Now we are sharing the same food. We eat the same food sometimes you do." They ate the fish, he ate the fish. Now he knew that the four-legged relatives are like human beings. They have compassion, and they have wisdom. He was not afraid anymore. The fear sort of vanished away. The distrust and the uncertainty went away. So he was not really in a hurry to get where he was going.

He spent over a month with them. Sometimes the wolves went out during the day. They would tell him to hide in the bushes. So he followed orders. He'd go hide, and they'd take off. He says, "Don't come out of this bush until we come back." Sure enough, when he sees them come back, he comes out. In the evening time, they'll bring him back food. So they were supplying him, keeping him alive. They would bring pieces of meat back for him, buffalo liver, kidney, the things that you can eat raw without getting harmed. The nutrients of these kidneys and the liver helped him survive. It's like vitamins.

Finally, he reached his destination. One of the wolves said, "Over this hill, when you go over there tomorrow, your people are going to be there. This is as far as we can bring you." He realized that the wolves took him there. So the next morning the wolves were howling around, and one of them said, "Don't forget us now. Don't forget us, and we won't forget you." He didn't.

So he received power from the four-legged as relatives, and he was finally able to find his people, his uncle, and that's how he grew up most of his childhood in Canada with the Húŋkpapha. When he went over the hill, he saw an Indian camp, a Lakota camp, and sure enough he found his uncle there. He made it to Canada on foot with those wolves. It was a long journey. It took him almost a year to get there because of the distance and being on foot. I think he left early in the fall and spent the winter with those wolves, and early toward spring he finally reunited with his uncle. So he spent a lot of time with those animals. And so when he finally reunited with his uncle, they all knew who he was. And what he was. He became sort of like a golden child growing up with those relatives in Canada.

He lived with his uncle, who raised him, but his uncle couldn't believe that Wóptuȟ'a walked thousands of miles all on his own to find him. Finally, Wóptuȟ'a told him what happened: "The wolves brought me here. I made friends with them." So his uncle helped him put a prayer of appreciation together. That's where the Five

Stick comes from. Each stick represents the wolves, the wolf people, his friends. That's where the Five Stick ceremony came from.

The Gray Hair People

The Five Stick ceremony honors the wolves, because they saved him. But the dirt that you put on there to make the altar, that's for the Gray Hair People, the *p̌ehíŋ sáŋ*. Those are the friends that he works with. They are ancestral people. They come from another world, a world that he visited, and that's what they call themselves. So that's where he got his power from, one of the eight worlds. According to Wóptuȟ'a, when God created this world, he started out with the sun. He put a tremendous amount of energy in the sun, but the energy, it blew up and the ball of flame carried a lot of electromagnetic energy and power. But in other parts of the universe, there are eight different worlds that exist out there yet to be found. Wóptuȟ'a visited these eight worlds before he came to this one on earth. But as we speak today, there are seven other worlds that have life, just like this earth. One of those worlds is the Gray Hair People's world. That's where Wóptuȟ'a made friends before he came to this world.

A lot of people today have no idea what the Gray Hair spirits are. Wóptuȟ'a was the only one who could have them, and then my grandpa Sam. Grandpa Sam is the only one that I know who still had that power. So the Gray Hair People came to Wóptuȟ'a, and they came to Sam, and they come to me. But nobody else knows these songs. They don't come nowhere else. They don't come nowhere else in the country, in this world, ever. When I'm gone and my son Bernard's gone, they'll probably never ever come to this world again. But for now, that's where they come from, the Gray Hair People. In Lakota, they call them *p̌ehíŋ sáŋ*, which means that they're elder spirit people, elder of the elders. Hardly anybody will ever know them.

The songs are different. Nobody sings those songs today. The songs remained kind of underground. There are seventeen songs that go with that altar, and they're all different. They're not the regular ones that people have been singing all over. There's also a good reason why they put seventy-five ties around the altar. That's how many Gray Hair People are out there, no more and no less. That's how that works. The Five Stick ceremony is about Wóptuȟ'a, his life, his connection to the Gray Hair People, and the wolves that saved his life. That was it.

In my experience with the Gray Hair People, they come to us as human beings, no different, just an ordinary guy, walking up to you and talking to you. But then you look around, and he disappears. They can shift themselves into anything. That's the spirit power of the Gray Hair People. The spirits that come to that altar are way different from the ones that come to the Yuwípi ceremonies. There's no relationship between these two. They're separate people.

So let's just imagine that you had the privilege to set up an altar. They give you certain instructions and say, "You're gonna call the Lakota people." And sure enough, some of us show up. But then you set up a different altar, and say, "I want to call the Navajos." Sure, the Navajos will show up. It's like that in our world with spirit people. They don't all come. If you need to do a nonhealing ceremony, you will use the Five Stick. If you do a *wóphila* ceremony, you will do the Five Stick. We have a spiritual calendar that we use. We live by the moon. So every new moon, we put the Five Stick ceremony up. Or for mourning, or new babies, or just appreciations, or to ask ceremonial questions, we go with that Five Stick ceremony. Each ceremony, different spirits come, those that belong to that altar. Even in the sweat lodge, the spirits that come to the sweat lodge are not associated with the other ones that I mentioned. They're all different. It's almost like you put this altar up, the Arapaho people will come. You put this one up, the Cheyenne people will come. You put this one up, the Lakota will come. It's like that in that world, it's all different. It's not generalized, no standardizations, all separate. A lot of people don't know that. There are different tribes of spirit people. They have different names, different principles, different nations. They're completely different, but to us normal people, we think they're all the same. It doesn't work that way. It's not like that.

The spirits that we have relationship with, they don't have emotions. They're just angels that have one-track minds: to be friends. When they tell you they're your friends, they're your friends. You can say anything you want to them, but they'll still be your friend. When you die and leave this world, maybe that'll end, but they have no emotions over it. So, for an example, if they tell you not to do something, "Don't do this," and you do what you're not supposed to do, your friendship ends. You can cry, sun dance, haŋbléčheya, appeal all kinds of ways to them, but they'll leave you forever. We humans, us guys, we're complex people, and when you dissociate yourself from a friend or companion, you might still have some feelings for him and you might even get back together again, forgive each other. Well, our spirit friends don't do that. When they tell you something, they expect you to do it. When they tell you something will happen, you can see it, they'll do it. Even if it takes a little while, you'll see it happen. So that's the nonemotional spiritual beings. They don't have feelings like we do.

Nothing's in it for them. They just do it for the love of God. And the friendship. They don't have to if they don't want to. There's really nothing personal in it for them. As far as they care, we can die. They couldn't care less. They watch you manifest, and they'll watch you unmanifest. They have no feelings about that. Nothing's in it for them. They just work for God. Imagine living in a world like that. What if you were like that? No emotional attachment to anybody. That's kind of like the world they live in. But if they say, "I'll come back for you later," they will come back for you later. There's no ifs or buts. No maybes. It's just it or not it, that's it. That's the kind of friends that we've got. And that's why we really have to be very careful about what we say to them, what we talk to them about. The Indian term for "without emotion" is called hiyá za. Hiyá za is a person without emotional love or understanding. He's a being. He's working for somebody to carry out what you want, because he chose to be your friend. If a friend asks you, if you ask a friend to do something, he'll never question you about it. You just have to say it once and it's done. He'll do it. He may advise you that what you want may not be good for you, but he'll give you a chance to change your mind. That's how they are.

When a human being makes friends with somebody, you both sort of agree that there'll be some principles that you both follow, like in a marriage. You both say you understand and will be together come rain or shine, no matter what the conditions are. Basically you're saying that your love for each other is final. You'll not back away from that. Those are principles and laws that you committed to together. You don't read it from a Bible, you say it from your heart. If you say it from your heart, it will work. But if you just repeat a Bible verse, you might not be telling the truth, because you're just reading it from a Bible. So when a medicine person makes his relationship with a spirit being to be their friends forever, there are certain expectations that they expect from you and there is something that you expect from them. It's a bond that's unerasable, it's together forever. So they might tell you, "We'll be your friends, we'll come when you call us. But don't ask us to do anything that we don't want to do." Like bad things. They don't like hurting other people. So they might say, "You've got to uphold those things from us. What we expect you to do is live a good life as well." The understanding is made, and then the friendship goes on for a long time. And it's not easy. It's a special relationship, communication, and commitment that you made with a nonhuman being that still can talk your language, so it's a really serious business.

They're nonhumans, but they're still beings. They come from a different world. I'm pretty sure they've got their own principles and laws that they've got to follow. That's their world. They don't have to be our friends if they don't want to. They have their own world out there. I think it's just a privilege that we're able to have connections with them. But we don't have a right to be in their world. One thing they tell us for sure is that the God that we pray to, that's their God, too. That's the God that they work for.

A lot of people think that they speak just like us, but that's not true. If you've never been around them, they could talk to you directly in broad daylight, but you'd never understand what they're saying. You'll hear them, but you won't get the message. You can't interpret for them. That requires internal energy. You have to work that energy in yourself. So that's part of the Native teaching, the interdependency of your own cooperation, your energy. And it's all designed and created by the spirit people. That's why it's really important that we stay in touch with them. They come from a powerful world, but the language they speak to us with may be completely different. The same words may be used, but the meaning is different. For example, when we say house, your home, we imagine a structure, with a bedroom, a living room, a home. In Lakota, we call that *thí*, as in *thípi*. But the spirits that Wóptuȟ'a and Grandpa Sam work with, their version of *thí* really meant *wahoȟpí*, symbolized by a bird's nest. So the bird's nest is supposed to be real sacred. It's a symbol of sacred home, because the winged people, whether it's an eagle or a hawk or a little tiny bird, they put a lot of work and prayer into their nest. Just with their little beak they bring back a twig and they carefully place it over and over every day until it becomes a complete nest. And then they settle in it, like a home. So to that world, that's what they call home. They symbolize the home as a nest. That includes the responsibility of the people who are part of that home. The man has to build that nest. So when the man makes that nest for the female, she really enjoys it. She takes it as her castle, her temple, and brings children into that home. It's a sacred place. That's their version of it, the spirit people.

So you've really got to pay attention. It's a spiritual language. Even our people often have no idea what that is. Nowadays if I say, "How's your nest?," I'm including *them* asking "How's your nest?" A guy will probably say, "I don't know." He'll probably think I was talking about a bird. If he understood what that meant, he would say, "Oh, my home, my house is good. I have enough wood. I have enough water. It's a comfortable place." That spirit feeling in that home is what is sacred there. So we know the Lakota word for home now, *thí*, but the spirits that come to us have a different word for it. They call it *wahoȟpí*, a nest. The *thuŋkášilas*, the spirits, they tell you about that. He says, "Every day you've got to work on your nest," your home. You've got to fix it up, keep it tight. A bird does that. Even the little tiniest bird works from day up, sunup to sundown. The deeper meaning requires interpretation from another world. They always symbolize something, but what they tell you may not be the way it is.

Another example. Back in the old days, if you had a set of horses and a son, the medicine man could tell your son, "*kih*," which is "team," "*lohaki waŋží ipachi etu elo*," which means "your team of horses, one of them looks the other way," which means that the child, the parent, one of them's cheating on the other. So that's a real deep language. You've got to know what you're talking about! They'll say it in a way where you really have to have your consciousness in order. That's why they call us "interpreters." Another example is "*híŋhaŋni ki aŋpétu wašté wanji wala kikyelo*." They'll say, "Tomorrow you will have a good day." And so tomorrow comes and you might have a blizzard. But to them, that might be a good day, because it cures all the bad illness in the air. It cleans more things in the world. But to us, a blizzard is like, "Aww shit, man, I got to stay home." So the language has a deeper, spiritual meaning.

It's all about the meaning. Somebody like my grandpa Sam, you can tell he has power because his language is mixed with their language, so you've really got to pay attention around him. Some of the things they say, nobody can hear it today. If I said it to somebody today, they'd have no idea. They're going to ask me, "What did you mean?" That's what they'll say. They'll want me to explain it in English so they'll understand. That happens to a lot of people around here. Even my own family, if I use some of the ancestors' words, they're going to ask me to break it down so they'll understand it. And their language changes all the time. There's a word for ceremonies. There's a word for social life. There's a word for war. There's a word for confidentiality, even marriage counseling. These beings don't care if you're cheating or not, they'll just tell you! Yeah. They have no heart. They just tell you how it is.

So Wóptuȟ'a had a total of eight ceremonies, but most of those were his personal ones. Seven of them he doesn't share with the family. The only one that he shared is the Five Stick. He passed that down to his children and grandchildren. But the other seven ceremonies, some of them are not good. Some of them are about war, killing people. Those are very dangerous. He works with animals. He works with dead people. He gave just a little piece of that power to his friend, Crazy Horse, and Crazy Horse's name went all over like a hero, a warrior, a killer. So it also involves death. But the purpose of the art of war was to preserve our lifeways, to protect our connection with the sacred world. That's why we went to war, to defend our relationship. So warriors had to be skillful. Lakota warfare was an art. It was not based on anger or hatred of the enemy.

The Lakota art of war was a way of life. They fight for good, honorable reasons. They have rules of engagement. They have honor. They don't just go mercilessly killing women and children and innocent families. They don't do that. They fight soldiers. And then if they get killed by the soldier, that's an honorable thing. That's a way of life. So that's the reason why my grandpa makes the *wóthawe* for warriors that go fight in war. They're not angry men. But they were skilled people and fought for a reason, to preserve our life. Nothing's personally in it for them, they're doing it for the love of the people. So the warriors that fought in the Little Big Horn or any other battles, they were not paid. There was no paycheck for those guys. Wóptuȟ'a was a very serious and kind man, but he was also a warrior. That's why they called him Wóptuȟ'a. He had a "chip" of power from every world that he visited. So we just stay with the good side, the healing side. It's impossible to describe all of him. People won't understand.

The Winged People

In his younger days, while he was in Canada, Wóptuȟ'a asked a question to his friends: "Where did we come from? Where did human beings come from?" So one day he had a visit from the winged people, eagles and hawks and different kinds of birds. They were all surrounding him. Back in those days, young men carried blankets or buffalo hides with them to wrap themselves up with. On this occasion, the eagles and the birds said that they're gonna take him on a journey. So they asked him to sit in the middle of that blanket, and the birds took each end of the hide and they flew away with him in the middle. As they flew away he realized that the earth was getting smaller and smaller, and as they passed the clouds, he arrived at another world. He didn't know where he was, but he arrived at another place and the winged people set him on the ground. It was a really beautiful place. There was green grass and children all over the place. Rainbows were in the clouds, in the skies. A really peaceful place. The children were sitting on rainbows, and they were happy. They were innocent. So he asked, "Where am I? Where did you guys bring me?" The whole world was filled with birds, everything from a hummingbird to a snow-bird to condors. The birds told him, "This is where human beings come from, before you went to the earth, this is where you came from. This is a sacred, heavenly place, where children come from. We prepare them here." The birds were given instructions to take care of humans.

The winged nation took him to that world. And the spirits of all those children that were there, they were innocent. They represented all nations. They were not just Indians. There were many different kinds of people, different colors, but they were all children. And they were all relatives. It's a beautiful place somewhere up in the skies above the clouds somewhere, where the birds land above the clouds. So they showed him where we came from. When the time comes, the winged will come and pick up one of those children, then fly off down toward the earth somewhere. At that time the child becomes a seed, it becomes a spirit being, and comes in between a man and a woman. That's how a woman conceives in her womb. That spirit places itself in there. That's the growth of a human being. That's where we come from. Originally all beings were born innocent. They weren't born bad. They didn't come here with hate. They didn't come here angry or mean. They all came as innocent children.

So the birds, the winged people, created that place. Children are created there. Before they come to this world, they go into the woman's womb as a seed, and a child is picked from that world and sent down here. So we come through the mother earth. We come through the woman, and we journey into manifestation, into the world that we live in now. Children are born innocent. They don't have any sin. They told him that it's us humans that made them bad. But every one of those children that came through a woman's womb and was born—they were born innocent. So even the worst criminal in the world that we live in today, when he first came here, he was innocent. There was no such thing as bad children. But it's the world that we live in, the earthly world, that makes people good and bad. So that was his experience with how the birds were given the responsibility to watch over the children. Then they sent him home. And part of the ways he was able to walk back down to earth. That was one of his experiences.

Crazy Horse

By the 1850s and '60s, Wóptuȟ'a started moving back this way, back with the Oglálas. There he met another man who had a story similar to his own as a young child. He had a pretty similar experience. So he became friends with that young man. His name was His Horse Good Looking, or His Good Looking Horse (Tȟašúŋke Oówaŋyaŋg Wašté), that was his name. His Horse Good Looking. They both grew up together. Later on he earned the name Crazy Horse. But his original name was His Horse Good Looking. They became good friends. They grew up as buddies. And then they grew so close that they made it a ritual. Back in those days, that's a real honorable thing. Nowadays, in English, we say "my friend," but maybe that's not true. Your friend might betray you. Friendship in the Native way is a lifetime journey.

Back in those days when they were teenagers, everybody wanted to be a great warrior. That was the dream of every Lakota—being a brave warrior. So His Horse Good Looking, or His Good Looking Horse, that was his dream. He wanted to be a great warrior. That's all he ever wanted. So when he went to *haŋbléčheya*, that boy had a dream. What looked like a hailstorm was coming at him, but none of the hailstones hit him. They surrounded him and hit the earth all around him. And when he came back down from the hill, he brought back a stone that had come to him after the hailstones all melted away. There was one stone left behind. So he brought that back, and Chips prepared it for him. He made a *wóthawe*, a medicine, for him, so he could become a great warrior. In his vision it looked like hail went to him, but if he wore this medicine, the bullets wouldn't hit him. He was hard to kill.

When he came to be known as a great warrior, his father, Worm, Waglúla, gave his ceremonial name, Crazy Horse, Tȟašúŋke Witkó, to his son. So he didn't use the name Good Looking Horse anymore. Now he took up the name Crazy Horse. And that's how he became well known, a war leader, a legend. So that was their story, the bond between those two. Later on, a lot of people wrote about Wóptuȟ'a-Chips being a friend of Crazy Horse. That's what kind of made his name come up a lot because Crazy Horse was a very prominent war leader, but what made him powerful was my great-great-grandfather Wóptuȟ'a. He got his medicine from there.

Today we all want to believe that Crazy Horse was a powerful holy man that came like a prophet and killed a lot of soldiers. In reality, it's not like that. The truth was he was just a regular, rough-around-the-edges kind of guy. He never wanted to be famous. He just wanted to fulfill his own personal dream of being a great warrior. He kind of accomplished that, and then he went home. The rest of it is fantasizing and romanticizing his life, Crazy Horse. He was never a holy man or anything like that. He wasn't into being a chief or a leader or anything like that. That wasn't on his mind. But his name made him powerful. My great-great-grandpa Wóptuȟ'a was a powerful medicine man, but he never said that Crazy Horse came to his altar after he was killed. He of all people could have said that and we would have all believed it, but he never said, "My friend Crazy Horse showed up." He never told anybody that. Maybe he did. Maybe he didn't. We'll never know. But if he did, I think he would have told us.

The Ghost Dance

Wóptuȟ'a's father's name was Iron Whistle, Tašiyótȟaŋka Máza. Iron Whistle's father's name was Walks with the Ghost, Wanáǧi ób Máni, or Ghost Hail. He was a holy man, but he wasn't like Wóptuȟ'a. They say that he encountered the ghost people and married one of them. A woman was brought back from the dead. So the children of Ghost Hail, his descendants, they don't talk about him. So we are prohibited from talking about them guys. We don't share that information. But that's how Wóptuȟ'a was able to obtain power, because his grandma came back from the dead. And Wóptuȟ'a's grandfather was the one that started the Lakota version of the Ghost Dance.

It wasn't originally called the Ghost Dance. Lakota people never called it the Ghost Dance. Most people have no idea what it really was. It's not a ritual that makes white men disappear. It was a sacred dance. The government was told that it was going to make the white man disappear. That came from the Indian Christians to make sure that the government used its authority to stop it. Instead of participating and trying to save that sacred connection, they condemned it. That's why people don't want to talk about the Ghost Dance anymore. It put a lot of fear into people. So a lot of our own people never heard about the true meaning of the Ghost Dance. They went along with the bad things that were written about it. That's why we're now in a world of confusion. That kind of happened with a lot of our ceremonies.

It was a powerful ceremony. It was a connection. And then it went underground.

Have you ever lost someone somewhere in your lifetime? If you've ever lost somebody, what if you had the opportunity to visit with them? What if you went somewhere in Indian Country, and they said, "Okay, you can talk to that person that you loved. Maybe you can ask them something. You can tell them that you love them and still think about them." The Ghost Dance reconnected people with their lost loved ones. It was a dance, but it was also a ritual. When you Ghost Dance, you have to pick one person out of your life. It has to be only one. You can't say, "I want to see all my people." You can't say that. That's a rule. You only get to see one person that went on to the other world. It was an honor to be with the relatives that went on to the other world. That's the only reason why we do it, to find out information, find out history, and renew the love that you have for your ancestors. It's like they're just in the other room. You just walk in there and talk to them and say, "I love you. How are you doing?," and they say, "I'm doing okay," and then they go back over there. There's more details about how it came, but I don't think we'll be able to share that. It's forbidden to be told.

So that is how the Ghost Dance was born. They say that it was headed in a different direction when it went underground. It was headed where you could see your future generations, your nephews, and grandsons, and what they were going to look like in the future, a hundred years from now. You were never going to meet them, but you'd be taken on a journey, and you'd be able to see what they look like. You could leave a message with them. You could write a message on the wall, saying, "All right, you can see that we both did it and we came back." It was headed that way. They say that Wóp-tuȟ'a made a sign on a hill. Wóptuȟ'a went on a future journey and saw all of us, what we look like, and what our voices were going to be like. And then he came back to his world. And then he went on.

The Ghost Dance stopped in the 1800s, when Ghost Hail passed away. He promised it would return someday. At first, they kept it going, but the magic started to go away. The connection with the ancestors didn't happen anymore. They were only supposed to do it once a year or once every other year. They weren't supposed to do it all the time. But they got addicted. They liked the power of seeing their relatives, so they kept it up, and pretty soon it got out of hand, so the ancestors from the other side said, "We're not gonna come anymore because you didn't listen to instructions." And then one day they tried it again, but no ancestors came. So they put it away for a while, and other people tried to revive it, with a lot of the dancing, but they couldn't do the ceremony where they got to see their relatives. They couldn't do that, so they were looking for the source that started it. Around the late 1880s, somebody tried to revive it.

Two guys named Short Bull and Kicking Bear were part of the Ghost Dance delegation. It was a society, and they were able to obtain traveling money so they could catch the train to look for a guy named Wovoka in Paiute country, Shoshone-Paiute country. They thought he had the power to do the Ghost Dance, just like Wóptuȟ'a's grandpa. They thought that maybe he might have returned in that tribe. But it didn't happen that way. Wovoka kept them for about a month over there, and they found out that he was kind of like a hoax. He wasn't the real deal. Wovoka was not even his real name. His real name was Jack Wilson.

So they had a new Ghost Dance, but it was a different version. But it came really strong. They started practicing this Ghost Dance everywhere, all the Húŋkpaphas, Oglálas, and Cheyenne River people, they were practicing this Ghost Dance. So the Christian Indians kept filing complaints against the Ghost Dance practitioners. They were naming off names and giving them to the authorities and government. Pretty soon the Christian Indians convinced the government that these were dangerous ceremonies, so they put a moratorium on Ghost Dancing. They stopped it, arresting people that kept it going.

It was the Christian Indians that sent out a telegram to Washington through their agent. And the Indian agent at that time, McLaughlin, they told him a lie. They said, "These people are Ghost Dancing so someday all the white people will disappear." At first he didn't really care. He thought that was just a myth. But they kept on him, and so finally he sent a telegram to the secretary of the interior in Washington and all the way to the higher-ups. So they issued an order that came all the way from the top, to arrest people doing the Ghost Dance. So they started arresting people whose names popped up. That's how Sitting Bull got killed, for supporting the Ghost Dance. He was one of the supporters of the Ghost Dance, so the Indian police went to arrest him in the middle of the night in

December. Something happened, and Sitting Bull ended up getting killed. And then they started arresting everybody. A guy named White Owl or Red Owl—he's also known as Bigfoot from Eagle Butte, Cheyenne River—took off toward the Pine Ridge Reservation, trying to seek refuge under Red Cloud. But they didn't make it. They all got arrested at Wounded Knee, and then they all got massacred. So the Ghost Dance became a controversy. People died. So they didn't want to talk about it too much. It stayed underground.

*

The teaching of the Ghost Dance was to let us know that when a human being dies, they don't die forever. They go somewhere. Our people never talked about "death," *wičhúŋte*. That's just a modern Lakota word that came out in the 1950s. Before that we used to say *ománi*, "we travel." We go to another world. When you *íníčhaǧe*, *oúŋčhaǧe*, this means you manifest. So when a child arrives from a mother's womb, they'll say, "*hey, ake onji he*," "somebody manifested," came into our world. And when somebody died, we don't say, "They died," we say, "*oh, waŋná kigle yo*," he went on to another world. That means it's not over, we still carry their consciousness, their voice, in our mind, in our consciousness, where it rests, loud and clear. It's like we recorded it, so when the time's right, you'll hear that voice again. *Hó*. Our voice is called *hó*. *Wičháhó* is a human voice. It's very sacred. Once you hear it, it stays in your mind forever, you don't forget. Sometimes when you sleep, that voice that you heard will activate itself in your consciousness and you'll have a dream about your relatives. They'll come into your dream.

There is a part of our brain that records and maintains sound, kind of like a tape recorder. It's like a little computer chip in your mind that collects voices. The sound goes in there, and it stays in there. Every day you hear thousands of sounds. Some of those sounds—you don't even hear it—but your consciousness still catches it. You didn't hear it, but you still caught it. That is our belief. That's what we were taught. So when they tell you to say, "Listen," they'll say *a*, and then they'll say *ná*, and *hó*, the guttural in there, *hó*, and then the last part of it is *pta*, so you say *a-ná-ǧo-pta-ŋ*. That's telling you to "listen." It means "listen," but the word *anáǧoptaŋ* is attached to the word *naǧóya*. *Naǧóya* means "recording, record." So the two are connected together. So they say we have a natural recorder in our brain. Sometimes an ear doesn't catch a sound, but the mind catches it. The white man calls it "unconsciousness." We were told that we collect our loved ones' voices. They spiritually stay with us. So when our relative passes away, the body is no more, but the spirit is alive. That's why they always tell us, "You walk with your ancestors, you walk with your people." When I first heard that, I was young, so I'd look around for them, but what they meant was that they're inside of you. And they'll stay there forever.

I can still hear my grandpa's voice if I want to. Or my grandma. Or my father. We don't do that, but if you ever miss your relatives, you can do what we call *tamahoon-wóčhekiye*, "praying inside of your body," talking to your relatives inside your body. But they discourage us from doing that. You want to let your relatives be at peace. Leave them alone. Don't bother them. There's a belief there that we don't talk about our ancestors too much. Because you're disturbing their rest. We mourn, but we end it. We put it away. We don't mourn forever. But of course we're all human. We miss our relatives. So when a relative dies, they never really die. They just go on a different journey. But we keep them in our consciousness. We carry their voice in our unconsciousness. Our relatives have never left us. They didn't die. They just went to another world. Their bodies stopped functioning and went back to the earth. But their voices live on in our memory, in our unconsciousness. Your mind and natural recording system kept those. That little place in our mind is a storage place for all the people we've known in the past. I know if I heard my grandpa's voice, I would know it's him. He's resting in there somewhere. That other world exists. We're in-between. I always hear about relatives who are dying. When they're near death, they can hear other relatives' voices or sometimes even see them. It's because their unconsciousness has awakened and sends out the signal that they're in distress and ready to make a journey.

And they appear. They reawaken themselves inside of you. You start seeing them. And when your body stops functioning, their voices become a reality. Then you will see them for sure. You'll join them. And then you'll go to the other world.

So we were taught that our voices are really sacred. The voice, in Lakota, is called *hó, wičháhó, wíŋyaŋ wičháhó, wíŋyaŋ tahó,* woman's voice, man's voice. *Hokšíla tahó* is children's voice. All sacred. So there's no word for orphan in our language. There are no orphans in the spirit world. So even though Wóptuȟ'a's dad died when Wóptuȟ'a was around eight or nine, his mother's brother, his uncle, raised him. So physically, biologically, he didn't have a dad, but at the same time he did have a dad, somebody that raised him like a father. And when Wóptuȟ'a passed away, I'm pretty sure he met his biological father. He reunited with him, but he also met more than just his siblings. He met relatives every day. Pretty soon, our world wouldn't even mean anything to him. That's the spirit world. We might look at a young child as an orphan, growing up without a mom and dad, but if you look at it again, he's not an orphan. He still has his mother's and his father's voices in his consciousness, in his mind and brain. They never left him. He has to figure out how to physically be alone in the world, but he still has all his relatives inside him. So he's not really a lost soul. So there's two kinds of realities that we live with. The first reality is that we're all connected with our ancestral world. And no one ever left anyone.

We don't realize that we're in other peoples' bodies, our spirit, my voice. That's the same way with all the people you knew in your life. We think that they're dead and gone, but a part of them is still with you. They never left you. That's natural law. We think we're alone, but we're not alone. We're carrying our ancestors with us. So if you have a grandma, or a great-grandma, or loved ones in your past life, they're all collectively resting themselves inside your brain. And when you're in a near-death situation like a life-and-death crisis, some of those loved ones are going to come alive and warn you. They'll come alive and say, "Hey," a little voice inside of you will say, "Watch out, hey, hey," or you'll even dream about them. You'll wake up and wonder, saying, "Gee, I dreamt about this guy." Or "I dreamt about my mom like she never left." That's because she never left. She was in your brain all that time. That's an old Lakota tradition.

When someone passes over, the spirit divides itself into four parts. It goes four ways. Eventually it all comes back together, but it goes four parts when you die. One of the four parts goes to your loved ones. Your spirit goes in there. So the voice that you carry from your ancestors, when that person dies, the ancestral voice receives that spirit, it goes right to that place. It just grabs onto that, and now that voice becomes a being inside of you. The other part of the spirit goes to the spirit world. Another part of the spirit goes to the places where you've been before. You travel for a while, and backtrack everything. The other one goes into the future. It just floats off somewhere out there. It goes off in four parts, but in time they all reconnect back together into one spirit being. That's why they call it *íčhimani*, a "journey."

Sometimes the spirit of a dead human still has some connection and attachments to the life he's left behind, so they stay in this world as a ghost. A ghost was once a human being, a human life, the inner life of the human being. So if they hear music that they used to hear, they'll go to where the music is at. Or if your voice is something that they're used to hearing, they might follow that voice, they might follow you. If you show an image, or play a voice recording, of a person that's left, because of the tone of the voice, if he's around that area, he might show up. He might be nearby, following the sound of his own voice or that of his loved ones. That's why we burn cedar to keep unwanted spirit beings from coming around, the bad ones, the unhealthy ones. Most ghosts have bad energy. Somebody might have lived a bad life as a killer, robber, murderer, or rapist. When he dies, his spirit stays with him. So being a ghost is being stuck between the ghost world and the human world. It's not like in the movies where ghosts look like horrible skeletons and ugly-looking monsters with blankets wrapped around them, floating around. It doesn't happen that way. That's just something made up. In reality, they'll show up like a normal person. They might show you the way they were in this world when they were alive. But it's their energy that you have to worry about. The common ghost is a human being. It doesn't mean that he's powerful. It doesn't mean that he's sacred.

Wóptuȟ'a's grandfather, Ghost Hail, was able to talk to the ghost world, the ghost people, but he wasn't a healer. He had a ritual, and he could do a ceremony that allowed people in our world to talk to relatives that went on to the other world, but that had nothing to do with healing. A ghost healer might be able to find the spirit of a human that could do some wonders or heal people, but that's really hard to find because most ghost spirits are around because they're not able to go to the other world. They're stuck here. But the spirit friends that Wóptuȟ'a had, they were nonhuman. They came from a different world.

A Visit to Washington

After the Indian ceremonies were outlawed in 1883, the intelligence department of the United States government wanted to know how the Lakota defeated them at the Battle of the Little Big Horn. Wóptuȟ'a was known as the master of the art of war. He didn't participate in the battle. He strategized. Lakota warriors were unknown, invisible people. They were not out in the front. Their names were never revealed. To this day, no one really knows who the warriors were that successfully defeated the Seventh Cavalry. A lot of people claimed to have participated in the Battle of the Little Big Horn, but many of the warriors, the people that actually went to war, remained hidden. And they died that way. Nobody knows. They were a mystery. None of them were ever killed by the U.S. soldiers. The U.S. soldiers claimed victory over massacring elders, women, and children like Wounded Knee, but those were after the peace treaties were signed.

So the government really wanted to find out about the power of Lakota warfare, and they searched for Wóptuȟ'a, and when they finally got a hold of him, they took him back to Washington. The government was full of questions. They could not understand

the power and the mystery of Wóptuȟ'a. So the government—
you know, they always have to test things, and research, and they
always have to have proof—put Wóptuȟ'a to the test. They brought
to him a blind kid from New York City and a boy who couldn't
walk and was confined in a wheelchair, from Philadelphia. They
planned it that way. They also brought a woman who was mentally
ill. They brought them to Washington and asked Wóptuȟ'a if he
could help them. They wanted to see how he worked and what his
methods were. So he told them that he needed to do a two-night
ceremony, that he should not be disturbed, and that the patients
be brought to him.

After those two nights were over, the blind boy could see, the
boy in the wheelchair could walk, and the mentally ill woman was
well. So the government was amazed by this, but they knew that
they couldn't own the energy of this man. Still, they respected him
and gave him an official government license, sort of like a procla-
mation that no one was to bother him or his children while they
were doing ceremonies. We still have that document license today
allowing Wóptuȟ'a to continue performing ceremonies. So even
though Lakota ceremonies were outlawed, Wóptuȟ'a was given a
license, a protection order, permission, a permit to continue his
healing ceremonies. And instead of sending him to Florida, which
they had planned to do, he was able to show them that his power
worked. So they sent him back home on a train as far as Omaha,
Nebraska. The government officials bought him a wagon and a team
of horses. They also gave him a bunch of supplies like tents and
cookware. Wóptuȟ'a, his wife, and his oldest son rode that wagon
all the way from Omaha back to the Indian reservation in Kyle.

After Wóptuȟ'a returned to the reservation, he settled in the area
east of Kyle. This became known as Wóptuȟ'a's medicine territory,
the Wóptuȟ'a zone. Anyone within those boundaries could not be
disturbed while they were doing ceremony. Outside of that, the
ceremonies were prohibited. Later on, Wóptuȟ'a's sons lived in
Wanblee, so they were also given that permission, too. So even
when our ceremonies were outlawed, nobody bothered our family.

Wóptuȟ'a was still considered a prisoner of war and was not allowed to leave the reservation. Sometimes he would sneak off and go to the Black Hills, dig medicines and stuff like that, but for the most part of his life he just stayed on the reservation.

Encouraging Bear

In the 1890s Wóptuȟ'a was in the Black Hills after a lightning storm had burned parts of the Hills. He was on his way back toward the reservation and his log cabin east of Kyle when he found a little dog, a little puppy that was whining around a tree, lost. It was a little tiny puppy. So Wóptuȟ'a looked around, but he didn't see the mother. No dog or nothing lying around. So he picked up the puppy and put him across his lap. When he was riding back, not very far from where that little dog was, he found a dead bear. Somebody had shot him. So that little puppy turned out to be a little bear cub! But now that he knows that the mother was killed, Wóptuȟ'a brought him back to the reservation and raised him, taking care of him. That little bear grew up to be a kind of pet, a friend. He behaved gently, but he was still a bear. That didn't change. The bear got used to humans, but he's still a bear, and someday in a bad mood, he might hurt somebody. There's a mystery about the bears. So they lived together in his cabin, and by the time the bear was a year old, he could understand the Lakota language.

Wóptuȟ'a knew that he was getting up there in age and he was not going to be able to take care of that bear forever, so he was preparing to take him back to the forest, to the Black Hills, and let him be. But the bear wouldn't leave him, he'd always come back. He would take him to the woods, and he'll go back to his cabin, but by the time he gets back to his cabin, the bear's already there. So he couldn't get rid of him. So he gave up the idea of getting rid of him. He figured, "Well, if he's staying, and if I ever leave this world, he'll just have to figure out a way to get along."

And here one of the Indian agents came from Washington to check on Wóptuȟ'a. They kept a close eye on him. He noticed that there was a bear in his house. So the Indian agent was really curious about that bear. He says, "How did you get it?" Wóptuȟ'a told him the story about how he saved the bear's life, how he was kind of like a son to him. But, he said, "I'm getting old, and I'm worried about him. We've got to find a better place for him to be." So the Indian agent said, "I'll take him from you, and I'll raise him. I'll make sure that he's well taken care of." So Wóptuȟ'a talked to the bear and says, "You have to go home with this man. He'll take good care of you." So the bear left with the Indian agent, but before he left, the agent said, "How can I repay you? How much money do you want for him?" Wóptuȟ'a said, "He's my son, I can't sell him. But you can take care of him, promising that you'll do good. But you can help us with one thing," he says. "You put us on the reservation and you took away our language, and our culture, and our way of life. Our people are sad all the time. So what we would really like is to have our powwow again, our Indian gathering. There's nothing threatening about that." So the Indian agent said, "What does it take to have your pow-wow?" He says, "For the government to not interfere with us getting together. We need our beads, and our feathers, and bells, and all the stuff it takes to have the powwow to come back to our reservation."

So Wóptuȟ'a said goodbye to the bear as they left on the wagon. They got on a train in Rushville, Nebraska, and went back east. He never saw the bear again. And here about a month later a big wagon train came from Washington and arrived in Rushville. Soldiers came with several wagon trains full of Indian stuff, bells and beads and feathers, and they returned the powwow to the Indian reservation. But the government wanted to make sure that powwows are managed according to government standards. They wanted to monitor it, so at every powwow, the government wanted the Indians to raise the flag signifying that there's peace between the nations. And the Indian veterans that were scouts back then were honored for their services. So around the 1890s, the powwow came back to Indian Country because of a bear. And Wóptuȟ'a earned the name Encouraging Bear. That was his Indian name, because of that bear.

The End of Wóptuȟ'a's Days

Toward the end of his life, around 1913 or 1914, Wóptuȟ'a stayed with the Randall family in Hisle and entertained children. That was how he lived his last days of life. He would perform tricks, magic tricks, for the kids, and folks from all over the country. Even as far away as back east, white people, Indians, they would come to see Wóptuȟ'a. So they built him a little shrine, like a little place where he could do that. He performed prayer services, and then he would entertain the kids. And the kids loved it. They came to get blessed by him, but he would show them magic. He would bring coyotes or wolves or animals, so the kids could pet them. They'd get their blessings that way, and then they'd go away. So a lot of people traveled to Hisle. That was what he was known for, entertaining children. So he pretty much retired, but that was his role toward the end. He really didn't do any ceremony or anything.

He was really happy living in Hisle. Both of his wives had passed away, so he was a single widower. He spent most of his time entertaining children. He became a renowned storyteller and put on magic shows. He'll have a drum there. One of his old wolf friends would show up, or a bear, or the birds, the eagles. And he'd let the children pet them. The snakes were his relatives, too. They also liked to spend time around him. And that scared people. They didn't want to come around him as much because there's always a snake wherever he's at, but they weren't harmful. He used their ability to heal certain illnesses, too.

A lot of people came to interview him. One of the last interviews that he did was in 1913. A *wašíču* guy named Rickerson was interviewing a lot of Indians across Indian Country. He interviewed Wóptuȟ'a about him and his days with Crazy Horse.

So that's how the end of Wóptuȟ'a's days were.

One of the things that he was also really well known for, according to my father and grandfather's stories, was his hackamore. They call it *šúŋka itéha wakȟáŋ*, hackamore, a muzzle for the horse's nose, a halter type, he makes those. The hackamore was used to put on wild horses, and once the hackamore was put on the horse, within a day that horse would be as gentle as a friendly dog. So because of that, a lot of the folks around here would bring their horses to him, borrow that hackamore, and put it on their wilder horses. And they said that within a day or so, the horse would be really tame like a dog. He would never get wild again. So it saved a lot of cowboys a lot of heartache. Instead of breaking a horse, they'd put that hackamore on there, and they'd get tame. So Wóptuȟʼa was not a cowboy, he's just an old man, but when he made that halter, he broke more horses than any cowboy in Indian Country! When he passed away, the Randall family kept that halter, but it didn't work anymore. They just kept it as a souvenir. Wóptuȟʼa never passed on the sacred hackamore teaching.

Around 1915 the government tried to force him to get baptized by cutting off his rations. Everybody got rations from the government, but they wouldn't give them to Wóptuȟʼa or provide medical care, and the family that was taking care of him got mad about that, but that was the policy with the government and the Christians, so he agreed to be baptized. He didn't resist. He was dying anyway. He said, "Go ahead and baptize me if you want." He had no idea what that was. He had no idea what was happening, so he agreed to it. One day they took him to the church and they baptized him. All he knew was they prayed for him, so he was happy. But he never practiced that religion. So in 1915 he was baptized in a Catholic church. With that baptismal card, the government issued him food. He never ate it. He never once ate issued food. He always had his own diet, but the family ate it, the ones that took care of him.

A few months later he passed away. He died in Hisle in 1916. At the end of his life, the Catholic church tried to claim him as a member of their church, to say, "Well, he was a Christian. Wóptuȟʼa was a Catholic Christian," that he renounced his Indian ways. But that kind of helped him, too, because when he died, it was the Catholic church that bought his headstone. They knew that he was important to the people, so the Catholic authorities bought a big, tall headstone. It came by train to a place called Interior, and some of the family members put it on a wagon and took it all the way to Hisle and put it up. That was in the 1920s or '30s. And it's been there ever since. So the Catholic church kind of helped keep him alive. That was a good thing they did, because if they didn't, maybe we wouldn't know where he was buried. If you go to Hisle today, you'll see it standing there. It's about four or five feet high.

That was the story of Wóptuȟ'a, about who he was and how he was able to make a difference in a lot of peoples' lives. I think his life is comparable to any holy man in the world. But he's still a human being. He's still a grandpa. He's still a husband, an uncle, a relative. But there'll never be another Wóptuȟ'a in the world again. There'll never be another one.

Fig. 1. Wóptuȟ'a-Chips and Feels Around the Pipe, in Kyle, South Dakota, circa 1911. Courtesy of Nebraska State Historical Society Photograph Collections.

Fig. 2. Richard Moves Camp, Wóptuȟʼa grave site, Hisle cemetery, Hisle, South Dakota. Photo by Simon J. Joseph.

Fig. 3. Tȟahúŋska, son of Wóptuȟʼa, circa 1890. Courtesy of Richard Moves Camp.

Fig. 4. Samuel Chips Moves Camp, 1910. Courtesy of Richard Moves Camp.

Moves Camp and Horn Chips   **3**

In the old days, it was normal for Indian leaders to have more than one wife. It was customary. It was not considered polygamy. Many Indian leaders had more than one wife. And not just Lakotas but many tribes. Quanah Parker had five wives. Spotted Tail had five wives. There's a reason why they had more than one wife. The role has a sacred meaning. It's not about sex. It's not about having a lot of wives. Back in those days, it's the wife that chooses the man. You can't refuse if a woman asks you to be her husband. That's how men ended up having more than one wife, because you can't turn them down. Nowadays in the literature, it's thought that the men picked their own wives and sort of carried them off. But it wasn't that way. If you earned the reputation of being a good man, a woman might ask you to become her husband. Leaders could have more than one wife. But each wife had a role and a responsibility, so there was no such thing as jealousy. They all understood that the family circle had many roles. Everybody respected each other. That came to an end in the 1880s. The Christians lobbied against it, and the government enforced it. Indian men were only allowed to have one wife, one legal wife.

Wóptuȟ'a had two wives and seven children. They all lived in one *thióšpaye*. The government gave him land east of Kyle. That was his territory. Wóptuȟ'a's second wife's name was Feels Around the Pipe. In English, they call her Gap. Wóptuȟ'a got along with both of his wives. There was no jealousy, but my great-grandfather moved to Wanblee, Lip's Camp, and relocated there. That's how my great-grandfather earned the name Moves Camp (Tȟoká Éthi). They moved his camp. My great-grandfather James Tȟahúŋska Moves Camp and his younger brother Horn Chips, and their mother and their sister, moved away from Wóptuȟ'a's circle. Even though Horn Chips and Ťhahúŋska were still part of his family, Wóptuȟ'a's second wife and his children from that marriage moved to the Wanblee area, around here.

His oldest son, James, was now the head of the household. They're still part of the family, but the family circle was disbanded. So he was given the name Moves Camp. He took his mother, brother, and sister, and they moved to Wanblee. They joined Lip's Camp. That's how my great-grandfather earned the name Moves Camp, because he moved away from the circle. His Indian name was Ťhahúŋska. It's a spiritual name, Ťhahúŋska. It means "Depends On Him," dependability. That name came from a spirit, from his friend. A lot of people misunderstand his name. They think it meant "Leggings" because back in those days people wore those pants. They called them *húŋsko, ťhahúŋsko*, which means leggings, the things that cover your legs. So they mixed up the two, and they thought he was named after some kind of leggings. But Ťhahúŋska really means being dependable because he was now the head of the family.

Horn Chips

There was a reason why Ťhahúŋska, my great-grandfather, moved away from Wóptuȟ'a's camp. Originally, Ťhahúŋska's brother, Charles Horn Chips, was supposed to be his father's successor. That was the original intention. His father picked him when he was a young man. Wóptuȟ'a loved his youngest son of all the five sons. That was his favorite son. Horn Chips was going to be his successor. He was going to take over Wóptuȟ'a's work. Wóptuȟ'a started to train him. He was Wóptuȟ'a's youngest baby boy. So he was really favored. Wóptuȟ'a had a *wašíču* friend, a fur trader. He was good friends with the family. He called Wóptuȟ'a "brother." He liked Horn Chips as a little baby boy running around. That was the fur trader's favorite nephew, so he bought the boy a toy buffalo headdress, and he wore that around. That boy really loved that headdress. He played with it, and he even slept with it on. He never took it off. He wore it all the time. And as he grew up, he outgrew it, but the trader bought him another one because he wanted another one. And here one day he lost one set of those horns. One of the horns fell off, so that headdress only had one horn on it, but he still wore it. He just kept using it. So that's how he got his Lakota name "Horn," Ptehé. Horn Chips. One Horn Chips. So his nickname was Horn, because of that headdress, and his last name, of course, was Chips, so that's how he earned the name Horn Chips. People started calling him Ptehé. Later, that became his spirit name, Ptehé. So Horn Chips and Ťhahúŋska, their names were given to them by their spirit friends. They got their names from the spirit people. But it was a secret. A lot of people don't share their names back then.

Horn Chips was going to be his father's successor, but it didn't happen that way. He made a mistake. When Horn Chips was about nineteen years old, he got married to a woman from Allen, and they had one son, who died. But while they were married, Horn Chips had an affair with his wife's sister and got her pregnant. They had a daughter. Her name was Suzy, Suzy Horn Chips. She started out as an illegitimate child. Back in those days, especially with Wóp-tuȟa's work, if you do something like that, it was unacceptable. So when Wóptuȟa found out what happened, he went to ask him, "I heard these words about you. Is it true?" And you know he can't lie to his dad because he's gonna know it anyway, so he says, "Yes, father, I did. I don't know what made me do that, but I did. I had a relationship with my wife's sister, and we have a daughter." So the old man got mad. He was really mad at him. He says, "There's only one thing I can say about that. You're not worthy to take over my work. You're going to always be doing that. You're gonna always be like that. This is not an accident. This is a habit you're going to have." Horn Chips always had a problem with womanizing. He was always accused of being with different women. He was a real nice-looking man.

So Wóptuȟa took his power away from Horn Chips. He hit him on the back, and here a white stone fell out of Horn Chips's mouth and landed on the ground. The old man picked it up and says, "From now on you're not going to have my power. You're not going to have anything to do with my work. You're not worthy to have my power." And it went away. He was not the guy to be his dad's successor. It was because of his behavior, the way he behaved. His desire, his weakness was stronger. So they had a quarrel. They had a falling-out, he and his father. And Wóptuȟ'a took his power away from Horn Chips at a young age, probably like fifteen.

So that was family history. You can't do stuff like that when you're doing the ceremonies. You've got to be careful. It falls back on you. I guess it kind of says the same thing in the Bible somewhere: If you do something to others, it'll come back on you. It's natural law, consequence. I think the old man Wóptuȟ'a knew that if Horn Chips still had his father's power, it would have been worse. He couldn't fight off the temptations from tempting women. And it probably would have been worse. That's why he had nothing to do with it. So Horn Chips got punished. He could never have his father's power. He's out of his father's circle. That's his punishment. Because of that quarrel, Tȟahúŋska took up for his little brother and they both moved away. But later they made amends and became good family again.

Yuwípi Man

Today, the majority of the healers on the reservations, they all do Yuwípi ceremonies. But they have no idea where the ceremony came from. They have no idea how Yuwípi came into Lakota country. A lot of people think that Wóptuȟ'a was a Yuwípi man, but actually it was my great-grandfather Tȟahúŋska and his brother, Horn Chips, who founded the Yuwípi ceremony.

Tȟahúŋska didn't really want to do any kind of Indian medicine work. Instead, he joined the Episcopal Church. I don't know if he was a priest, or whatever they call them, lay readers or ministers or practitioners or something, but he was doing that for a while. That was how he earned money to support his younger brother, sister, and their mother. So they were taking care of the church in Wanblee. That church is still standing there, since the late 1800s. It got remodeled a couple of times, but it's still standing there. Then he joined the Indian police. I don't know how they got paid, but it was from the federal government. At that time the captain of the Indian police was a man known as Sword, Captain Sword of the Indian police. There were a lot of former Indian scouts and warriors that joined the police force. They were given a rifle, a pistol, a horse, a badge, and a uniform. And they patrolled on horses. So Tȟahúŋska worked around the area of Kyle and Manderson. They kind of scattered all over.

And here there was a medicine man. They didn't call them medicine men back in those days. He was just a man with special power. His name was Holy Arrow. Waŋhíŋkpe Wakȟáŋ. He had different names at different times, Holy Arrow, Points Arrow. He got the name Waŋhíŋkpe Wakȟáŋ when he realized that the spirits he worked with were sacred and could do good things. Before he knew that, his name went by Points Arrow. He lived by himself, and he kept his secret power to himself. He lived in the Manderson–Wounded Knee area. But he was a single man. He didn't have a wife. Earlier in his life, Holy Arrow and his family were attacked by Pawnee warriors. His wife and children were killed. But somehow Holy Arrow managed to survive. He was left for dead, tied up in a tree, but after a while, he came back to life. His heart started beating again. He was barely alive, but he was still there. He came back to life. And here, he felt that some people underneath him noticed that he was breathing, and managed to climb up the tree, cut him down, and bring him down. So they dragged him along for a while. He felt like there were a lot of little people, hundreds of them holding him up. He was only above the ground a few inches. But they were taking him somewhere. They took him to what felt like a cave in the mountains. He heard the river down below. He lay there for a while, and pretty soon, they were doctoring him. They were fixing him, little by little. Pretty soon they started unraveling him.

He noticed that the people who saved him were not human. They were different beings. At night he felt like there was a whole bunch of people around him, but during the day they'd be gone. At evening time, they'd come back. That went on for days, weeks, and months.

Eventually, he was able to recover and started to make relationship with his new friends. They helped him survive. Eventually they became friends. By that time, he really got to know them. He knew then that they weren't human. They came from another world. It took a total of 405 days for him to fully recover. They brought him fresh water and made him different herbs and teas. They brought him different kinds of food. Later on, when he recovered and was able to get around on his own, he was able to go hunt and provide for himself. But he carried a lot of pain and sorrow, because his wife and his children were killed. He felt the guilt of surviving, but after those 405 days they told him, "Go back to your people. You can't stay with us forever." So they helped him out, brought him back to the world.

Finally, he made it back to Oglála country. By that time the reservation was established, so he moved back with his band. People were surprised that he was alive, but they were also not very surprised, because that was common in those days. People sometimes died, but they don't bury them right away because sometimes they come back after a while. So he came back and moved to the Wounded Knee–Manderson area. He built a cabin and lived a regular life, but he was very resentful about not having his family. He was full of anger and resentment for losing his wife and children. He carried a lot of pain. So even though he had friends, he never thought about doctoring or healing anybody. He would just have them do things that he wants. He'll have them go get stuff that he wants. And those little people, they will get it. They will steal him a horse. They will steal him some good items that he likes. They will go get it. If he likes money, they'll find some money out there and they'll sneak it back to him. His friends would also steal other people's women. He would have his little friends bring women to him. So a lot of people don't like him. That's why he stayed alone. I guess he wasn't a good-looking guy, either. He just had his friends. Some of the prettiest girls in Lakota country, he could somehow use his magic to bring them to him. He'd be with them for a little while, and then he'd let them go home. So he was kind of known as a dangerous person.

Nobody liked him. He was not a friendly guy. Nobody can just go out there. But he was still a tribal person, so he's still entitled to his monthly food rations, but it took the police to take care of him. Even some policemen would come back and say, "Wow, I'm not going back out there again. He chased us off. He's not a nice guy."

One day they chose my great-grandpa to go out there and help him, to deliver his food. Tȟahúŋska took a wagon out there and delivered food for him. But Holy Arrow wasn't mean to Tȟahúŋska. He was okay with him. He allowed him to come in the house, drink coffee, and talked to him. Tȟahúŋska checks on him and brings him his mail, food, and rations. He managed to get along real well with him. The guy never had a family, so Tȟahúŋska was a good candidate for a *huŋká* son. As time went on, they became good friends. Holy Arrow was an older person, and Tȟahúŋska was a young man who became like a son to him. And he trusted him more and more, so when Tȟahúŋska goes out there, he's welcome. It's kind of like his second home. Pretty soon the relationship got even better, and Holy Arrow started to trust him with his friends. He allowed Tȟahúŋska to see his friends come around and do this miracle, magic work. Moves Camp realized that this Holy Arrow had some power, a different kind of medicine. It wasn't about healing, but when people went missing, Tȟahúŋska would go ask him, "What happened to this person?" Because he was also a policeman. So he convinced police officials to go over there and give him money and ask to have a ritual, and Holy Arrow would find these people for them. He solved a lot of crimes in those days.

One day there was an epidemic. Everybody was getting sick from tuberculosis. Tuberculosis was killing everybody. So Horn Chips and Tȟahúŋska both went out there and helped him with ceremony, and they had a sweat. Tȟahúŋska asked him, "Uncle, have you ever asked your friends if there's any kind of medicine for this tuberculosis?" They call it *hoȟpa khuže*, the "coughing illness." Holy Arrow said, "You know, I never thought about it, but let's ask them." So they had a ritual, they had a ceremony, and these little friends brought an herb from somewhere. And they said, "Give this to one of those people that have the illness." So they gave it to somebody who had the illness, and that person got well. Just like that. They got well. So then more and more people started going to Tȟahúŋska. They'd say, "Wherever you got this medicine, it really works," even the doctors. Tȟahúŋska would say, "It wasn't me, it was my uncle, Holy Arrow. He's the one. You have to get the blessing from him to get this medicine." So they asked Holy Arrow in a good way, and he authorized them to use that herb as a cure. And sure enough, within a year there was no tuberculosis on the reservation. It was a final cure. So that put Holy Arrow into a different position. Now he was important. He cured a lot of illnesses, and he became known as a doctor, an Indian doctor, because he took care of a lot of people and got them well.

As Holy Arrow grew older, he became well known, well respected, and needed. Toward the end of his life, the people around him realized how important he was. They needed his help. So now the government said this guy might be really useful. So they kind of made him like an official healer. He was not to be disturbed. So even though the ceremonies were outlawed, he was respected. But he was still angry. He was still bitter. So Tȟahúŋska said, "Uncle, you don't realize what you're saying, but your words are hurtful. And your attitude is hurtful. People are not going to like you. Not that it matters to you, but what you do is very important to the people. So you must find some healing for yourself." Holy Arrow thought about it for several days and said, "Nephew, you're right. I've been really angry for a long time. I need to get well."

So Tȟahúŋska and Horn Chips helped their uncle Holy Arrow. They put him on the hill. But it was his friends who came and doctored him. They fixed him up. He received a visit from the deer, the deer people. When he was on the hill, he had a visit from his wife who had died, who'd been killed. She came to him and says, "You really have to make peace. I'm in a good world. I'm doing well. Our kids are doing good in another world. But you're bitter. You're still stuck in those days, and you're not able to be happy. So you really need to come out of your anger." So she healed him. She showed him that she's not dead. She's just in another world. And then she turned herself into a deer and just walked away. But one of the things that she left for him was the tail of a blacktail deer. She left that on the ground. So he took it. And knowing it is from her, he held on to that for his healing. And from that day on, in Holy Arrow's tie-up ceremony, on the altar, you'll see the tail of a blacktail deer hanging there.

And the children that he was missing, those who'd been killed, they were eagles. They flew around and said, "We have always been watching you since we left you. You didn't know that. You were in a different place. You didn't know that. A number of times we've come to visit you, but you totally ignored us. But to let you know that we're here." The eagles were flying around him, so a feather, representing those two children, was placed on his altar as well. So now he had a personal healing. He had his family back now in his work. And those little rattles that rattle around represented those little men that come to him.

That's how the tie-up ceremony began.

The original name for the Yuwípi ceremony was hardly known. Nobody knew what that was. It was called the Little People's ceremony, the Little People's altar, because the man that started it, he had encountered some friends from that world, and that's how the whole thing came about. They're people just like us, except they have power. They have a tremendous amount of power, but they're curious about us. That's why they picked him. He died, but they saved his life, so he was no longer the same person that he was. He kind of became one of them.

In the Yuwípi ceremony, the man gets tied up. Being tied up represents being a dead man. When people died in the old days, that's how they'd tie them up and put them away. They'd put people up in a tree. And the person that founded the ceremony, he was dead. That's how they tied him up and put him away. So when he's released, he's back from the dead. He's freed. He's not tied up anymore. That's how it went. In the ceremony, they sing the songs and those little friends come over and do what they have to do.

But when it was time for him to pass in his eighties, he taught his adopted son, Tȟahúŋska, and gave the whole ritual to him. He gave him the power. He said, "You'll take over my work. But don't do any of the bad things that I've been doing. Stealing, stealing people's wives," and all that stuff that wasn't good. But he healed himself of all that. And he remained a good man when he finally passed away.

So Tȟahúŋska was kind of like the original founder. He made relatives with the person that really owned the Yuwípi ceremony. He was the one that really broke the barrier about making relatives with him. But Tȟahúŋska and Horn Chips were inseparable. They loved each other. And Horn Chips was supposed to be Wóptuȟ'a's successor, but it didn't turn out that way. So Horn Chips was really sad. He was heartbroken. He was crying when Tȟahúŋska came back from work. He says, "Who made my brother cry? He's crying all day." Nobody answered him. So finally he asked him, "*Misúŋ*, my brother, who hurt your feelings? What happened? Tell me what happened." And here he told his brother, "Our father took his power away from me. That's what really breaks my heart." Tȟahúŋska told his brother, "You know better. You're not a kid anymore. Those are not things to do. And you know he's right, you're no longer capable of doing his work, so I can't help you there." But because Tȟahúŋska loved his brother, he said, "You may not be able to use our father's teachings and medicine, but you can come with me and we'll learn from Holy Arrow and you'll still be able to do the things that you want, your dream to become a healer." So Tȟahúŋska introduced him to Holy Arrow. Both of them became friends.

Later, Tȟahúŋska put Horn Chips on the hill for three days, and at the end, Horn Chips was able to do the tie-up ceremony. Tȟahúŋska gave him the feather and tail. That all became Horn Chips's stuff. Tȟahúŋska loved his little brother, so when he was given the power to be Holy Arrow's successor, he turned some of that power over to Horn Chips, so Horn Chips could fulfill his desire to become a healer. As his older brother, Tȟahúŋska was kind of like his guide. He also played the role of a dad in his life by keeping him in line. So that was Tȟahúŋska's story.

Wanblee

After Wóptuȟ'a passed away in 1916, Ťhahúŋska and Horn Chips both went the Indian way, permanently. They lived in the Wanblee area most of their lives. The original founder of Wanblee, or Lip's Camp, was a man named Breast, Makȟúla. He had two sons. His oldest son's name was Lip. Phuté. Lip was Breast's successor. When Chief Breast passed away, Lip took over. Between Kadoka and Wanblee, there's an area of the Badlands where Lip's Camp first started out. Later, they moved because of a lack of adequate water. They moved upward toward the plateau where Wanblee's at now. But the original camp of Lip was on the Rosebud Reservation's boundaries, so they're Rosebudders, but then they moved to Oglála. So the Oglála band adopted the Lip's Camp into the Oglála band where Wanblee is located today.

It wasn't called Wanblee back then. It was just called Lip's Camp. The story was that Lip traveled to Washington DC and asked the Indian agents to help him establish Lip's Camp. A church, a school, a trading post, a post office. So they granted him permission to start it, and they sent some Indian agents to help set him up. So they had a post office in Wanblee, and a church was donated. That church was really old, from the 1890s. It was donated from some folks in Kadoka, and it took several teams and wagons to get that church across the river and moved to Wanblee. And then it stayed there ever since, and it's still there today. So that was an old Episcopal church. The first church. And then the first school was a few white buildings. It was real small. My dad was one of the ones that went to school there.

That was how Wanblee community or Lip's Camp started. And then after the school was started, the church, and then the post office and a blacksmith—those places where they work on horses—and a gas station, a little store, and then more and more non-Indians moving in town, so there was a pool hall. On the reservation, early days, even though alcohol was banned, beer was legal. Selling beer was like soda, because the beer at that time only had 3.2 alcohol, which is almost nothing. Nowadays if you drink beer you'd probably have to drink a whole case in order to get a little buzz off of that, but that's what they used for socializing. So Wanblee had a pool hall where people come and play pool and they sell 3.2 beer. And nobody ever got drunk, but what they found out was that the guy that was selling 3.2 beer was selling real beer on the side, under the table, black-market bootlegging real beer, so everybody was getting drunk. So that kind of ended that whole idea of a pool hall. But people used to come in town and do all that. Wanblee was a regular town. They had a theater, too. There was a time in the 1940s, Wanblee had its own theater. People go to movie nights. The first black-and-white movies and a gas station, and they had a hotel there, and they had two grocery stores and a restaurant. Somebody in Wanblee still has pictures of the old town site. So that's how it all got started.

A lot of people don't know that our high school wasn't named after Chief Crazy Horse, the war leader. It was originally named after Nellie Larrabee, Nellie Crazy Horse. When Crazy Horse was killed, his wife was a widow. Her name was Nellie Larrabee. She married White Squirrel, Wóptuȟ'a's half brother. So Nellie Crazy Horse and White Squirrel joined Wild Buffalo Bill show in Europe, and White Squirrel changed his name to Crazy Horse. He borrowed Nellie's name. So he was known as Crazy Horse. They got married later on and had children. So instead of all those children being named White Squirrel, their names were all Crazy Horse. So that's how the Crazy Horse kids came about. They moved to Wanblee, where the present-day Crazy Horse school is built. They lived right there. They had a cabin and an old homestead. So in 1974, '75, Wanblee was going to get a new high school. And I was on the student council. I was still in high school. So they asked us to come up with a name for a high school, so we were digging up names. We were going to call it *Phuté Owáyawa*. "Lip's School." Or somebody said to name it "Brown's." Or "Long Commander," all the original founders of the school. And then we interviewed an elder. His name was Ellis Cutt. He was ninety-nine years old, and he talked to us about history. He didn't speak English, and I was glad that I went because I heard most of it, and most of my classmates, they recorded it, but they didn't speak Lakota, so I understood what he was saying. But right where the high school is being built is where Mrs. Crazy Horse and White Squirrel lived. That was their home. And all along that hill there were many log cabins, so he said the appropriate name for the high school would be "Nellie Crazy Horse High School." So hearing it from him, the student council all voted, agreeing that our high school would be named after Mrs. Crazy Horse. And that's how that name came about, Crazy Horse High School.

In the 1880s the government issued an allotment act which cut up pieces of land and gave it to individual Indians instead of the whole reservation being reservation territory. They called it the Dawes Act. Horn Chips was given part of the butte. He had a big chunk of land, and then right next to it, his brother, where we live now, inherited about 480 acres. So all of that western part of Wanblee, all the way to the Badlands, that was Horn Chips and Moves Camp property at one time. That's how we ended up with the land west of Wanblee. That's how my grandfathers Ťhahúŋska and Horn Chips earned their community residence in Wanblee.

Eagle Nest Butte was a sacred mountain to the people. The guy that took care of that butte, that was his name, Waŋblí Hohpí. He was the original caretaker of that butte. People checked in with him before they'd go to use that butte in prayer. Then in the 1930s, the Christians, the Episcopal church, also started using that butte, so there was a road that went up there and a tower. The government used the tower as a fire lookout. They also put a phone line up there. So there was a tower in Rosebud, one in Wanblee, one in Allen, another one in Porcupine, and one toward Oglála. They kind of put them all across the reservation, those lookout towers. And they said that they were looking for fire. So in the 1930s, the Episcopal church put up a concrete altar on top of that butte. The remains of that altar are still up there today. It's just like a little cement block. The church used to gather up there and have services every year. Then they'd have a picnic up there. So they did that for a while until a child died of food poisoning and the church ended that whole idea of having services up there. But the Indians still secretly have their prayer, *haŋbléčheya*, services up there. They did it hidden, under the radar. So they named the Wanblee community after that butte. They changed the name from Lip's Camp to Wanblee community. So that's how we earned the name Wanblee.

Back in those days the white people and the Lakota got along well. At one time, everybody was on the same page, even white ranchers. They protected the medicine man. They understood that he was important and that he needed to be protected. That's what the white people and the Indians had in common back in the 1930s and 1940s. What brought them together was their belief in the Creator. That didn't cost any money. They didn't say, "Oh, that's for the Indians only." They didn't say that. They just said they were glad that they had something in common. They understood each other and they knew that God was real. They saw it. Some white people even spoke Lakota. It was a good generation. You didn't see much racism. In the 1930s and '40s, the whole world experienced the Great Depression. Everybody was broke. Everybody was poor. Everybody worked together. They all accepted each other as human beings. Back then, the white people living on the reservation, they shared the same land. There were no fences. So they came here and raised their cattle and they drew water from the same well. We understood each other because we all struggled. It was a difficult time.

So that's how I grew up with most of the white guys around here. They're all farmers. I went to school with some of them. And I rode horses all over the Badlands with a couple of them. They're no different from me. These white guys around here struggle with problems, too.

In the 1930s and '40s, Horn Chips made a *wašíču* friend. He was a white man. His name was George Frost. Somehow Horn Chips managed to give him the power to do ceremonies. He let him speak to them. So now there was a white man who could speak with them guys. He can talk to them. He can set up the altar. He'll call them and they'll show up. You can see them talking to him, but he didn't always know how to interpret their teachings to the Lakota. I remember seeing him come around in the 1960s. He was a good guy, probably one of the kindest men you'd ever meet. And Horn Chips had no problem making him a medicine man.

That proved that anybody can practice our spirituality. Anybody can do it. He spoke real well. If you closed your eyes, you probably couldn't even tell it was a white guy speaking. He spoke Lakota real well. It was always good to have him around, because he and his wife always brought stuff to cook. He likes to barbecue a lot. He loves ceremonies. So it was kind of fun to have him around. The bad side about it is that he'd buy liquor for the Indians because they couldn't buy liquor at the liquor store. So he became more than one kind of useful person! We loved him for the ceremonies, but on the other hand, our alcoholic relatives loved him, too!

He preached against it, though. He told them, "It's not good for you." He heard that from them, the spirits, so he would tell my relatives, "I can't be buying this for you forever. They're gonna get mad at me up there, you know." So they'd say, "Okay, George, just this one time only. We'll never ask you again." I was a little guy when all that was going on, seeing him around. I liked it because he brought me candy. He brought me goodies. I liked him for that. But he healed people. He was a bridge between two worlds. He spoke to the white people. He explained it real well, about these ways, whereas our people had a hard time explaining it. White folks knew. So when he showed up, they'd come around, too. He had a tent full of white people living outside, the other part Indian living on this side. But they all shared the same ceremony. They all had a good time. It was fun because when they all got together, time wasn't a factor. They could sing and pray all night. As long as those guys from the other world come, that's a blessing. That ceremony kept going on. Sometimes they'd take a smoke break, and they'd go back in there again, and start doing it again. People would take part in it, then go back to their house and sleep all day and try to get in the next night. But he had to earn it. There's no free ride for that. That guy went on the hill for four days. It didn't just come to him because they liked him. He had to qualify for it. But he had great teachers, though, Horn Chips and Ťhahúŋska.

The two brothers always got along real well. They grew up together. Horn Chips was never meant to be a Yuwípi man, but Ťhahúŋska loved his little brother and helped him through it. That's how much he loved him. As a matter of fact, he gave almost all of his power to Horn Chips. He says, "You do it." Ťhahúŋska does it, too, but not very often. He just kind of kept it low key. Horn Chips was the one who went to town with it. Toward the end of his life, Ťhahúŋska mostly kept to himself. He quit the police force and married a woman from Rosebud. That was my great-grandma Helen Kills. From that union, Ťhahúŋska had four children. His first son was my grandpa Sam Chips Moves Camp. Sam married a woman named Winnie Iron Rope. That's where my father came from. My father was the oldest. They all lived where I live now. In the 1930s, Ťhahúŋska's first wife, my Grandma Helen, died. So he married another woman named Walking Bull in the 1940s. She already had several children from another marriage, sons named Charlie, Henry, Daniel, and George, and a daughter named Victoria. They lived together here in Wanblee until Ťhahúŋska died when he was eighty years old, in October 1949.

The End of Horn Chips

Horn Chips got really actively involved in public. He was pretty famous. He was well known everywhere. He went around Rosebud and everywhere like that in Indian Country. People called him "the *Yuwípi* man." That was Horn Chips's name. It's not the method of the ceremony. Today the ceremony is called Yuwípi, but it was only Horn Chips who had that name. It was the Christian Indians of Wanblee who were making fun of him, giving him a hard time whenever he goes to town to buy supplies and food and stuff. They'll make fun of him: "Oh, there's that man that gets *Yuwípi*," tied up. In Lakota, *Yuwípi* describes somebody that's been wrapped up, tied up. So that was his name. That's how he was known. That's how Horn Chips earned the name "*Yuwípi* man." It's sort of like a nickname because he was made fun of, ridiculed for being tied up in that ritual. But it was the same people that run to him when they were sick and going to die, then they come to him. When Horn Chips goes to check his mail, or do business at the store to buy supplies, they'd make fun of him and say, "There's that man that gets tied up like a mummy. There's the man who likes to get tied up." Pretty soon he was known as "the *Yuwípi* man." Everybody kept saying, "Hey, *Yuwípi* man," "Hey, *Yuwípi*," "*Yuwípi wičháša*, come over here." He never put up any protest. He went along with it. He let people call him whatever they feel. When he started healing people, the white people that hung around the reservation in those days gave him the name "Doc," Doctor, "hey Doc," and then pretty soon his name was Dr. Horn. So he had that name for a while, Doctor Horn. A nickname, a household name, Dr. Horn Chips.

Horn Chips did a lot of miracle show–type things when he was in power. He did a lot of things that convinced people that the spirit power was real. That was his specialty. He helps you restore your faith. A lot of Indian people were caught up in the Western world. It was easy for them to lose touch with the traditional medicine, and they really didn't understand the Western teachings either, so they were lost. Horn Chips helped them come back to the faith of their own world. That's what he's known for, building relationships with people and God. He reconnects them together. One of the highlights that made him famous was one night in the 1940s, his *kȟolás* took him to three different worlds in one night. When Horn Chips was tied up, his *kȟolás* took him to the Cheyenne River reservation where they had another altar like his set up. So he arrived, they took him there. And they turned on the lights and he ate supper with them. And then they turned off the lights and they took him to the Rosebud Reservation, and they did the same. He had lights and showed people. They gave him gifts and blankets and stuff. They put them on the altar while they were retying him up and he ended up in Wanblee with all these gifts and stuff like that. All in one night, he was able to do that. So he immediately became a legend. Everybody knew that Horn Chips was able to go to two different reservations in one night to do his job. That was a miracle. If you were there, you would become a believer for sure.

There were four things that Horn Chips kept in mind whenever he prayed, four principal spiritual values that constitute what it means to be a "common man," *ikče wičháša*. There's four things that a person must know to be able to live a life of *ikče wičháša*. Number one is a person has to believe in God, Wakȟáŋ Tȟáŋka. God is the most sacred being. There's no power other than God. Number two is that the body, our human body, represents the earth, Uŋčí Makȟá. The *ikče wičháša* must respect the mother, the female. Number three is the *wakíŋyaŋ oyáte*, the lightning power. We're alive in this world because of the lightning power. Lightning power goes into the spirit of the person and then we have energy, the energy that keeps on moving. And the fourth one is the *íŋyaŋ oyáte*, the rock nation. That is how we make relatives with the winged, the four-legged relatives that live in water and underneath the ground, the spirit beings. These are the four things that Horn Chips always keeps in mind whenever he prays.

So all of the non-Indians, the white ranchers that lived around the reservation, knew Horn Chips for his abilities. Half of his followers were white people, local white people, ranchers and farmers. They would come and they would take care of him in the winter. He never had to worry about anything. He always had food. He had heat. And he had a car. He was well taken care of. He never needed any money, because everything was there. Part of the Indian community and the white man community took care of him. If he was alive today, he would be known all over. There would be books about him, movies about him. He was a great man, Horn Chips. People gave him gifts. Nowadays, a medicine man, they'll give him money, but back then they'll give him horses. A white man gave him a semitruckload of cows, just gave them to him, they were all his. Three hundred head of horses and three hundred head of cows. A lot of farm equipment. He had five brand-new cars parked in his yard. If you go to that land now, the house is still there and you can see all these little bumps like that, fields of them. Those are all Horn Chips's gardens. He did that himself. He made one of the largest gardens in Lakota country. Corn, squash, potatoes, and then he'd have a festival where people could go out there and get sacks full of vegetables and go away. He'd just give them all away. That was his habit. He likes to garden. He was a unique kind of person.

But he's a human being, too, so people also bought medicine from him. They could buy an altar from him. And he'd do it. He'll let them have it. I think one of Horn Chips's weaknesses was that he had a taste for that gold. And that's what kind of messed it up for him. There's a lot of people in Rosebud who are doing ceremonies because of Horn Chips. If you come to the reservation today, most everybody does Yuwípi. They get tied up. They all do the same thing. They imitate. All the medicine men that I knew were doing that. They were getting tied up. They probably don't even know where they got it from. It started out with Horn Chips.

In 1943 those Little People that come to the Yuwípi ceremony told him that they're not going to come anymore after he and his brother pass on. From that day on—the rest of the Yuwípi ceremonies across the country—it is very unclear where they got their altars from. The Yuwípi was generalized, standardized. Everybody does it, but it's a mystery. It became a mystery. They probably have different spirits that come to them. It's unknown. But as far as the Little People that originally came to the tie-up ceremonies, they said they weren't coming anymore. The only reason why my grandfather Sam was able to continue that Yuwípi was because he had friends from his grandpa, and those friends were the ones that hosted those Little People to come back to visit their altar and then they go back to where they come from. We're not doubting anybody else, the rest of the people that conduct Yuwípi ceremonies. They probably have different spirits that come to them, or maybe they become the spirit in helping people. In the Lakota way, we believe that sacred power, the *wówakȟáŋ*, comes through the bloodline. Wóptuȟ'a's altar required the bloodline. The Yuwípi altar was different. It didn't require the bloodline because Tȟahúŋska and Horn Chips got that altar from someone else. That's why a *wašíču* guy like George Frost could do the tie-up. Horn Chips sanctioned a lot of people to do it before he died. But when Horn Chips died that ended the original tie-up ceremony. The power sanctioned from Horn Chips ended when Horn Chips passed away.

When Horn Chips was going to doctor somebody, he'd get tied up. But when people just want some information or a thank-you ceremony or something other than doctoring, then Horn Chips won't get tied up. He'll just do a regular Lówáŋpi. That's how they usually operate. The only time they get tied up is when they're going to doctor somebody. So they'd tie up Horn Chips. Every time they'd tie him up, the way we interpret it, is that he died. He put his life away for the purpose of healing somebody, giving them life. And then when his friends come in there and they doctor that person, that person will get well. But there's always a price to pay. So before they untie Horn Chips, they'll give that family instructions to compensate for his life to come back. Before they untie him, somebody from the family has to commit, maybe a *haŋbléčheya*, or something that they have to do to compensate so they won't cut another year off of Horn Chips's life. So that's why they untie him that way. So some people got what they wanted, but they never paid the price. They forgot about the thank-you ceremony, they forgot about healing him, so it fell back on him.

Horn Chips did a lot of wonderful things, but what people didn't know was that his powers were limited and his *kȟolás* didn't want him to be doing that. He was just supposed to keep it simple and doctor people. But he went far beyond his working limits to convince people that he was a great man. And that's how he was known, as a great medicine man. But that cost him. Everything has a price. It cost him his life. You can only do certain things. You've got a limit on everything. You've got a limit. And by overextending his authority and his work, he cut his life a little shorter. He should have died when he was eighty years old, but he died when he was seventy-one years old. His life was cut short every time in his work. It's kind of hard to understand it, but that's how it went. He was still in his seventies. He had nine years cut out of his life. So these things are good, but you have to keep it real and safe with common sense. But he did that at a time when everybody knew how the spirit works. If he did that now, just think what would happen. He would have a whole city built around his house. People would be around him every day. He'd have a whole community out there. People search for something *wakȟáŋ* every day. They hear somebody, they'll follow him all over. That was part of Horn Chips's life. But the power has its own limits. You don't want to abuse that either.

Horn Chips authorized or put medicine on two people while he was still alive. This was in 1944. A guy named Roy Stone was five years old when he was ill. So they took him to Horn Chips. And Horn Chips cured him. But at the same time, he put medicine into that boy. He said, "Someday, he's going to be working for the spirit people." He was only five at that time. He said that he's going to live to be in his seventies, but that someday in the future he has to pay them back by working for them, like ceremonial ways. So he did that to Roy Stone. And then another one was Adam Bordeaux. Adam Bordeaux was doctored when he was a boy. Horn Chips told him that someday he's going to be taking over, using some of Horn Chips's power. So there were three men who had Horn Chips's power. Roy Stone, Adam Bordeaux, and then Godfrey Chipps. Godfrey sort of came later, after Horn Chips died, but somehow Horn Chips's friend chose him.

During those times, only a few people sought power. Everyone hid from the Lakota ways, especially from the Lakota Christians. So Horn Chips would travel to Rosebud under the radar. He was arrested a lot of times in Rosebud for the crime of ceremony. He would be arrested, and then he would be escorted back to Pine Ridge. The Indian police would arrest him and escort him back to Wanblee because Wanblee, Kyle, and Hisle, that zone was given to his father, Wóptuȟ'a. Nobody's supposed to disturb him when he does ceremonies in that area. If you step outside that area you can get arrested for doing ceremonies. Tȟahúŋska and Horn Chips operated under his license, but Horn Chips was brave enough to go to Rosebud once in a while. The Indian police were pretty strict over there, and some of the prominent Indian policemen would arrest Horn Chips. They were all Catholic traditionalists, so they had a lot of reasons to go against him. They're well known for arresting him. Horn Chips lived in Rosebud for a while, but he rarely did ceremonies. Maybe once in a while he'd discreetly do something, but for the most part the Indian police kept a close eye on him so he was never able to be active over there.

*

Horn Chips had a lot of stepkids. One of his stepsons was named Jessie Standing Buffalo. He was the son of Horn Chips's second wife, Maggie Thunder Horse. Jessie was an artist. He made stuff from leather, little deer animals or man-animals, little ritual-like things. They kind of looked like horses or elks, or whatever. He made a lot of them. And he put it out there that these were old Grandpa Wóptuȟ'a's ritual stuff. He put it out there like that. He said they came from Wóptuȟ'a. He was selling them in Rapid City and the Black Hills, saying that those were Wóptuȟ'a's stuff, so people were buying them, thinking that they belonged to Wóp-tuȟ'a, those little dolls and little things. Well, somebody told Horn Chips that his stepson was selling ritual items and claiming that they belonged to his father. So Horn Chips, Ellis Chips, Henry Walking Bull, and several others found him and confiscated that stuff. They confronted him and said, "This is what you're doing! Give those to us!" So they took those away from him. Now Jessie feared for his life. He thought he was gonna get killed or something, so he took off. No one saw him again. He felt ashamed and embarrassed, so he took off and he wasn't seen for a long time. I think he was gone for about ten years or something. Every once in a while he'd appear, here and there, but he was ashamed, so not much is known about him because he stayed away.

Horn Chips wanted to burn that stuff because it didn't come from his father, but he never got a chance to get rid of it. Around that time, Horn Chips's own son Ellis, from his second marriage, went to prison at Fort Leavenworth, Kansas, for manslaughter.

He was a bad drunk and accidentally killed one of his babies. So that broke Horn Chips's heart. So he carried that for a while until his wife passed away. Then Horn Chips remarried somebody from Rosebud, a woman named Maude Jack. Like Maggie, Maude also had children from a previous marriage, Eugene, Viola, Francis, and Victoria. Those were Maude's own children and Horn Chips's stepkids. So he moved to Ring Thunder to live with Maude and he took those items with him, but he never got rid of them. After Horn Chips died, Maude and her family kept that stuff. They didn't throw it away. Later, Maude's daughter Viola turned blind, so she didn't really know what was going on, but she had a family member who sold that stuff to a guy in White River, saying they had Wóptuȟ'a's medicine items and stuff like that.

So Horn Chips married Maude while Ellis was in prison. They lived in Ring Thunder for a couple years. But when Ellis got out of prison, he came after his father and took him back to Wanblee. I think Horn Chips was in love with Maude and wanted to spend the remainder of his life with her, but when Ellis came back, he went over and brought him back to Wanblee. He took him away from his new family. He says, "He doesn't belong here. He belongs in Wanblee." Ellis said, "We're going to start over. We're going to do okay again. Things are going to be back the way they used to be." Back in those days, everybody was afraid of Ellis Chips. He was a man to be feared. So nobody said anything to him. So he brought Horn Chips back to Wanblee and promised that he'd rebuild everything and everything would be back to normal.

In the course of Horn Chips's work, people gave him gifts. He never asked for money. But the farmers and ranchers gave him livestock. So there was a time when Horn Chips had over three hundred head of cows and three hundred head of horses, farm equipment, and a lot of cars. He was wealthy and had the biggest garden in the community, but when his wife died and all these things happened, they sold all his horses and cows and cars, and nothing was out there except for the house. Ellis brought his father Horn Chips back to the house and went back into town and picked up his old habits, started drinking again. It was just Horn Chips and his grandson Vincent out there. Horn Chips was really sad that his first wife had died and he'd lost all his household stuff, and now even more they took him away from the love of his life. They took him away from Maude. He felt like there was nothing left for him in the world anymore.

One day in October 1945, he filled his pipe and went to the sweat lodge and called his spirit friends. He said, "Come and get me now, I don't want to be here. I'm through." He didn't want to live in this world anymore. The pain was too much to see his young son go through all these problems. His grandson Vincent witnessed it. He saw the whole thing, where Horn Chips asked his friends to come and get him. He didn't want to live. That happened in October of 1945. And it worked. He started getting sick. They answered his call. They came after him. So Horn Chips slowly got sicker and sicker. His health declined. And in January 1946, he passed away.

One of the reasons why Horn Chips left this world was because of an old belief that our ancestors had, that we pass on energies to the future generations. So when Ellis killed that little baby, there was blood on his hands. And Horn Chips really couldn't take that anymore. That was the last straw. So on that afternoon in 1945, when Horn Chips filled his pipe and asked his spirit friends to come and get him, it was also because of what Ellis did to that baby. That energy would be passed down to the next generation. Horn Chips didn't want that to happen. He wanted to stop it right there. He didn't want that blood on his son's hands to be passed on to the future generations. So he voluntarily left this world. That was one of the reasons. Horn Chips sort of took that bad energy with him so it wasn't passed on to the future generations. The second reason was because it was impossible for him to find a solution to Ellis's problem with drinking and destruction. He didn't want to be around that anymore. Those were the two reasons he told his grandson Vincent why he wasn't going to be around anymore. He was only seventy-one years old. People had all kinds of ceremonies for him. Different medicine men tried to save his life while his health declined. None of them were able to carry through.

One time they were doctoring him, and the next day he felt good. So he decided to lay in the other room. He was singing some songs, just happy, singing. So my father asked his grandpa, Tȟahúŋska, "Well, looks like there's light at the end of the tunnel. The old man's singing. Does that mean he's gonna get better?" And my grandpa Tȟahúŋska said, "Nooo, that's a ghost singing right there. He's gonna die. There's no way around that." That's when they found out that he asked them to come get him. He thought that they were gonna change their minds when he said that. He really thought that those guys said, "Oh no, we're not gonna do that to you, you're gonna live a little longer because people want you to live." Now that's a human talking. A spirit friend will never say that. He says, "Oh, you wanted to come with us? You are coming with us." That's just it. No matter how many ways you appeal, you've already told them that. You said it with the pipe that you want to go with them. Well, you are gonna go with them. That's just cut and dry. Yeah. I wish it wasn't like that. That was the life story of Horn Chips.

*

Ellis never really recovered. He kept on that rugged life, drinking. I think mostly everybody was afraid of him. He appeared to be a killer. Even though it was an accident, back in those days, if you kill somebody, you're not really welcome anywhere. You're a person to be feared. Your negative energy will ruin Indian ceremonies. There were also some good sides about him, too. The good side is that when he sings spiritual songs, they were really good. He's a great song maker. I think all of the sweat songs and the ceremony songs sung today, he made all them songs. When he was sober, he made all the Yuwípi songs around today. And the Sioux National Anthem, he composed that during the 1940s. He had a beautiful voice. The other side, though, is that you don't want to be around him when he's angry. He had no limits. Everybody was scared of him. Even today some of the white folks around here that grew up around him tell me, "I used to be really scared of that guy." They're all old now, too, but they have a memory. They had a good experience with his father, Horn Chips, but his son, Ellis, pushed them all away.

Horn Chips had a lot of friends and relations, but I don't know what happened to the power when he passed away. In 1942 Ellis got married to a woman named Victoria. Her last name was Lodge Skin. They had three boys, Charles, Philip, and Godfrey. For a long time they were without ceremony. They'd been trying to get some kind of power for a long time and finally around the early 1970s, Godfrey started doing ceremonies. He did that on his own. He didn't get help from anybody. He just all of a sudden started doing it. They thought Charles was going to do that, but he was not able to do it. So Godfrey took it from there. He died on July 6, 2014. The day before my birthday. He was young. He was only fifty-eight years old.

*

Horn Chips led a good path. He never drank. He never did anything wrong. He had a lot of white people believing in his ceremonies and they followed him, but when he passed away, all that energy went with him. All that good energy died. The white people knew it too. They backed away. And they also died out, too, by old age. Today, the younger generation, their fathers who were close with Indians, they're all gone. It died out. It never happened again. So we're hoping that someday when Horn Chips's power comes back, it'll be done in the way he did it.

Horn Chips gave up on life in this world, but his *kȟolás* never gave up on him. So they honored his request. But they didn't let him go to the spirit world. They took him into their world, the Little Peoples' world, so he became one of them. That's how we get our information, because they pass that information to us. They tell us ahead of time what's going to happen, where they're going to go. That's how we know that Wóptuȟ'a is with his own people, his friends. That's how we know that Grandpa Sam is in another world and doesn't come back around. Tȟahúŋska, he went to another world. Except for Horn Chips. Horn Chips was an exception. He had a hard life. Even though he was a powerful medicine man, things didn't go too well for him. So he asked his *kȟolás* to come and get him. He asked a big favor. He says, "Well, come after me. Come and pick me up. I can't handle it here anymore." He had no attachments to this world. He didn't see himself in this world anymore. He wanted to go with them. But when he went with them, they learned that when he was alive, he did a lot of good deeds. He saved hundreds of lives, so he earned some privileges. He earned some respect from his friends. So they made an exception for him. They allowed him to come back to our world through ceremonies. That's a big move. He became one of the helpers from the other world. He became one of them. They transferred him into that world, so he comes to our world, into our ceremonies. He'll show up. He earned that, though. He earned it. It didn't just happen.

Wóptuȟ'a would never come back to this world, not in our lifetime. But maybe Sam, or maybe Tȟahúŋska, maybe they can do that. They can show up somehow through a messenger, but it's very rare. Tȟahúŋska didn't really pass on his Yuwípi teachings to anyone except his brother Horn Chips. He wanted my dad to do it, but my dad didn't do it. He just stayed a singer. That's how the story of Tȟahúŋska went. Most of the time he was just helping people. He died when he was eighty years old. That's all I kind of know about my great-grandpa Tȟahúŋska Moves Camp and Horn Chips's life. So that was the life of Tȟahúŋska and Horn Chips together.

Grandpa Sam   4

My grandpa Sam's Indian name was "Four Altars," Hóchoka Tópa. That was his name. "The One with Four Altars." He was born somewhere near Eagle Nest Creek on the Pine Ridge Agency in April 1891 to James Tȟahúŋska Chips Moves Camp and Helen Kills. He was the oldest of four children. At the age of seven, Sam was taken from his family by his grandfather Wóptuȟ'a. Wóptuȟ'a raised him to be the successor to his work and teachings. At the age of nine, Sam began singing for his grandfather. He learned how to prepare herbs and medicine for his grandfather. My grandpa had to earn his privilege and power. He had to work for it. It didn't just come to him. In his younger days, he had to spend thirty days out in the wilderness all by himself. He had to live off Nature. Imagine being alone for thirty days in the wilderness. You miss people, but the longer you're away from human civilization, the more the other world starts to come to you and make connections with you. The trees and the plants and the water. You learn to be as one with them. And then when you have that gift, it's permanent. No one can take it away.

Wóptuȟ'a took Sam from Tȟahúŋska at a young age and raised him. That's why he knew a lot of Wóptuȟ'a's life stories. Wóptuȟ'a passed most of his work to his grandson Sam, my grandpa, so that's how we ended up with a lot of information about Wóptuȟ'a. He also passed some of his abilities to my grandpa Sam. So they called him "The One with Four Altars" because he practiced four different ceremonial altars. First, he was practicing his grandfather Wóptuȟ'a's altar. He doesn't hardly ever use that, but he has it. And then his own personal one. And then there's the Five Stick ceremony. Wóptuȟ'a was the only one who was connected with the friends that come to that particular altar, the Five Stick. And then my grandpa Sam. Later on, Sam kind of sanctioned Tȟahúŋska and Horn Chips to put up the Five Stick, but their father's friends never came to the altar. It was only their own friends that come there. And then he had another form of doctoring with stones, the *íŋyaŋ waphíye*. He also ended up practicing Yuwípi, in later years, so that became a fifth altar. But he didn't do that until later on in the forties. The reason why is because his sister was passing away. She told Sam that she wanted to live, but for some reason, my grandpa couldn't use his original altar to fix her, so he had to do something different to help her. That's when he used his father's altar as a backup, a different altar. It helped. It saved her life, and she was able to live for a long time afterward. That's how he ended up with that altar, the Yuwípi altar. So he actually ended up with five altars before he passed away.

The Seven Medicine People

One of the stories my grandpa learned from his grandfather Wóptuȟ'a was how there were only seven medicine people in the original Teton Sioux nation. The first medicine man was long before Wóptuȟ'a was born. It was a buffalo *waphíya wičháša*, a buffalo medicine man. One day a Lakota man was on a journey. They say that he was on a journey all by himself when he came across a young woman in the middle of nowhere. He just met a woman down by a creek. He was surprised and looked around, but there's no other camps. But the woman knew where she was at, and she was comfortable there. They both got along. They became real good friends. They stayed together for about a month, and then as a couple months went by, somehow the man knew that there's something unordinary about this young woman. She was not a regular woman. She was strange or special. She had a tremendous amount of power. She was stronger than a man, yet she was a woman. So knowing all that, he really kept his boundaries and respect. And here one day she said, "Let's go meet my family. It's time for us to meet my family." So he did. He followed her to a crowd of people in the Plains, and she introduced him to her father, and her mother, and all the kin around that area. And the old man that's supposed to be her father said, "We're gonna give her to you. You're gonna make life and generation. But always respect her. Don't disrespect her. She's a woman. She's our daughter. And if you take good care of her, you'll live a long time." So they made an agreement, and the man said, "Yes, I will do my best to honor her. I will not disrespect her in any way." So they walked away with a marriage. So they walked away, and they heard the ground shake, like a rumbling, like the world was coming to an end or something, the ground's all shaking. And he looked back, they both looked back, and all those people that they met, they were buffalo. They turned into buffalo, and they just rolled over the hill.

So the man's conclusion was that this woman was part buffalo. She just turned herself into a woman. So he was very honored by that. He took care of her. And they had one son together. He was a very good boy. Knowing that he'd come from a different generation, that made him an even more special boy. Like Wóptuȟʼa, he had supernatural power. As the boy turned ten years old, sometimes he would disappear, nowhere to be found. At first they were real worried about him, looking for him, but then they realized that this boy had a purpose in life. And sure enough, when the boy came back, he had spent time with the buffalo and he had power.

But there was a problem. The woman was not an ordinary woman, so she would not socialize with his people. When they gathered around, she would go with him, or when they lived together, she would live in her own *thípi*. Once in a while she'd come out, but she very much isolated herself from the people. She wasn't sociable. She was hard to figure out. So pretty soon, the family didn't like her. They just despised her. They thought that "she thinks she's different, that she's better than all of us." So they didn't have anything good to say about her. But she never bothered anybody. She just kept to herself. That went on for a while. The man would get in trouble, because he'd take up for his wife and get mad at people. So things like that happened, and finally one morning the woman said, "I'm going to go back to my people, because your people are not nice to me. They don't like me. I don't feel welcome among your people. So I'm going to leave that boy with you. You do your best to raise him." So she started packing her stuff and walked off into the prairie. The man and his son followed her. And as they followed her, she started walking and then she acknowledged them one more time and then she joined a herd of buffalo waiting for her and took off. The man and his son didn't get sad, because she wasn't dead. She just went back to another world. But they didn't know what to feel. They couldn't mourn, and they couldn't grieve. She did not die, but she's alive somewhere. The boy wasn't sad, because he knew that he could be with his mom anytime, but the man couldn't. He's human.

So the man and the boy grew up together. He raised the boy, and when the boy was in the early ages of manhood, he got married. And from there, they had two sons and a daughter. And here those young children, they also had power. One of them had power with the horse people. And the other one had power with the eagle. The girl had power with the deer and elk nation. So now there were four medicine people, the buffalo, the horse, the eagle, and the deer. There were four medicine people that people could go to. Each had different kinds of healing power. If you had mental health problems or bad dreams, the horse person would heal you. The buffalo would heal body illnesses, and the eagle relates to the people's ancestral connections. The woman had power with the deer, with the energy of the deer. So those four helped the people for a long period of time. So even today when the Lakota people pray, they pray to the west, to the horse; to the north, to the buffalo; to the east, to the elk and deer; and to the south, the eagle nation. So that became a way of life. Years later, there was a bear medicine person. Then the man who started the Yuwípi ceremony. And then Wóptuȟ'a was born. So there's a total of seven types of healing in our history. A lot of people don't know that today. They think we're all the same.

Wóthawe

One of the rituals my grandpa Sam learned from his grandpa Wóptuȟ'a was making *wóthawe*. A *wóthawe* is a medicine pouch that guides and protects an individual from harm. Sam made many *wóthawe* for men who went to war during World War II, the Korean conflict, and the Vietnam war. I witnessed some of his ceremonies making *wóthawe* for soldiers who were going to Vietnam. The soldiers would come from all over, even white people. He had them pick two kinds of sage. Grandpa would then sit them down in a circle. This was during the daytime. He lit cedar and smudged them and talked about his grandpa Wóptuȟ'a as a master of the art of war. He told them that this medicine wouldn't be effective if they violated the ethical rules of war, but that it would prevent them from PTSD. He had them roll the sage into a ball and hold it in their hand. Then Grandpa would sing a song, and when he finished the song, those balls of sage had turned into stones, some black, red, brown, and so forth. Another time two men came to visit Grandpa from Rosebud, Roy Stone and Adam Bordeaux, to go on the hill to fulfill their dreams. Their parents accompanied them and pitched their tents by the white house at my grandfather's place. These men received *wóthawe* from Grandpa Sam to do the Yuwípi ritual.

Lakota Spirituality

Lakota spirituality is about energy. Natural energy, the wind, the trees, plants. We recognize that every plant has energy. The Lakota point of view is a spiritually based understanding about energy, *wówašake*. The plants that my great-great-grandfather Wóptuȟ'a and my grandpa focused on, and the basis of their healing, are about energy, the power of the plants. It's a 180-degree difference between the Western herbalist and the Native Indigenous use of plants. Of course there's some valid things about the herbalists' understanding of plants and how they work, but the Native way is much deeper. I can't speak for other tribes, but for us, every plant is like a person. It's got feelings. It's got ears. It's got language. And what makes my great-great-grandfather Wóptuȟ'a a special person is that he was able to make connection between the plants and the animals, even the water. He was able to communicate with them. The medicine people don't just go out and dig an herb. It doesn't work that way. They have to understand what it's for and who it's for. This process is included in the ceremonial ritual. But I used to think that Western way, too—that I could just go out and dig a whole bunch of herbs out there and store them and go get them when I need them. It doesn't work that way.

A single plant can do many things. My grandfather works with plants. But he doesn't work with thousands of plants. I used to think like that, too. One day I told my grandfather, "Wow, you must know a lot of plants!" My grandfather sat there for a long time and said, "No, I just only know about two or three." I said, "What? Really? I thought you knew a lot of them." He said, "No, I only have three or four plants in my whole life." So I thought about it for a while and realized I need to learn more. What I found out was that those four plants that he works with are his friends. They are powerful friends. He digs them up from the ground, but before he digs them, he talks with them in his mind, he communicates with them. He takes out the plant while it's still alive for whatever patient that he's working with and says, "This person is sick. He's got that illness right there. I'm asking you to help him on that one." So this plant might work on somebody who has a heart condition or some other condition, but this plant can work on many people with many different problems. He just has to understand why he's requested to give his life to help others. But in order to have that ability to connect with the plant, you've got to earn it. It just doesn't come to you. It doesn't come from a book. You've got to meet it halfway. For the plant to work effectively requires some physical work on our part.

Back in those old days when there were *thípis* and tents, the energy was well protected. So when a patient visits my grandpa, and the healing starts from offering tobacco, the protocol, the next level of healing with plants, is that this person has to isolate themselves in a tent or *thípi* or home, log house, or whatever. He can't be around other people. He has to totally isolate himself, go through a sweat lodge. It's because of the sensitivity of the energy. The plant energy is vulnerable. So if you're not healthy, clean, physically clean, and spiritually clean, and you come across this plant, your energy will contaminate it. It'll kill that plant. It'll just die, because your energy is not in tune. It might have come across a woman who's on her monthly moon or a person who's been around a certain kind of animal. So you have to protect this plant so it stays alive while it does its work. So this plant will work, it'll meet you halfway, turn into power, and work miracles. Whatever illness that you have, this plant will do everything it can to take care of it.

In his compound, there was a cabin that he uses for patients. He keeps them there. Nobody visits them. Somebody cooks special food for them, and he'll administer the medicine herbs to them. And they get well. They'll get well. He was the last to have that connection. This practice was normal among the Lakota. They had mental health, physical health, emotional health, and spiritual health. But when Wóptuȟ'a passed away, and the next generations were dealing with the colonialized world, the practice of isolating our patients in a special place and preserving that kind of energy went away. Even today, now, my generation, they think that the medicine man can take care of everything, like singing a song and then say, "Okay, you'll be all right." That'll probably never happen, because the energy of the traditional process never happened.

Back in the old days, you really put your heart into the belief. If you choose to go to a medicine man, your whole heart has to be in it for it to work. If you don't believe in it, then it probably won't work. That's the understanding between you and the medicine man from the beginning. You've got to meet me halfway, he'll say. But if you're sitting there thinking that it's not gonna work, with that attitude, it's pretty hard to do the job. Even Indian medicine has its limits. Some patients do come, but when they go back home things aren't right, and the energy dies off. So the whole family has to be really careful. They should have faith in the medicine. How badly do they want to get well? I think if you went to the Western doctors and they prescribed you some pills, you'd have to have some faith in those pills, too. You have to play a part in it for it to work. If you don't have much faith in Indian medicine, just don't go to them. Go somewhere else. You're just wasting time.

When Grandpa Sam was alive, he could cure diabetes. He found a cure. But the instructions are almost impossible to follow. It is possible, but it's difficult to follow. You have to change your whole lifeway. My grandpa cured about 150 people who had diabetes. He cured them, but he also gave them instructions, twofold medicine. One with the herb, the other one is the diet. They both have to be balanced for it to work right. The medicine that he has cleanses the pancreas, and then when it's clean, it starts all over, but now you've got to cut out certain parts of your food. Your whole life has to change.

Earth People

Lakota people, we called ourselves earth people. Originally, our genes, our bloodline, the way our body functioned, our healthy lifestyle was based on what we ate. We ate a lot of fish, buffalo meat, elk, prairie chickens, pheasants, ducks. We ate plants, vegetables. Our people ate buffalo and fish and other kinds of animals, and they knew how to eat it. It's one thing to kill a buffalo, but it's another to know how to process it and keep it. Imagine back in the 1800s. They didn't have refrigerators. They had to process food so it lasted them a long time. So what they did is they cut up beef jerky, *pápa*, hung it up, and dried it. There's only certain ways you can eat *pápa*. One of them is to make a stew. Another one is to roast it and make *wasná* out of it, the natural way. The only way you can preserve fruit or vegetables is to dry them and preserve them. So that really made their lifestyle a disciplined and different way.

That was a way of life that's really hard to understand, but it was natural and it was beautiful. You eat enough just to keep you going. The rest of your day, you will experience hunger-like symptoms. Imagine waking up and having breakfast, but afterward you're still hungry. And that hunger is a way of life. You have to accept it. The Native people learned to appreciate what they had but not to overdo it. Just enough to keep them going. They learned how to eat just enough, not till they're full, but just enough to keep going. Imagine a life where you wake up hungry, go to bed hungry. You live your life sort of hungry, but it's not because of lack of food. It was a matter of keeping your health and the discipline that goes with it.

There was never a time when our people starved. They had access to a lot of vegetables, wild potatoes, carrots, onions, and berries that our people totally forgot about, living on the reservation. During my grandfather Wóptuȟ'a's generation, their diet was dry processed food. They're gonna take it and keep it. Like turnips, potatoes, they were all harvested and dried, even fruits, dried plums, chokecherries, buffalo berries, strawberries, Cheyenne's turnips, *thíŋpsiŋla*. There was even food that used to grow in the river, along the creeks, *sinkpila ta-thíŋpsiŋla*, onions that grow along the creeks. That's the kind of lifestyle that they lived in the old days. Their bodies were tough. Their bodies were really strong. It affected their spiritual well-being as well. They weren't sick. We had countless vegetables that grew on the land that we were supposed to eat, but that changed when the government gave us domesticated food. Canned food. Flour. And a lot of starch. Our diet changed, and a lot of our illnesses started from that, our daily diet.

My grandfather was supposed to be on a special diet. He has his own special diet. He can't eat processed food from the can. He has to have meat from a cow, buffalo, or elk. And he can't use regular cooking utensils. He can't use metal plates or metal silverware or cups. Everything has to be done with wood. And that's a mystery. None of us will ever know why. It's a secret. He never shared it with us. But I imagine it had a lot to do with his energy and power, the way he works. Because he handled his grandpa's altar, he had to have a restricted life. I guess if you didn't know him, you could consider him like a magician, he can make things appear and disappear. He can make things happen. But he's not a magician. Those are real things. If you really pay attention to him, you'll see that there's a lot of special things about him. Hanging around him will make you a believer. So my grandpa had to use wooden plates, wooden spoons, wooden cups. Even while he's preparing medicine, he couldn't use a metal aluminum or metal saucepan to boil herbs. The exception was that he could use enamel because it's got that special coating.

So when he eats daily meals, my grandfather can't use metal. The energy that the metal gives off conflicts with his body, and he starts choking. He starts losing wind. He has a hard time processing his food. Being around it for most of my life, I took it as normal. At the time, people followed his ways. So everybody that came to Grandpa Sam's ceremony, they knew to bring their own dishes. It's usually a wooden bowl, wooden spoon, wooden cups. And then after a while, the wooden bowls, spoons, and cups would get old so they started using plastic spoons and plastic, disposable ones. But people avoided metal plates and cups.

His spiritual life and his physical life were supposed to be restricted, everything from his diet to being around women on their time. There's certain things he can't do, will not do. He says, "If I do those things that you ask me, my friends won't be so friendly anymore. They won't come around." So he has restrictions, too. Limits. And so that was his way of life. He had to earn it every day. The work that he does is really hard. He has to have a sweat all the time, because when one of the women on their time goes by him, he starts getting really sick. He can't breathe. So it was hard for him to go anywhere. He fixes himself up so he's protected before he goes. He likes to go to Kadoka a lot. He likes to go and sit with his friends, but if the bartender's on her moon, he'll come back and get sick. A woman might be on her time, but they want to come talk to him. Then it'll affect him. So he always has to have a buffer around him, somebody that keeps an eye on him. For a while, that was my job. I kind of had to screen people. Like if it's a woman, I'd say, "Well, are you, you know, on your monthly cycle?" Some don't want to tell. Some say, "No, I don't want to tell you that." "Well, it's important for him to know that, somebody's got to ask you. He's not going to ask you." So they'll say, "Yeah." "Well, you can't talk to him." They think that he's going to get hurt by them, but it's the other way around. It's the woman who gets hurt. It really doesn't hurt the medicine man. It twists around and shoots right back at the person. So that's the reason why they don't want women to be around ceremony stuff, because the women can get really hurt.

Even though their energy overpowers that stuff, the woman pays the price. I don't know why it's like that, it's just Nature's law.

Trying to live a normal life was a challenge for him, real hard. We didn't know how to take care of him too well. Well, I was too little, but my aunts, my grandmothers, and the people that fed him kept him alive by feeding him food. Either they didn't care or they didn't know. Somebody didn't tell them. They tried, but it didn't really happen. So he would eat processed foods, canned foods from the commodities, sweet stuff. He just had a normal diet like everybody else, which was real bad for him. He tried to live a normal life, but if he had that strong diet, I think he would have been healthier. He always kind of got sick, because when he'd go visit somebody that didn't know about his restrictions and they'd give him dinner with a metal plate, coffee with a metal cup, when he gets home, he really gets sick. But he would never complain. He would survive and continue.

*

One time me and my nephew were sitting in our cabin and all of a sudden the radio just turned on by itself. We had a beat-up old radio that ran on batteries. But as me and my nephew were sitting there, it just came on. We looked at each other and said, "Did you see that?" "Yeah, wow, jeez, I don't know." We turned it off. Then my nephew said, "Hey, there's no batteries in this radio!" So we were blown away. Now I've got something to tell my grandpa! Here an hour later he showed up. He told my dad—he didn't tell me, he told my dad, even though we were all sitting there—he says, "That pickup." I used to own a pickup, a 1957 Chevy. Me and my nephew would drive around in it all day, and when we ran out of gas we'd just leave it there till we got gas. He said, "Today that pickup doesn't go nowhere. Don't drive that pickup today." So we listened to him. When he says something like that, we don't doubt him. Then he says, "You guys heard something today." So we looked at each other. We didn't tell anybody about that radio. But he says, "They heard something today. That pickup. If they don't listen, if they take off, that pickup will wreck." And then he named my nephew who I was with, he'll die. So he wants my nephew to make tobacco ties before the sun goes down. And so he did. We didn't do anything. We just made ties. We didn't touch that pickup for a whole week. He just said "today," but we waited a whole week. And we thanked him for that. We gave him gifts, for saving our lives. He wasn't even there. He just came over and told us what was coming.

*

One day my grandpa Sam didn't have any money. He didn't have anything. And some of his relatives from Nebraska were stranded. They didn't have any gas money. So they asked Grandpa, "Do you think you could help us with some money? We want to get home." My grandpa reached in his pocket. He had one dollar. One dollar bill. I saw him tell one of my uncles to lay that dollar down and trace it, make an outline around it. Then he told him to cut it with scissors, so there's a piece of white paper, and then the dollar. Then he put it together. He had a white cloth around there, and he smudged it down. He didn't let anybody see it, just me and my other uncles. I think he sang a song. The folks were all sitting in the other room, drinking coffee and waiting for my grandpa. He opened that white cloth, and it was a stack of hundred-dollar bills in there! My eyes—I couldn't believe it! He said to them, "You only have one hour to spend this. Once you pass the hour, if you have any left, throw it away. It's no good." So he had them go into town and fill up their tank with gas. Some of them didn't believe him, so they held on to it, but by the time they came back to the house to thank him, it was just paper. Just paper. Now that's an illusion! Only a magician can do that. I told my dad and them, "Grandpa went to the bank real quick like in his backyard." But only he can do that. It's like he went to the instant ATM. I was blessed to have been around him, because I've seen some of the things he could do. Sam used that power to help people, but sometimes, once in a while, he'll put on a show.

*

One morning in the 1940s during World War II, Grandpa Sam woke up and went outside, drinking his coffee. He heard some children in the creek laughing, and he thought that was pretty early for children to be playing down there unsupervised. So he got concerned about it and started walking down the creek. Sure enough there were two little kids. He couldn't tell if they were boys or girls. They were just children with long hair. They had found some boards, just small little boards, and they made them look like they were boats. They put sticks in the middle of the boards. They put some little flags on there and made them look like sailboats. They were little homemade toy boats, and they were making them float along the creek. Those kids were following their boats and running along the edges of the creek. And then one of those boats sank right into the middle of the creek. It was kind of deep so the boat went right straight down, and there was only one left. So one of the kids started crying. He says, "My boat," *wáta*. The boats are called *wáta*. He was crying, saying, "*Wáta*." Grandpa said, "What's happened?" And those little kids were surprised. They were startled. They looked at him, and then they ran away. They disappeared in the creek area. He couldn't find them. They were nowhere around. They disappeared right in front of him. So the little boat was still left in the middle of the creek, floating away, and then finally disappeared. Later, he found that boat washed ashore. It was kind of sitting along the creek, so he took the boat and he walked back up to the house with it. And he said to his wife, "I saw some kids playing in the creek, they made some toy boats and one of them got sunk in the water and the other one I managed to recover, but those kids disappeared." So they were talking about it. Nobody had kids out there. All the kids were home. It's a mystery.

So they decided to put on a Five Stick ceremony that night. The message was that those two boats represented two ships. Uncle Jimmy was on one of those ships, an aircraft carrier. And my cousin Silvester Bad Cob was on the other ship, an ammunition carrier.

They were on two separate battleships, and one of them was going to be sunk by an enemy attack. So the two guys, Uncle Jimmy and Silvester, one of them's not going to come back. So they were really worried. My grandpa was really concerned about what he was told. He asked his friends, "What can I do to save it from happening?" And they gave him instructions. His friend said, "In order to get them back, you have to die. You have to die for a little while. And when you do that, your friends will help prevent this from happening." So Grandpa Sam filled his pipe and wrapped himself in a blanket and was buried in the ground overnight. They made an airhole for him out of tree bark and put some willows across the grave, and he was all covered up in the dirt. He stayed there early in the evening, all through the night, and the next morning. Somehow when they went after him he was already outside the grave. He was sitting there. He said, "Before the sun goes down, we need to cover this grave." So they did. They covered it all up like it never happened. And sure enough, Uncle Jimmy's and Silvester's lives were saved. They both came back after the war. So that was kind of interesting how the water people delivered a message. The Wiwíla Oyáte, the water people, delivered a message to my grandpa. They showed up as little children, as little kids.

*

After Horn Chips passed away in January of 1946, Uncle Jimmy was still in the Navy. He was stationed at Treasure Island, close to San Francisco. One morning they had an R and R day, and most of the sailors went into town for the weekend. But Uncle Jimmy happened to stay at the base, and out of nowhere, an Indian man showed up looking for his grandson. He walked through the gates. They didn't object. They let him through. So they told Uncle Jimmy that he had a visitor and he went outside. He went to the gates, and here it was Grandpa Horn Chips. He said, "I've come by to check on you." He said, "I'm going on a journey." So they visited. He said, "Everybody's fine at home, everything is okay." And he says, "I'm going on a journey, but I just wanted to let you know that we think about you. We pray for you that you'll go home. When you go home, you've got to pray." He gave him instructions that way. And then he went back through the gates and disappeared. He said he was going west, so Uncle Jimmy figured he was gonna go into the city. Jimmy thought that somebody was waiting for Grandpa outside the gates to take him into the city. Later on he wrote a letter to my father. He said, "Grandpa Horn Chips came to see me. That was a big surprise." My dad wrote him back and says, "Your grandpa died. He passed away this past January." That was in midsummer that he wrote the letter. So even while they're gone, they still manage to appear. So that was an interesting story, that my grandpa visited my uncle while he was in the Navy on his way to be with his friends.

*

One of my uncles had bladder problems. He was really embarrassed to talk about it in ceremony, because he didn't want to let people hear it. So he told my grandpa in private, "This is what's wrong with me." My grandpa said, "Okay, during the ceremony, after you pray, you'll go outside and we'll wait for you." Back then we didn't have electricity, so when it's dark, it's really dark outside. But he made my uncle go outside. He gave him a piece of white cloth and said, "You're gonna find an herb out there and when you find that herb, tie this cloth around there and tomorrow at daytime you can go get it." So we had the ceremony and when we stopped, he prayed and then they opened the door for him and he went out. He asked for a flashlight. My grandpa said, "No, you don't need no flashlight. You just need to use your natural eye." So he went out there, and he asked me to go with him, too. He was almost my age. I said, "No, I don't have any problem. You go yourself." But he was scared, so he asked me to go with him. So my dad said, "Go ahead and follow him." So I went out there and here the whole world was dark, but then we saw a light. It looked like somebody had a green security light inside a blue light, like that, and here it was a little plant all lit up. So he tied that cloth around it, and we came back inside. The next morning, that white cloth was hanging on the plant. So he dug it up and took it home and took care of himself that way. That's how he does things like that. Only my grandfather could do something like that. I saw that happen, growing up.

*

One time we took my grandpa to a wake. He had a nephew who got killed in Kadoka. There's a railroad track just before you get into Kadoka, but there's no lights on that railroad crossing. So when the nephew was crossing over, the train came and hit the car, killed him. So they brought the body back. My grandpa hardly ever goes to wakes or funerals. He stays away from them. This one he went. And we were with him. It was in a church. There was a chair, so we sat behind him. He got up and he went to see the body. The body was laying there, and he had a bandage or a cloth around his head. He was laying like that, and my grandpa was looking at him, paying his respects. My grandpa had a five-dollar bill, so he laid it on his chest. And I swore I saw it. I don't know if my grandpa saw it, I think he was praying, he just kind of had his head down, but that dead guy looked up and smiled at him—like "thank you"—for that dollar. And then when my grandpa walked away, he just lay like before. So I said to my nephew sitting next to me, "Did you see that?" He said, "Yep, I saw it! He's not dead, he's alive!" So I asked my grandpa. I said, "Hey, did you see that guy when you were giving him that money? He looked at you and smiled at you." He said, "Did he do that?" He looked at me. I guess he wasn't watching. So I said, "Yeah. Maybe we ought to go check. Maybe he's not supposed to die." He said, "Well, it's too late. He's gone already." So even dead people react to him when he shows up.

*

One night, two brothers got into an argument with a guy from Wanblee. They were fighting over a girl, that guy's sister. The two brothers went into town and stole her, took her back out in the country. I think people thought it was against her will, so her brother went after his sister and I think he beat them both in a fistfight. So he rescued his sister. As they were driving back to Wanblee, those two brothers got into a car and chased them. When they got closer, one of them peeked out with a .22 rifle and shot into that car. Here that bullet hit that guy behind the head, went inside, and lodged right up there right inside the nose. So he fell over and went unconscious. The two brothers took off. Back in those days, they could have called the police, but that guy's parents and the two brothers' parents got along real well and knew that this had happened over drinking and women. So instead of taking the injured guy to the hospital, one of them had the idea, "Let's take him to Sam." So they showed up at our house late at night asking for an emergency ceremony. The guy was still breathing. His heart's still pounding. But he had a bullet in his head. The family said, "We want him to live, and we don't want no charges. This is just over a stupid thing, so we want to end it."

So Grandpa Sam had to do the ceremony. My dad had to get up. We all had to go. They brought the guy into the ceremony room. He was unconscious, laying there. They woke him up, and here he's up, but he can't talk. So my grandpa Sam had a ceremony, and his friends came and they pushed that thing out of his head. He had them bring a wooden bowl and they put it on the altar. My grandpa Sam blew into that hole with a whistle and here that thing came out and hit the bowl. It was a bullet with a blood clot in it. As soon as that metal left his head, that guy was okay again. He could talk and he was all right. So they were really thankful. They thanked my grandpa Sam for taking that bullet out. No charges were filed. The two brothers apologized, and they all remained friends after this. They never talked about it again. But a lot of people knew about it. A policeman came later. They couldn't believe that Grandpa Sam took the bullet out. But there was no death and no injury, and the victim was talking. He said, "I don't want to file charges." So they couldn't arrest anybody. So they just let it go. The next day he just lived a normal life. A lot of people had a lot of respect for my grandpa Sam after that. He became an instant surgeon! We all used to talk about that, not in a bad way, but when we'd talk about some of the stuff that Grandpa Sam could do, that was one of them. But he told us, "Just because I can do that, don't go around shooting each other. I might not be able to save you next time."

*

My grandpa Sam married my grandma Winnie in 1909. Her maiden name was Iron Rope. She was a humble woman. They stayed together until my grandpa died in 1973. She died in 1977. I always say that she was the medicine person. She handled all the herbs and took care of his pipe. She looks after him. She tells him when he needs to clean himself. She was a really quiet, humble person. She don't talk too much, but she takes care of my grandpa. They stayed together for a long time. It was good stories they had together. They joke about each other and stuff like that. I think they were married for over fifty years. Back in those days, marriages last. When you have a wife, that's a blessing. You depend on her as a partner. She shares the same medicine. She knows how they come to him, those visitors from another world. She too got used to that world. She tells a lot of stories, grandma stories. She prepares the herbs. The spirit will tell my grandpa, and my grandpa would tell my grandma, and she'd say, "Oh, that's the one they're talking about!" So she'll tell my dad, and my dad will go get the medicine. She has her favorites, though, her favorite grandchildren. And I wasn't one of them! She treats me good, though. But she'll have candies—you know how grandmas have their little snacks and goodies—I know they're not for me, but I never ask. But when one of my cousins will show up, she'll say, "Oh, I have something for you." She's a good lady, though. Everybody likes my grandma. She's quiet. She's humble. She's not outspoken. She likes to do stuff on her own. She talks to somebody. We don't know who she talks to, but she complains to somebody while she's doing work.

A lot of people think that Indian medicine men can't doctor themselves. That's not true. My grandfather's friends come and doctor him all the time. They take care of him. It's just a matter of people coming and offering tobacco to him. They'd say, "Well, we're gonna put on a ceremony." He'd ask them, "What is it for?" They say, "No, we want your friends to come and doctor you." And he'll accept that. So every so often, maybe every six months, he had to have a ceremony to doctor himself, focused on himself. His friends would come and work on him, taking the bad energy, the negative energy that he encountered away from him, and fix him up. So that's how he survived. He has to take care of himself, too.

*

My grandfather was a human being. But he loves his wine. He doesn't get drunk, but he'll have it once in a while. When he was getting older, he drank more wine. He feels like he's retired. He'd drink more often, but I never saw him drunk. He drank wine, but he never did anything bad. I never saw him staggering around all over the place. He managed his life with it until he died. He was eighty-two years old. He never had any health problems related to alcohol. We realized that he was on his way out, so we just let him. We just let him drink his wine, eat his olives, and all that stuff. But most people misunderstood. They thought that his drinking wine was valid, was okay. So we followed him. My uncles, my aunts, my cousins, they drink beer and whiskey. And then they ended up in a horrible way. We try and talk to them. I had a big round and round debate over one of my uncle's drinking habits. He's drunk almost every day. Pretty soon I said, "You know, you've got to sober up sometimes. At least spend a day sober. You've forgot what it's like to be in the real world." And then he started yelling, "I don't want nobody to preach to me about my drinking, my father drank and that's good enough for me." I said, "Well, my grandfather did a lot of good things. He earned his cup of wine once in a while. He works day and night helping somebody. Sometimes he loses his sleep, and sometimes he loses freedom in going on the hill for several days, and being gone, and all that stuff." I said, "Uncle, you can't be like him. You can never walk in his moccasins. The only thing you can do is at least live up to his teachings. You could at least become some kind of spiritual leader or singer or something. But you chose to pick up his other habit. You chose to pick up his drinking habit and let go of the good parts. And that's not what your grandpa's all about." But he just went on and on, and finally we just stopped talking to each other about that subject. My uncle died of drinking.

My grandpa Sam really loved his family and he was a generous man, but he likes his wine. And that kind of hurt our family in the long run. To this day, our families still suffer from alcohol. There's a number of people that died like that. He knew that, too. He knew that it was wrong for him to start touching that alcohol. Because everybody that looked up to him thought it was okay to drink. People misunderstood that. They can't be like my grandpa, even if they want to. They thought it was valid, but it wasn't. Drinking's not good for anybody. Even my grandpa knew that. You're not supposed to overdo your drinking. Alcohol—that's the greatest enemy of natural law. We didn't know how to handle that. It's the worst diet ever. But it's a very powerful spirit. A lot of the troubles that we have in Indian Country have to do with alcoholism. The Lakota name for wine was *mni šá*, the "red beverage." Whiskey was *mni wakȟáŋ*, "sacred beverage." That doesn't mean it's a good beverage! That doesn't mean it's a good sacred, but it is powerful. It will definitely take you on a journey! You end up doing some of the worst things in the world. And beer. We call it *mni pȟíǧa. Mni* is "water" and *pȟíǧa* is "boiling water," the suds it creates. It was never considered anything bad. It may not be a bad spirit, but it's a very powerful spirit. It depends on how you use it and how you get mixed up in it.

I think part of the reason why Grandpa drank his wine is that he wants to take a break for a few hours. He doesn't get drunk, and he doesn't raise hell or anything. He just takes a couple glasses and eats some of his snacks, and then he goes to sleep. I think the important part is that he gets to sleep. That's one of the things about living this way. You don't get sleep all the time. So part of the reason why he drank his wine is that when he drinks, his friends go away. So he drinks that, and then he goes to sleep. He sleeps all night, and then he wakes up in the morning. But he doesn't do it all the time. I think he's using the wine as a medicine to take care of himself without getting woken up in the middle of the night, somebody yapping away in his ear, you know. They bothered him all the time. All the time. They bothered him all the time. They don't like it, either. I heard them chew him out. I heard them complaining about it.

*

I'm named after my uncle Richard. He died when he was thirty years old. That broke my grandpa's heart. He lost his second son. For about a year or so, he just didn't do any ceremonies. He was drinking then. It broke his heart that he couldn't save his own son. So he stopped doing ceremony for a while, and he just started drinking really heavy. That's right around the time that my dad's first wife got sick. Those were dark times for the Moves Camp family. My dad was really upset that my grandpa can do all these things for people—he's well known for curing dangerous illnesses—but he couldn't do that for his wife, his own daughter-in-law. That really didn't sit too well with him. In that way, my dad lost both his wife and his daughter.

My great-grandfather Ťhahúŋska raised my father when he was a boy. He was going to pass his altar to my father. My dad was going to be his successor, but his first wife got sick and passed away. He wanted her to live, but it didn't turn out that way. Right around that time, my grandfather Sam was drinking a lot, so Sam didn't doctor my dad's wife. And she ended up passing away. So I guess my dad was really angry for a while. He was heartbroken. He was disappointed. I think he believed that if Ťhahúŋska was still alive then, he would have had a chance to save his wife, but that didn't happen. Ťhahúŋska died in 1949, and my father's wife died in 1951. So that was kind of difficult for him. I guess he was kind of mad at God for a while. He gave up on ceremony. My dad had two daughters from his first marriage, Evelyn Silvia and Elsie. Those are my half sisters. The oldest, Silvia, was only twenty-eight years old, but she got sick with cancer. She had a miscarriage that caused cancer in her stomach, and she passed away. That broke my father's heart again. He was really disappointed in the ceremonies. He just let everything go. He just left it until he met my mom.

My mom, Esther, was my dad's first wife's sister. That's how I was born in 1956. I was the only child. I don't have any brothers or sisters. I had two half sisters, but they both died. So that's how my family came through. My father never did do ceremony. He never went there. He just sang. He was just a singer. So that's the story about my father. He came back around after a while. Somebody came and did a Wiping of the Tears for him and put things back in order. I was feeling bad for my dad for going through all that, his pain, but then in the end I said, "Well, if Grandpa had saved her, and she got well, and they lived, I would have never come!" Things just happen the way they are. They're just meant to be that way, I guess. My mother met my father, and they stayed together until they were both really old. My dad was eighty years old when he passed away, and my mom was eighty-five years old when she passed away. So that's how things went on that one.

Toward the End

My grandfather was able to talk to four different people. That's what made him special. He had four friends. He had that special friend with him all the time, animal friends, a bird, and a stone. Around 1967, his friend came to him in front of me and my grandma and said, "Our relationship is coming to an end." Shortly after that, the bluebird that always used to come around him disappeared. We found it dead somewhere. That was his friend. That was a signal, a sign that his life was coming to an end. So I guess he was waiting to put me on the hill. My biggest fear growing up was that when he left, they're all gonna leave. So I didn't want that to happen. I didn't care if it was me or somebody else. I just didn't want it to be gone, because not having them in our life would be impossible. So we tried to help our grandpa when he was here. We use the house that he lived in now for ceremony. It was built in 1938. We call it the *thí ská*, the "white house." Toward the end of his life, he started having ceremonies in the same house where he lived. He didn't want to go out somewhere. He'd say, "Oh, just bring your stuff in here, we'll have it right here." Nowadays when I look at it, I can't believe how many people would sit in that room. It used to be packed, really packed. That's where I grew up.

By 1971 my grandfather was slowly dying. He told us he was dying. You could tell. He was slowly going the other way. So he started to give away his stuff. He wanted us to take him to a town called Wall, South Dakota. He had Wóptuȟ'a's pipe. He passed that on to my aunt, my dad's sister. Her name was Rose. She married a Bad Cob. Rose Bad Cob. Since she was the oldest daughter, my grandpa said, "You're the oldest daughter. I want you to keep this." He gave her Wóptuȟ'a's pipe. He said, "Don't use it. Keep it as a memory for the family, but don't use it. It's too old. It's real fragile." So she took it. She took it with great honor. After that, my grandfather's health started declining. In the spring of 1972 he started to do things showing that he is preparing to make his journey. He started giving things away. He started preparing himself. One morning Grandpa came over to our house and gave my father some ceremonial items that belonged to his father, Tȟahúŋska. He also gave my father a black book. He kind of didn't want nobody to see it. It was sort of like a secret. He said, "Don't just leave this laying around." The book was thick, like a Bible. It was his daily diary. He always kept track of daily events. He'd be sitting there, writing down what happened. My grandpa Sam used to keep track of all the relatives, the time and the date they died. I never did know why, but that's what he does. He gave it to my father. And after my father passed away, then I ended up with it. I didn't pay attention to it until one day I was reading it. And here it was his, my grandfather's diary. So I sat on it for quite a while, but I figured that this was the time to bring it out.

On April 21, at noon, Grandpa Sam made his journey home to the Gray Hair nation. That same day, his dog died too. He was really old and mangy. But he passed away on the same day. So we buried the dog's body behind the house. That was his best friend. They called him Toby. He was a good dog. We call it fate, but all of Wóptuȟ'a's children working with medicine ways, they don't live beyond eighty years old. Some die earlier, but that is their destiny. They can't pass eighty. But my grandfather Sam was lucky. He died when he was eighty-two. My father died on his eightieth birthday. I'm going to be sixty-five this summer, so I'm kind of looking at that eighty years old a lot and going, "Gee, it's getting close." That's why I end up not sleeping at night sometimes. But that's kind of the way our family history is set up.

I was about seventeen years old when my grandpa passed away. I didn't really do the ceremonies that he taught me right away. I kind of stayed back for a while. I didn't really want to do it right away either. After my grandpa put me on the hill, he gave instructions to my dad that I'd have to do some more *haŋbléčheya*. So after he was buried in April 1973, that summer I had to go on the hill. I had his instructions. I had to go to the old Horn Chips place, where Grandpa Horn Chips used to *haŋbléčheya*. It was northeast of his place in the creek. It's dry now, but it wasn't dry back then. It was a little island surrounded by water. You had to have a little bridge to get across there. I thought I'd have to go on the island, but I had to stand in the middle of the water, *haŋbléčheya* inside the creek. So Grandpa Ellis Chips, my dad, Uncle Godfrey, and another uncle of mine put me in the middle of the water up to my knees high. That was one of my grandpa's instructions to *haŋbléčheya* overnight standing in the middle of the water. I had to wear cloth wrapped around my feet, ankles, and thighs. Standing in the middle of the water was one of the instructions to make relations and hear the voices from the water. The next morning they went after me, but my legs were pretty numb. I couldn't feel anything in my legs. It was so cold. That same day Godfrey Chips took me into one of the hottest sweats I've ever been in, just him and myself, and he restored the feelings back into my legs. But part of the reason why I had to do that before I started doing ceremony was because the water is sacred. I had to communicate with the water, to have that connection with the life within the water. I had to do two *haŋbléčheyas* in one summer to fulfill the teachings, to be able to have them friends of his continue to come to me.

When my grandfather passed away, I felt empty for a while because I knew that nobody could ever do what he did. His teachings are as deep as the bottom of the ocean. When he died, I knew that there was no one like him in the world. I already knew that. So I never looked. When we lost our grandpa Sam, we didn't know where to go. We just kind of stayed away from everybody. I saw my grandfather do some wonderful things. I witnessed it. I heard it. He brought life back to a lot of broken people. He revived them, made them look alive again. But when he died, we fell short. We no longer had that guidance. We had to figure things out by ourselves.

Present Times

I was named after one of my grandpa Sam's sons. His name was Richard. He died when he was thirty years old. He drank himself to death. That broke my grandpa's heart. He never did get over that. I was named after him. My uncle was really a blessed person, well-to-do. People still talk about him today even though it's been over fifty years since he's been gone. I still hear stories about him. When the old people come around, they say, "Hey, Richard, are you the old Richard's boy?" I'd say, "No, that's my uncle," but they talk about him. He had an injury, a horse injury, and he only had one hand. One of his hands was amputated. So back then instead of giving you an artificial hand, they'll put a hook on you. I guess they use it to pick up certain things, and stuff like that. That's what he was known for, being a one-armed Indian cowboy. But he drank a lot. He died at a very young age and was buried here in Wanblee.

I used to hang around young teenagers that did a lot of rodeos. I had two buddies that I grew up with. They're cowboys. They rode broncos. So I'd go with them. They'd pick me up. I was about eighteen years old. That's how I got to know a lot of rodeo people. I didn't ride any broncos or anything. I just hung out with them. I dressed like them. I wear a cowboy hat and boots and all that stuff. But I never rode a bronco. I just help them get ready. Most of the time I'm sober and I'm the designated driver. These guys were cowboys. One of them was a bull rider, and the other one was a bronco rider. So for about two years we'd go to just about every rodeo on the reservation and off the reservation, too.

That's how I started drinking. I followed in the footsteps of my uncle, I figured. After the rodeos, they'll have tailgate parties. They'll drink and when everybody passes out and gets better, they go home.

So the rodeo is long-ending for us guys. After everybody's all gone, we stay at the arena with other cowboys and have our own party, drinking and stuff. One night around the Fourth of July, I was eighteen years old. I got carried away drinking. I drank one too many beers. I thought I fell asleep, but I blacked out. I came to, and I was walking in a field out in the middle of nowhere. I was walking in a field with another person, who was holding on to my arm. I guess I was lost and wandering around, so he found me.

We were walking. It was nighttime. I had no idea where I was at. I said, "Where's my friends?" He said, "They're somewhere back there. I just found you wandering around, so I'm taking you home to a safe place." So I said, "Who are you?" But he didn't answer me. I noticed that the man had a hook on his arm. I didn't know who he was. He was just another cowboy. And then we came to a place where there were lights and people with spotlights around. He said, "Those are policemen. Let's hide right here." He told me to lay down. There was a lump on the ground, a bunch of lumps, but I lay down there. He sat right next to me. He said, "Well, they're really close by. Don't move. Nobody's gonna look for anybody in a graveyard."

I was at a graveyard. I passed out again, and my face was all hot and sweaty when I woke up. Here the sun was already up early in the morning hours. I got up and I looked for my buddy, but there was nobody around. I woke up in a graveyard, right in the middle of the graveyard west of Wanblee housing. Just right there in Wanblee. I don't know how I got from Interior to Wanblee. It was a mystery. But I got back there. I woke up, and I looked at the cemetery, and then I looked at the cross where I was resting. It had my name on it. It said, "Richard Moves Camp" on it. I was shocked. I was like, "Gee, did I die? Am I gone already?" I started touching myself and looking around. But I looked at that cross again, and here it says "RIP, 1951 June, June 15, 1951." Whoever that person, Richard, was, died then. That's him. So it wasn't me. But I was at my uncle's grave. He took me to his grave, to rest. And he saved my life.

So I woke up, and I walked across the housing and went back to my house where my mom and dad lived in the housing. My dad was up cooking for himself, and I sat next to him at the table. He fed me, too, so I was eating. It really bothered me, so I told my dad. I said, "Hey." I told him in detail how everything happened and how I ended up. He said, "That was your uncle. That's my younger brother. He died in 1951. That was him who probably took you to his grave. There's a message behind that," he says. "You better pay attention." So I took the message that if I don't stop this drinking, I'll end up like him. It's a symbol, a sign. So that was my last drink. I never drank anymore after that. I put it away. So that was when I was seventeen, eighteen years old. I never drank again. So that was the story of how I became sober.

A year later, on the same day, the Fourth of July, my buddies came after me to go to the rodeo. My dad was working on the garden. We lived out in the country. I looked at my dad, and I remembered what happened. I said, "You guys go ahead. I'll stay. I got something to do." They looked disappointed, but they took off. And here the next day I got notice that those two were killed in a car accident. They died at the rodeo. That would have been me. So I got saved by my ancestor. Ever since then, I've gone the other way, worked as a counselor, and tried to help people sober up. Because I always remember that from time to time. I never met my uncle, but I met him way later. He was never married. He died young. But his grave is still here in Wanblee.

*

I met my wife, Arvella, when I was nineteen years old. I was gonna go on the hill. They took me to a place in the woods where people went to *haŋbléčheya* since the 1920s. I was getting ready with my father and my mom and two of my uncles and one of my cousins. They were there helping me get ready. And out of nowhere—I didn't see it right away—I was down there, preparing, getting my stuff ready. People were doing things, building a sweat fire, but then all of a sudden, a girl showed up out of nowhere. She just sat above the hill where we were getting ready. She sat down and was looking around. Everybody looked at her and said, "Where did she come from? Who is that?" And then she got up and walked down the hill, down the creek. So my uncles and my aunts chased her, but there's no person there. So that was a mystery.

After I went on the hill, a whole summer went by. I went to a sun dance, and there was a powwow after the sun dance. And here I saw that same girl walking by. I said to my brother Tim, "That's the girl. That's her, the one we saw out there." He said, "That's right, that's her!" Tim, my brother Tim—he's not shy—so he went up to her. "Hey, what's your name?" She was only sixteen, seventeen years old. So I met her. I met her then. I didn't get together with her yet. I just met her. And I said, "That girl that I saw at the *haŋbléčheya*," I told my parents, "I saw her at the powwow." She never did say anything. She didn't know I'd seen her.

And then about a year after that, we got together. We've stayed together ever since. We always do things together. She sort of runs the family now. She's sixty-one. She'll be sixty-two this year. She's a grandma who's totally in charge! We got married the traditional way. We didn't go to a courthouse or stuff like that. But later on we did. We went and got a license from the courthouse. We got a license a year after we were married. There was an old man at our wedding. He was congratulating us, but this old man—he's a white guy, but he's married to an Indian—he says, "It seems like it's a bed of roses, but it's not. It's got its ups and downs, too. Just hang in there. That's all you can do." That always stayed with me. After we got married, we moved back to where I grew up, right behind the cabin. We put a trailer house there. We only had one daughter at that time. We lived there for about fifteen years. When my dad was getting sick, we moved into town where he was living in the housing area and stayed with him. And when he passed away, we moved back into the country, and then finally we ended up with this house here. I did my first ceremonies in the house that I grew up in, the log house. I think I was about eighteen. Then later on when they gave the white house to me, I rebuilt it, remodeled it. We started using it around the mideighties all the way through the nineties, till today, present times.

Spirits and Ghosts

The things that we know are very sacred. It's real. It's powerful, but it's hard to describe. In English, the word *spirit* is very broad. In the Indigenous world, it's very complex. In the everyday world, most people have no idea that the ghost world and the spirit world are two different worlds. They think everything is the same. And that's where everybody gets confused. There are different sets of tribal spirit people. They're not all the same. There's a maze out there. You've got to have the right connections. That's what people don't know today. Sometimes you don't see them. You can just hear the voices. There's a song about this. It says they live in four dimensions—one you can't see, one you can, one you can feel, and one just silent. But they show up whenever they want to. I don't need to put up an altar. I don't need to put up ceremonies. When I'm driving by myself, somebody will show up. They don't just appear. They show up in the real world. The other day I was driving. I picked up a hitchhiker coming back from Rosebud. It was one of them! So I said, "Good thing I stopped!" They show up that way.

They can follow you everywhere. They can show up and talk to you wherever. You can sit in a restaurant with a hundred people, they'll still show up. And the people will not even know that he's walking up to you and he's not real. Some people will see them, too. But the people who see them have no idea he's not real. They have no idea. They think he's just another Indian guy showing up. Sometimes they show up as white people, too. They show up any way. I used to think I was the only one seeing them. But other people see them, too. Anybody can see them. If need be, anybody can talk to them, too. It's just that you'll have no idea that they're spirits. If you have that knowledge and connection, then you'll know it's one of them. They can just turn around and disappear, like that. They're really tricky, though. They'll show up anywhere. They have no boundaries. But there's always a rule: If you do this, they won't come anymore. If you do that, they might not come. So it's kind of like walking the fine line. It's like a contract. They have a right to terminate the contract anytime they want to. And once you lose it, it's pretty hard to get it back. You won't get it back for a long time.

That's something you've got to earn. You have to earn it to see them. They don't cut corners. If you want a college degree, you have to go to school. Same way with our world, you've got to go to school for it. There's some do's and don'ts. But there's nothing in it for them. They have no feelings. All they're doing is helping their friend with a request. They don't care if you die or not. But if you ask them to watch over you, they will watch over you. They will do their mission. But in the world they come from, it doesn't matter if we live here or not. So that's why we pray and ask them to help us to have somebody stay around a little longer. You got to be specific about what you ask them for. They don't care. They just work for God, whatever God asks them to do, they'll do it. I don't even know if they have any compassion or not. If you want them to help you, they will. But you've got to ask them. And that's why we pray and ask.

There's nothing in the book that says the angels who work for God are loving angels. They're just God's servants. They answer to God. It's just our idea that they watch over us and love us to death. That's what we want, but they're just servants of God. It is only the living that have compassion and sensitivity. We understand emotions, mentally, connections, us humans. And the trees and the four-legged and the winged nation, they have the same feelings as we do. But the gods beyond the living, they have a different world. And that's why we do these ceremonies and sacrifices—we're showing them that we really mean it from our heart when we ask for something. They have that power to give it to us. For most people, they make that call but nobody answers. And so you get disappointed and wonder if there's really a line on the other side. But they don't know the right number. The privilege is sacrificing. My grandpa used to say, "Anybody can do it. You can do it, too." And he's right. He allowed some of us to see what he saw. We don't hear it, but we saw what he saw. We saw them talking to each other. We saw them take him away and bring him back. And he even allowed some of us to talk to them.

He didn't just get that because he was cool or because they like him. He had to earn it. Sometimes when you call them, they don't show up. You're living on their time. So they don't always answer. They have their own minds. So if they're not in a good mood, they won't come. You've got to do everything in order. It's kind of like the way my dad describes it: "If you want a car to run good, you make sure you have the right kind of oil, the right kind of gas. Put all the parts together, and it'll start up and take off. But if you cut short on some of these tools, it might not even start. It might not even go. If it goes, it might break down. Ceremonial life is that way." Everything's got to be done in order, to preserve that energy. Everything has to be done. That's the sacrifice. You can't cut corners on these ways. So that's what it's like living in that world.

It takes sacrifice. It takes sacrifice to earn that privilege. They don't come to you because they love you. They come to you because you've earned the right. You've earned what it takes to get there. Sacrifice. Everything requires sacrifice. Nowadays everybody wants the goal, the spiritual connection, but they don't want to sacrifice. They just want to get it. And they fantasize about how it comes to them. But my grandpa Sam had to sacrifice. It required a lot of hard work, a lot of lost sleep, a lot of sacrificing, a lot of good suffering. It's the only way to break that barrier between us and the invisible world, the other side. You can't just get it. You have to go, step by step, over the mountain, come back down, maybe swim across the river, to catch it. But when you get it, it's permanent, permanent. They will come when you ask them. The power of the sacrifice, the payoff, is that when you dial that number, and place that call, somebody will pick up on the other end. But even with that privilege, you're still just a human being, you're still gonna die someday. I wish it wasn't like that, but it is that way. God made it like that. The greatest men in my life, I saw them die. It makes you disappointed. Why is God doing this to us? But that's just the way life is. Beautiful flowers bloom to their best and then die off.

There's some danger that goes with this, too. Just because you can talk to them, other unnatural beings will try to sneak in that door and come to you. You've got to watch yourself. Back in 2010, I was living in California. The room that I was staying in had a phone in it. That phone rang at four o'clock in the morning. It's a motel room. I looked at the clock. It says four in the morning. So I picked it up, and here it was my mom. I said, "Why are you calling me this early, mom?" She says, "I want to ask how you're doing." I said, "I'm doing okay." "How's the grandkids?" "They're doing fine." "How's everybody else?" "Everybody's doing good." "You need to stay home once in a while. Don't be traveling all the time." Just like a mother would talk to their son, you know. I said, "Yeah." And then it occurred to me—just that minute—that she died back in 2006! I said, "Mom, you're supposed to be dead. Where are you?" And then the phone went dead. So I said, "God damn it, that woman's sneaking around on me again."

I hung up the phone, but then just before daylight, my face was starting to tingle. My eyes were watery. I'd had a ministroke. I was in trouble. My whole body was tingling. She called me for a reason, to take care of myself, look after myself. So I canceled my events that day and made arrangements to catch a flight home. I barely made it to Rapid City. Arvella came after me, but I only made it as far as the river. I couldn't drive anymore. Pretty soon the highway split into two highways. Everything I saw was double. I was in deep trouble. So the next morning, my daughter was the first one up. I walked in the kitchen. She looked at me and said, "Oh dad, you're in trouble. You better get yourself to the hospital right now." So I ended up in the regional hospital for ten days. I had a stroke. That phone call messed me up. During that time, my friends never showed up. I was calling them, but they never showed up. So I felt like I was alone.

So just because you're open to that world, the no-good ones are waiting along, too. You've got to always watch out. You've got to be careful. But I got over it about a year later. It took me almost a year to get back to normal. But my health started going downward after that. I started getting diabetes, high blood pressure. They couldn't control it. The Western doctors said my blood pressure was too high and my diabetes was out of control. So that caused the Bell's palsy and the stroke. Some of my friends took me to a therapist in Chinese medicine. They do acupuncture all over your head. They did that for about four treatments, and then after that, it worked. I got better. I took control over my diabetes and took all kinds of pills to make my high blood pressure go down. I learned a big lesson. You've got to take care of yourself.

I think my mom was standing by someplace. She had to intervene. That was my mom, but I don't think she was a spirit. She was a ghost. I wasn't in good health, but her energy, wherever she was, I was aware of it because she was my mom. And something inside of me was triggered by reviving her voice in my consciousness, it welcomed her back. She came into my body through the voice. So she woke me up and became part of me by telling me that I've got some health problems, and that if I don't take care of it, I could die. Sure enough, that almost happened! After she made the call, I got really sick. She was a *wanáǧi*. She came into my world because I was in a state of mind receptive to see ghosts. So that was kind of like a weird experience. Now if I stay someplace and the phone rings, I don't answer it!

Another time I was driving. This was only a few years ago, I think 2017. I went to the store, me and my relative. It was winter time. We went after bread and different things, getting ready for supper. It was drizzling outside, and we were coming back. We turned into the junction, and here, there's a man standing on the road. He looked like a monk. He had a brown, canvas-like hood on and a rope tied around his waist. He was facing the other way. So I said, "Somebody's dressed weird, got a weird raincoat on." My relative was sitting in the back. We pulled in there, and that guy got in the passenger's seat and pulled his hood down. I looked and here it was my uncle, Godfrey Chips. He died back in 2014. He came back in real life. He just showed up on the road. I accepted it because I thought he was with his friends that he works with, but it wasn't that way. Still, being Wóptuȟ'a's grandson, I think he earned the privilege of being able to relay a message back to our world. He says, "I've been waiting for you right here." I said, "What do you want?" He said, "I don't want this to happen to my son." He pointed at the driveway. I didn't even see him. So we both got out and walked over to the approach, and here one of his sons was laying there. Somebody killed him. He was all beat up. I was looking at it. He said, "I don't want this to happen to my son. I want you to put on Grandpa Sam's Five Stick ceremony to prevent that from happening." Then he walked across the fence without even climbing it. He just walked across. And then he started going up in the air. He started getting smaller and smaller and then disappeared. My relative was all freaked out. He said, "Hey, who was that? Who was that?" My relative even saw it. So we drove a little bit farther, and we both vomited. That was too much. Now my relative don't want to go around with me no more. But we did the ceremony, though. Godfrey's son was in prison at that time, but he got out and sure enough, he was found like that, all beat up, but he didn't get killed. You kind of open yourself to that world, so you've got to watch out for the good and bad. You've got to be ready all the time.

There's a story about an old man who lived west of Wanblee. He was doing something late one night and was going home on a wagon. He stopped to open a gate and drove his team and wagon across. He closed the gate and got back on the wagon, and here there's a person with a hoodie on sitting next to him, looking straight ahead. Just sitting there. He don't know how he got on there. So he says, "Where did you come from? Who are you?" But the man didn't say anything. He just sat there. So they took off, but the horses were nervous, jumpy. They went five yards, and the guy just jumped off and walked away. But those horses kept going. The old man thought they were taking him home. But after about less than half a mile, the horses stopped and didn't want to go anymore. He was whipping them and trying to get them to go, but they wouldn't move. Then he realized that the horses were standing on the edge of a fifty-foot cliff. So now he was totally confused. That wasn't the road that he was supposed to be on. So he turned the wagon around and started taking off, and here he saw a man over the hill calling his name. It was one of his relatives. He'd been gone for two days!

So real ghosts have power. The *wanáǧi*. They're not spirits, but they're the spirit of a human. And that can be dangerous. They can take you away somewhere. That old man didn't realize he'd been gone for two days. He had no idea how he ended up way on the other side of the Badlands. So they did a ceremony for him, but he was never the same. That bad energy can be dangerous if they come to you. They have that power. They don't even have to talk to you. He can just walk by you, and your mind will be gone for a while. Imagine waking up one morning and you realize that you're all alone in the world. You go outside and there's nobody in your town. It's just you and the buildings. No cars. No dogs. Just totally empty. So you go over to the next town, nobody. You find yourself totally alone in the world. And for the rest of your life it's gonna be like that. Yes, you do go somewhere, but sometimes you don't get anywhere.

Bad Medicine

There's a myth about Indian ceremonies that still affects a lot of people today. Everybody thinks there's "bad medicine." That's what they think. Bad medicine. Everybody asks me about that. I've been asked that too many times! I always tell people the same thing. There is no bad medicine in our world. In our ceremonies, sweat lodge, *haŋbléčheya*, sun dance, the pipe, and the Lówáŋpi, there is no bad medicine. It's a myth. It doesn't happen that way. There might be bad medicine in other parts of the world, like witchcraft or devil worship, that's probably still out there. Maybe there are devil worshippers or witchcraft people out there, but that has nothing to do with Lakota medicine ways. In these Indian ways, there is no bad medicine. That's what I've been telling people, all the time. None of these ceremonies were intended to be anything bad. I've always said that. I don't really buy into it. I don't think that was part of our ways. For one, I don't think there's a medicine man alive who can do that. Maybe a long time ago they might have been able to do that, but not today. But people really believe. I don't believe it's possible. People probably do pray against each other, but they're not supposed to. That's against the ways. Nobody's supposed to be praying against each other. I've never heard anybody praying against anybody either. There's no method out there that can do that. None of the Indian ceremonies I've ever been to had anything to do with bad against anybody. It's not supposed to be that way.

The spirits understand the difference between good and bad. If you're doing good to people, they'll bless you with something good. They'll give it to you. If you dish out something good, they'll give it to you. At the same time, if you dish out something bad to others, they'll give you something bad, too. The consequences will come back on you. So it would be unethical and wrong for a bad person to have that spirit connection. They know the difference between good and bad. So if your intentions are bad, they won't even come near you. You can talk good to everybody, but if you're a mean, bad person inside your heart, they'll know what's inside of you and they'll stay away from you. They're lenient toward good behavior and good things.

When my great-grandpa Wóptuȟ'a was young, he would make protection medicine. It's called *wóthawe*. It protects you from anything from physical bullets to physical hurt. It's a protection, but it also serves a purpose of avoiding getting hurt and winning a war. It also protects you against what we call *waȟmúŋǧa*. *Waȟmúŋǧa* is a bad spell or a bad energy that you put on somebody physically. People used to have that power back in Wóptuȟ'a's generation. When Wóptuȟ'a was young, many other people had power like him—probably not as strong as him—but they had power. I think the energy's thinned out nowadays. It's weak. Back in the old days, different tribes used to go against each other, *waȟmúŋǧa*-ing each other. They used different ways. It's real scary. I'm glad nobody can do that nowadays. Back in that generation, if they wanted you dead, you'd be dead. I think that's why they gave us all these rituals, to protect ourselves from that energy that way and you refrain from getting involved in bad things.

But when the ceremonies went underground, a lot of important information went missing. That bad medicine concept came out as something that belonged to other nations. A lot of tribes believe that. It was the Christians and the government who made our ceremonies look bad. They did a good job condemning our ceremonies, saying they're bad medicine, witchcraft, and stuff. Christian society came in here and denounced our culture, saying it's bad medicine and witch-doctoring. The Europeans, when they came over here, they automatically labeled our ways heathen. They made a lot of Native people believe that. A lot of Native Christians today still believe that the Indian ways are bad energy, bad medicine. They look at it that way. Those people are in between Christian and Lakota. They use the ideology of the Christian teachings, and then they kind of apply it to the Indian stuff. That's what I call colonialism culture.

People in the modern generation think that Indians can do that to each other. Today, as we speak, many of our tribal people believe in that. If you go outside and you slip and fall, they'll make you believe that somebody put a curse on you. That's a fear factor that they put on each other. But it's just a myth. They even came up with a word for it that never existed before, *wákúŋza*. That word is an Anglicized cultural teaching, an Anglicized Lakota word. It came when the Christians came into our world. It means cursing, wishing bad on someone. *Wákúŋza* is something that is contrary to good things, wishing bad things on someone. People try it. People scare each other. Even medicine men sometimes say, "Somebody put bad medicine on you." So I don't believe in bad medicine. But you do have to look out for bad medicine men. We have a lot of those out here. Maybe the person drinks a lot. Or he doesn't do things right. He's not 100 percent there. He's not in a good place. That happens a lot in Indian Country today. It's disappointing. No wonder a lot of our people are turning away from medicine men, because some of them are not real. So you have to educate yourself about how it's supposed to be.

Back to the Old Teaching

We have to change our way of life, go back to the old teaching. Our culture almost became extinct. A lot of our ceremonies, the way of life that we lived, vanished. Colonialism killed a lot of our people. Colonialism caused us to lose our family values. Our Indian way of life changed. If you're an Indian, some of your own people are not familiar with their identity.

I'm not against any church or religion or anything, but the Catholic Church is one of the richest corporations in the world. The church is an organization meant to control the world. One way they did that was to send the churches onto the reservations. They used force, too. They took kids away from their parents and sent them to Carlisle Indian School. They taught them to be anti-Indian. They didn't want them to speak their language. They wanted to wash out their insides and put the white man's thinking inside them. So they might look like normal Indians, but inside they follow Christian teachings. They don't even understand it themselves. They just do it because they want to belong and they no longer see themselves fitting in the traditional world. They go to church so they can belong to something.

So if you're Indian, but you're not baptized, you belong to that class over there. You belong to the sticks. You don't get the rations like everybody else. They hold them down out there, the people in the wilderness. But the Christian Indians who left the Indian ways, you live in a nice house over there. And you have a better job. That's classism. And that was the reality on the reservation for a long time. And that's what our grandpas hated. Classism destroyed our people. That's the teaching that came from our grandpas. Tȟahúŋska knew that real well. He was just trying to make a living. There were hardly any jobs, so he was a practitioner of the Episcopal Church. He was a church man. He wasn't really seriously into it, because he left the church and went back to the Indian ways. But it was an organization that hired people to spread the word of God. So he started out that way, but it didn't last very long.

Many Indians believe in Christianity. These are real lovable people, too. But when it comes to the topic of spiritual ways and beliefs, they're curious about it, like how it works, but they stick to their own Christianity. A lot of our own people, registered members of the Lakota tribe, have no connection with this culture or spirituality.

So when the ceremonies started coming back to the surface, they snuck back in some really unusual, interesting ways. The ceremonies came back with colonialized teachings, colonialized ceremonies. The original teaching kind of stayed hidden.

In the precolonial Lakota world, it was all about coming from your heart. We strayed off from our original spiritual thinking. Today when we try to make relations to the Creator, the ideology that comes with most people is "What's in it for me? What do I get from this relationship?" That offends *those* guys up there. That's not spirituality. Wóptuȟ'a, Tȟahúŋska, and Horn Chips, they never say that. They never said, "What's in it for me?" If they want friendship from you, then it's friendship. There's nothing in it for them but friendship. *Wólakȟota*. You never ask for anything back from what you give that person.

We've been practicing our ceremonies in a colonialized way for a long time. Most of us have no idea what the original teachings were. But my grandfathers understood those things. They embedded themselves in that. There are still some teachings that kept going. But there's another part where there was rebirth during the sixties and seventies. So there's two different cultural teachings going on here. There's two types or versions of every ritual, a colonialized one and a precolonialized one. And there's a lot of information missing on the precolonialized teachings.

We're still living on a Christian's agenda. It was all about demonizing our culture. We were born into this society, but we didn't realize it wasn't our society. We still have powwows. We still have ceremony. We still have schools and kinship. But these things were done in colonialized and Christian ways. So we were sort of lost and didn't even know the difference for a while there, in the 1960s and

'70s. We've now just sort of reached a plateau, where we recognize that we had a history and a culture in precolonialized times.

So we want to go back to those ways. That's our goal, to go back to those ways. A lot of good people on our reservation are really hungry for spirituality. They're really hungry for something that will bring them closer to God. We're at a crossroads where we want to go back to precolonialism times, which make sense about our culture and our proper identity, to learn our ceremonies. We have to relearn the prayers and the pipe and stuff like that.

Wóptuȟ'a's generation, those guys never went to school. They were still roaming the Great Plains. I consider them civilized. When they took the culture away from the Indians, we became uncivilized. The more we strayed into the modern world, the more we became uncivilized because we're living in a foreign world, a colonial world. We're culturally handicapped, because the majority of our students can't speak Lakota and our original way of life became foreign. Everybody used to think that our ancestors never went to school and never had any education, but according to the records in Pine Ridge and the federal government, all of our ancestors, including my great-grandfathers, they all finished school. They weren't dropouts. They finished school. The government made sure that everybody went to school. Back then the schools only went up to sixth grade, so once you made it to sixth grade, you finished school. You're considered a graduate. My grandpas finished sixth grade and went to work afterward.

I used to think that my grandpas never had an education in the Western world, but they all finished school. The old people honored the agreements made between the two nations and still held on to their cultural competency. They still held on to their language and customs. It's only a myth that our people were uneducated and uncivilized until the Europeans came. We considered ourselves civilized. But when the Western way of life came, we became uncivilized. We lost our way of life, our world. We lost the language. We lost the teachings. The generation that came after me, they knew all about the Western ways, but they became culturally incompetent in their own culture. Many of our kids today are culturally incompetent in our own culture.

It's been like that since the 1940s and '50s. There was a lot of shame. Psychologically, Natives were driven to be ashamed of their language and identity. Many people wanted to be modern, Western-type people, so they learned the English language but denied their own identity. That happened through the 1950s and '60s. Substance abuse affected a lot of people. Alcoholism became a norm, drinking. Even though it's wrong, they still do it. And that changed the lifeways of our people. We lost our way of life. In the early part of the 1970s, that started turning around. The social movements helped turn that around. Now, they want to go all the way back to the old ways. Now, more Indians want to go back to the Indian ways and forget about the white ways. Now we even have white people that want to learn about the Indian ways, sweat lodges and sun dances, ceremonies. But the problem is we try to learn it through the colonialized process. And there isn't much written material about precolonial times in the literature.

The Pipe

Today everybody thinks that what was written in *Black Elk Speaks* is the way it was. They say that White Buffalo Calf Woman brought the pipe, the ceremonies, and our teachings. But it didn't happen like that. Before the pipe was received, we already had these rituals, *haŋbléčheya*, Wiping of the Tears, Inípi. These were here long before the pipe came. So it's important to tell people the stories about our rituals and ceremonies. They've been here long before the pipe came. The pipe came way later. Our ceremonies were here long before the pipe was ever given to us, but since the pipe was the last thing that came from Creator, they use it in all ceremonies, all gatherings, because it represents peace, *wólakȟota*. And because it was sacred, the people used it for personal prayer and ceremony, but not enough knowledge about it was taught to them.

The version that I learned was that the woman who brought the pipe was on a journey. And the two men who met her were helping her get to her destination. It wasn't just an overnight thing. It took a while for them to get to know her. And when they got to know her, she was very tempting. She played all the roles in a man's life, in their minds. She spoke to the men in a sacred way, but as they carried on, she also tempted them because she was a woman, just simply being a woman. They saw her legs, they saw her body, and that energy tested the men's minds, their sanity, it played with it. Both men were strong physically, but one of them was weak in the mind. That man decided to cross that boundary and fulfill his desires. But he didn't get anywhere. He ended up dead.

That is the story of the pipe. The story of how it was brought is the life we're living today. Men suffer when they lack spiritual strength and are ruled by their desires. What makes men weak today is alcohol and drugs. It causes them to go the wrong way. It started from back in the day when the pipe was first brought to our people. We say women are sacred, that women are the center of the world, but after we were colonized, it was the men who were considered important. This modern world that we live in today really changed our thinking and behavior.

Everywhere you look, women are being abused by men. Every day, as we speak, a female somewhere is being violated or abused because a man is mentally ill. When we became colonized, we lost our values and principles and we began to abuse our women. Women are sacred. In Grandpa Sam's ceremony, Grandma was the center of it. She sat with the pipe. She took care of Grandpa. Everything was about Grandma. She smoked the pipe first. She drank the water first. She gets served food first. She's the one that takes care of the medicine.

A woman brought the sweat to us. A woman brought the pipe to us. A woman brought us into this world. In our ceremony culture, the female is sacred. Women are the center of the world. So we've got to watch out for our women. Today, people carry the pipe, but that's all they know. They think it's a spirit god or something like that. But it's got a real purpose. Back in the old days, it was a very honorable thing to possess a pipe, to carry it in a good way.

Our interpretation is that the pipe was given to us to prevent and repair broken marriages for the sake of the children. *Wičhóuŋčhaǧe*. *Wičhóuŋčhaǧe* means "a generation of life." A continuation of life. A child's healthy life. The second reason is peace. To make peace, with yourself, and with other families. The pipe was given to us to focus on family dynamics, family life, to repair broken homes, broken relationships, and broken circles, community circles, to repair marriages. It brings peace to what is broken in that way. That's the only reason she gave us the pipe. That's the purpose of the pipe. That's the only purpose of the pipe.

The pipe is used all over, but what it's really here for is to resolve conflict. That's what its original power was for. When you believe in that pipe, you want to be peaceful with everybody else. The pipe can help straighten us out. The pipe can bring us back to reality. That's what the pipe is for, but a lot of information about the pipe is gone today. It's supposed to be the center of the families coming together and living good, healthy lives. Conflict resolution. My grandpa talks about that. Every Lakota was familiar with that. That's what the pipe was for. That's why the pipe was given to us, to make peace with people, to honor that peace. As a pipe holder, you have responsibilities. You're supposed to pray for people to live together, resolve problems, to pray for the younger generation. It's supposed to deepen your faith in Creator and yourself. It's to help us stay focused on what is real. That's what the pipe carrier should be concerned about and trained about, restoring peace, resolving conflicts.

The problem is that today half of our people went Christian, so they don't know too much about the pipe. They kind of make it look like a hobby, carrying the pipe. It's just a ritual item, an artifact. So along the way we lost the meaning about almost everything that we possess, the sweat lodge, the pipe, the songs, the drum, the ceremonies. The original meaning was that you've got to put your heart in it and take good care of it. The ceremonies each had their own individual songs. There were no standardized songs. And the medicine men each had their own dreams. But when the ceremonies went underground, a lot of those songs didn't come back. So now we're doing the best we can with the songs we have. We're doing the best we can.

I used to witness the Tribal Chairmen's Association. They used to have an annual meeting. So I was invited to their meetings to say a prayer, but none of those tribal chairmen fully understood our pipe. It was a colonialized possession. One of them even had a trunk full of pipes in his car. He was doing some kind of publicity stunt and presenting pipes to senators or congressmen who came to visit. This guy would go to the trunk of his car and get a pipe and say, "Here, I want to give this to you." I was too young to say anything. He was way older than me, but I watched him do it. I don't know where he got his hands on all those pipes, but he passed them out without even telling them anything, just "here you go, have this." Those white people would say, "Oh, okay, thank you." They probably took it home and hung it on the wall.

*

Today, as we speak, white people are coming to our reservation because they're looking for spiritual sanctuary. On Pine Ridge, Rosebud, and probably Cheyenne River, most of the sun dancers are white people. And they're good people, too. They come with a good heart. They're trying to learn. But that just shows you how much they've lost of their own ways, that they're looking for answers from Indian Country. And they all carry pipes, too. The majority of them are pipe holders. Every one of those white people that come to the reservation, if they were taught right, it would be a better world. They're hungry for spirituality, and they're trying to get whatever helps them, but there's a lack of teaching.

Anybody can hold a pipe, but if you didn't go to school for it, what's the use in holding it? You have very little information about it. You just have it because you know it's sacred so you're holding it really tight, but there's a lot of information that you need to know about it first. That's my thought about it. Learn about it. Go to school about it. Have some idea what it's for. I know a lot of people come today to seek answers from the pipe and our ceremonies. There's nothing wrong with that. They just have to learn the right way. I'm not against anyone holding a pipe. You can be a white man. You can be an Indian. You can carry it, but you've got to learn. And if you learn more, then you become very humble and respectful and mindful about using it.

*

In the teachings from Wóptuȟ'a, Grandpa Sam, and Tȟahúŋska, the pipe isn't the center of our world, but because it was brought to our people by Buffalo Woman, Wóptuȟ'a and Tȟahúŋska held that responsibility sacred and honored it. So they used it in their ceremonies, and they taught about how sacred it is. But if it wasn't here, the ceremonies would still continue. They hold it sacred, but they also know that it's not the center of our spirituality. It plays an important role, but the main reason it's here is for families and children. *Wičhóuŋčhaǧe.* The families. And peace, *wólakȟota.* These teachings are missing today. People like Tȟahúŋska and Wóptuȟ'a had a close relationship with the people that watched the pipe. They would come to Wóptuȟ'a and Tȟahúŋska and ask them for guidance, how to take care of the pipe. So they relied on them. There was even a time when they tried to get Tȟahúŋska to be the caretaker of the pipe. But he refused because he said that's not my family. But when people asked Wóptuȟ'a for his services, they offered a pipe. So he decided to work with the pipe, even though he didn't have to.

When people offered him the pipe and asked him for his services, it was kind of like a three-step process. So when you want to ask him for healing, you ask him, and he'll prepare himself. You'll take him the pipe and he'll smoke it, and then after he finishes smoking it, he'll ask you what you want. Then you tell him. And then he'll figure out what kind of ceremony you need. And then he'll give you instructions. That's step number two. He'll give you instructions and he'll say, "You need this, this, and that." And then we pick a time and date, and you'll do it on that day. Step three is when you actually perform the ceremony. Afterward, you can give him a gift. It's called *wóȟeyaka*. It's not a payment and it's not compensation. *Wóȟeyaka* is an offering. That's giving the medicine person a gift. Back in the old days, it used to be a horse, a blanket, or a buffalo hide, something of value. And then he'll accept that. Nowadays, people will give money. Money is sacred. You can give him whatever. People give him money or a blanket. Different things. It doesn't matter. As long as it comes from your heart. And his friends will be happy because you paid him. You can give that to him right there, but you also have to have a *wóphila* later, a thanksgiving, a kind of putting a closure to that.

Tȟahúŋska and Horn Chips had different ways. Each ceremony required a different way of offering that pipe. They're not all the same. So for Yuwípi, the tie-up, you fill the pipe and give it to him. In one shot, he'll just take it. For Grandpa Sam's ceremonies, he has four different altars. Each one requires a different way of approach. For his Five Stick ceremony, you have to hold the pipe and point it in all directions, and then you go in front of him and give him the pipe. Then he'll accept it. But if it's for another ceremony, like a Yuwípi, you just give it to him. If it's for another one of his other ceremonies, he'll tell you how to give the pipe to him. You don't give it to him. You just set it in front of him. You put it on the ground in front of him. And then he'll take it from the ground and smoke it. How you present that pipe affects the ceremony, affects what you want. So that's how it went, all the way through three generations, up to today. Lately, since the 1970s, when people present the pipe, they do it four times. That's something just recently made up. They do that during the sun dance. People don't know that, so they think that's the way to do it. So the protocol kind of changed after the sun dance came back.

Ceremonies were never public. They were always private. It was just the family, the medicine man, and a singer. That's it. But nowadays, a lot of people show up in the ceremony house. I think it's because people today are starving for spirituality. And they compare ceremony with the church. In a Sunday church, everybody's welcome. The door's open. But ceremony's different. It's private. It's like going to a doctor visit. It's supposed to be private, confidential.

That kind of changed when Ťhahúŋska and Horn Chips came out. They used to have packed houses, a whole bunch of people. Today the medicine man won't complain. The more people, the better for him. He became a show-off. So a lot of people show up, but a long time ago it wasn't like that. It was very private, just the families and relatives. But nowadays everybody shows up for a ceremony, and then they talk about what that guy wanted in the ceremony. They say, "Well, we had a ceremony, thirty people showed up, we helped that guy out. He wants his wife back." It became a public thing. It's not supposed to be that way. So now since the seventies and eighties, they have packed houses, packed ceremony rooms, over a hundred people. Open house. But that was never part of the tradition. Sometimes it might be just four people in a ceremony. Unless the person that's putting it on invited all their relatives, family members, then you see a lot of people in there. But it's not an open house to everybody.

Sometimes, in a real heavy case, if somebody's really sick, then the person that's offering the pipe can have four nights of ceremony, but it has to be four. It takes four nights to help that person get well. But nowadays people don't know that, so they just have one night, thinking that's gonna take care of it. It's not like that. It requires four nights. It also involves honor. Let's say you met my grandpa Sam. You asked for his help. You gave him the pipe. He's going to ask you where and when. So you say, "Oh, next Saturday. Let's do it around evening." He's locked in there now. He accepted your pipe, so he can't accept another one until he finishes yours. Come rain or shine or blizzard, he's going to show up over there at that place. Saturday afternoon, he will show up. That's honor. You've got to stick to your commitment, so it has to be done at that time. Nowadays we just call each other and say, "Let's move it to next week. We're not ready." It's not supposed to be like that, especially when it comes to a ceremony. So that was the way Grandpa Sam, Ťhahúŋska, and their father, their generation, do ceremony. It's supposed to stay that way. When you do it that way, the energy and the power are there.

The Seven Ceremonies

We have seven ceremonies, represented by the seven stars in the Big Dipper. That's how we interpret our star knowledge. Our ceremonies came at different times. But what's important is to recognize that some of them are still usable today. According to my grandpa, the sweat lodge was the first ritual that came to the Lakota. It was given to a woman. It came from another world called *thuŋkáŋ oyáte*. The woman was given instructions to build a temple to clean the men, to keep them pure. Women don't need to do that for themselves, because they get cleansed every month by the moon. So a woman developed the sweat lodge and put it together, and then introduced the *thuŋkáŋ oyáte*, the *thuŋkáŋ* people. They came from another world. That's how the sweat lodge started out. A woman was visited by some people from another world, and they introduced themselves. That world was known as the *thuŋkáŋ oyáte, thuŋkáŋ* people. We use stones to represent them, but they're not actually "stone people." They're just like you and me, a nation of people, but they have power, more power than we do. Their connection with the Creator was much stronger, so they have abilities to do miracles. They gave the woman instructions, and they emphasized that the dome of the sweat lodge represents a family, the *thiwáhe*. They told her that whenever the temple is built, they will come and they will do the healing. The word *thi* means home. So the Lakotas will ask you, *tuktél yathí hwo*, "Where do you live?" They'll say, "Where is your *thi*?" The *thi* represents your home, a sacred temple. So the sweat lodge represents that. And the first two willows of the doorway, they represent the father and the mother, the man and the wife. That's their beginning. That's their center. And then the next willow represents the girls' kinfolks' mother and father. The next willow on this side represents the men's folks, so the in-laws cross each other on the other side. And then their ancestors, and the other's ancestors, they crisscross. So each willow represents a member of the family, and the willows that wrap around the circle represent the children, the future generation. The second row of willows represents the second generation, third generation, fourth generation, it goes until there's no more willows. So the whole dome, the whole temple, because it came from a woman, they also say it represents a woman's womb.

Over the years, the sweat lodge came to represent all the other ceremonies. Other rituals came to us, but we all have to go through the sweat before we go to ceremony. That's why people do that. So the fire that's built is the fire of life, Creator God, Wakȟáŋ Tȟáŋka. And the little mound that's in between the fire and the sweat lodge, that represents the generations, what kept us together. The sweat lodge represents the power of the Creator. When it first started, the *thuŋkáŋ oyáte* would come and sit in the middle of the lodge and take care of people. But after a while, that didn't happen anymore, so then they began to use stones to represent them.

Today a lot of men and women sweat together. It's a bad practice. I come from families that didn't do that. My grandpa Sam never did that. Horn Chips and Wóptuȟ'a and those guys, they never sweat with women. They never did that. Grandma Winnie goes in there all by herself. She sweats by herself. She even hauls her own rocks. I never seen her go in with anybody else. The only time my grandpa would go in the sweat with a woman is when she's getting ready to go on the hill. But other than that, there's no social sweating. I can see why men sweat with women now. The songs you sing together, it's like a choir. I feel uncomfortable doing it, but I think it's going to have to be like that forever. It's a modern world now.

The second ritual that came was the *haŋbléčheya*, the fast, going on the hill. If you do it right, you will receive something from the other side. There's no other way to be a medicine person or go after power. You've got to go on the hill. It's a sacred ceremony. Even in the Bible, Jesus had to go away for a while before he started working for his father. It's powerful. It's about knowledge and understanding what that is. It's a real important part of our lives, to have that connection, that *haŋbléčheya*. It's really making connection between your dream and yourself. It makes you understand what spirituality is. It's not what you might expect. We're conditioned so that when we say God, we automatically look up, but when we learn to cooperate with that energy, God is everywhere. Everywhere. God made it like that. So the only way to reach him is to go through the natural process. You can't go directly to him. He doesn't allow it that way. It's like a school of medicine. If you want a degree in medicine, you've got to go to college for it, right? In the Indian world, it's the same way. If you want to become a medicine healer, or work with herbs, you can't get to it just like that. You have to go through the whole thing, make some sacrifice, go on the hill, spend a lot of time with Nature. That's how you earn that status. *Haŋblečheya* is where you're going after power, an energy, a power, an answer. So you have to be precise and detailed about how you prepare to go on the hill. Going up on the hill still remains very powerful if you do it right, if you follow instructions. To better understand *haŋblečheya*, my recommendation is to learn how to meditate; even if it's ten minutes, meditate. It takes patience to go up on the hill. To this day, anybody can earn the privilege of contacting the spirit beings or the ghost world, but you've got to earn it. You've got to go on the hill.

The third ritual was the Wiping of the Tears, *ištá pakhíŋta*. The Wiping of the Tears is a ritual that helps you stop mourning and grieving. But it covers a lot of things, not just death. Losing loved ones is a pain that stays with you, but if you learn how to control and live with that pain, eventually it will just turn into a spiritual scar. The memory's there, but it becomes an honorable state of mind. If your mom or dad died ten years ago, then you can talk about it now. The first year, it'll be hard to even go there. The pain is too deep. That pain stays with you if you don't take care of it. That's why it's important to have a Wiping of the Tears ceremony. You let your spirit accept that the person is not going to be in your life forever. It's also for families that are no longer gonna be together. The children get a Wiping of the Tears. The ceremony puts to rest those voices inside your mind so they don't interfere with your daily life.

The ceremony of spirit keeping falls under the Wiping of the Tears. It's an addition to that ceremony. When a family loses a loved one, they can do that Keeping of the Spirit because the person was too young to die. That spirit might be wandering around, so they do that to keep it secure. And then one year later, they'll make their journey. But they don't do that for everyone who dies.

The fourth ritual was the *huŋká*, the relative-making ceremony, making relationship, *tȟiwáhe*, family. *Tȟiwáhe* means family. The *tȟiwáhe* is supposed to be sacred, a sacred union. It's a lifetime ritual. Why did they call it *huŋká*? It really means paint. They paint themselves. They draw symbols on themselves. Each symbol is a statement. *Huŋkákáǧe*. You see those Indians who have paint on their faces. That means something—your status, your society, your community. So making a relative is when a family member puts a mark on another person, and that sign means that he or she now belongs to that family, that clan. The *huŋká* ceremony makes you a sister, or brother, or aunt, or uncle, or whatever role, you become a relative, a family member. *Huŋkákáǧapi*. The painting means that you are a member of a family.

Another side to that is friendship, *kȟolá*. Friendship is deeper than *huŋkákáǧapi*. It has more status and power. It's difficult to say you're friends with somebody. You have to have a ceremony to prove you will be a friend. In English, friendship is a cheap word. It's dishonorable, because you can't trust anybody nowadays. They call you a friend and then stab you in the back, sell you down the road. So friendship is a real hollow word. But in the Lakota world, it meant life and death. When you make friends with somebody, under any conditions you have to stand by your friend. That's hard to do. My great-great-grandpa Wóptuȟ'a was friends with Crazy Horse. It's deeper than a relative, deeper than *huŋká*. Because you smoke the pipe and you do the ritual of making friendship. And they both held their honor. They honored that with each other, even after death. When Crazy Horse was gonna go on to the other world, he let his friend Wóptuȟ'a know, "Don't let nobody see my body again. Nobody will know where I'm buried." So he did. He buried Crazy Horse in a remote, secret place, and he died with that information. He didn't give him up. And to this day, nobody knows where he's buried. That's the meaning of friendship. Wóptuȟ'a didn't even share that with his own family, because they might give him up, they might dishonor him. So it's better to just take those commitments to your grave.

The fifth one was the womanhood ceremony, honoring the women. Women are very sacred to our people. The woman is the foundation of every family. Our belief is that women have a guardian angel who watches over them. That guardian angel is called a *womb*. The womb is placed inside the woman. She takes care of the woman. Some women may not have a womb, but the spirit of the womb is still in there. So the womb watches over the woman all the time: asleep, awake, whatever she does, that spirit of the womb goes to work. It cleans all of the toxins from the woman, and after a certain time of the month, it drains the woman's used blood, like changing oil from a car. When a woman is on her time, she's really sacred. She's more powerful than all these rituals that were given to us. So she prays on her own. In Lakota, they call it Išnáthi, which means "a woman stays alone." She has to because she's very powerful. Her words can affect other people. That womanhood ceremony lasts four days.

There's also a ceremony called the Throwing of the Ball. When a woman completes her womanhood ceremony, and she's ready to move on with life or career, they do a Throwing of the Ball for her. The families will bring gifts, representing her. There'll be a circle, and a bunch of gifts—like a giveaway—and then the relatives and all the people will stand around the circle. The woman and all the gifts are in the middle, and the circle is all the relatives, and all the families are facing the woman. They sing songs, and the woman will throw the ball backward toward the family, and whoever catches that will go out in the middle and pick out a gift. And then they walk away. They do that until all the gifts are gone. That's honoring the woman. It's a real good feeling for the young girl to be recognized that way. So after she finishes that, she moves on with her world. That was all part of the ceremony, the Throwing of the Ball.

The sun dance, the Wiwáŋyaŋg Wačhípi, was the last of the seven ceremonies that came to the people. The guy that started the sun dance was called Nažútala. His English name was Neck. He was half Cheyenne and half Lakota. One day he went out hunting for buffalo. Back in those days they didn't use guns. They had to run buffalo herds over a cliff. So he was in the middle of a buffalo herd and found himself surrounded, heading toward a big cliff. He tried everything, but those buffalo were all around him. So he went with that herd over the cliff. He died. The buffalo all died, too, and hit the bottom. So they buried him right there. They found a tree and laid him up there, and wrapped him up. They took their meat, went home, and told people what happened. So from time to time, people would come and visit, but after four days everybody was gone.

And here somebody found him and knew he was alive, moving around up there. He heard a bunch of songs, like people singing. And he realized that when the wind stopped blowing, the songs went away, too. So he realized that the songs were coming from the leaves of the cottonwood tree tingling like that. It sounded like a song. And somebody was underneath the tree there, moving around, and finally managed to get up there, untie him, and bring him down to the bottom. It was an old lady. She rescued that warrior. She healed him. She gave him medicine, herbs, and water. She took care of him. She took him to a safe place, fed him. It took a couple months to revive him and really fix him up. She told him, "This is a story. The power of the sun gave you life, so you must share this with the people." And the message he got was that he had to die for the people to stop suffering. And he renewed his life. God gave him a chance to have a new life and start over. One day before he returned home, he noticed that the woman was singing and drinking water and here she turned into a deer. She shifted into a deer and walked away. So a Deer Woman saved his life. So to our people, the deer is real sacred to us. And the eagle-bone whistle that they blow, the sun dancer blows that so that that grandma will listen.

The sun dancer has to go without food or water for four days. That means that they've stepped into the spirit world, a different world, and their old life is gone. It's like they died and then they came back with a new life after four days. That's how the sun dance got started.

Our Sun Dance

When the sun dance and the ceremonies were outlawed, they all went underground. The sun dances were kept secret back in the day, real secret. They didn't want to expose the sun dance to many people. They thought it was going to be gone. People were afraid to talk about it. In 1928 the government allowed us to have an open sun dance, but they knew it was not going to be a real one, just a modern sun dance, something that showed people that we used to have a sun dance. It was the semicentennial celebration of establishing the reservation, so they celebrated that in 1928 on the Rosebud Reservation. Then it just kind of went away. Only a few did it underground. They went into the Badlands and kept it up, but by that time a majority of the people were Christianized, and it was the Christian Indians that were really against these ways. So there was one that was done publicly like a powwow, and there's a real one, but the real one was hidden. It was done in a secret way. They kept it alive. You'd never find it. You'd have to know somebody to go. But it was under the radar. It was secretly done. A few people would gather together, word of mouth, they'd gather in the Badlands. Nobody knew. They didn't have any publicity. They finished their dance, and they quietly went their separate ways.

In 1969 the government allowed the Oglálas to have a sun dance at Pine Ridge. But again it was a mock sun dance, more like a show. They have the sun dance at six o'clock in the morning, and it ends at noon. And that was it. Then in the afternoon, they'll have a big powwow. People will come back through, regular dancing contest and stuff. They had a carnival right next to it, too, and a rodeo. So it's a mixture of everything. A lot of people didn't want to go into the real ritual, like the fasting. They didn't want to do it that way. So after the day, the sun dancers would go eat and socialize and then go back into the arbor. So that threw a lot of elders' support away. They liked the sun dance and the songs, but they got turned off by how it was run, how it was carried out. They didn't want to talk about it right away, but from time to time they'll raise things about it, comments. But nobody wanted to listen. They don't want to go there. So everybody knew about the sun dance, but they didn't know the sacredness involved in it. The sun dance was like a powwow. They didn't know the details and the protocols of sacredness and prayer. They looked at the sun dance as more of a show or a powwow.

My grandpa was alive when the sun dance came back in Pine Ridge. He was alive, but he never went to any of them. He said those are all crazy. He never went. The first time we became aware of it was when we saw a pretty big poster at the post office. It said, "Welcome to the blah-blah-blah annual sun dance and powwow." People were pretty impressed by reading it: "Come and watch the sun dance. They're gonna pierce and powwow." I was pretty little, but I wanted to see it because it's an open sun dance. People can go there. Fools Crow and a guy named Bill Schweigman, they were running it, but we didn't go right away. We went a year later, probably like around 1970 and '71, we went to the sun dance in Pine Ridge. Me, my mom and dad, my uncle Dallas, we drove. We had to save our money, because back in those days when you go from Wanblee to Pine Ridge, that's pretty expensive. That's a long way. Our cars weren't that good, either. So we really had to prepare ourselves. We were limited in our resources, so we made our own lunch, too. We ate boiled eggs, sausages, and bread, a thermos full of coffee. And then we had enough money for gas to get there and come back. We took off about six o'clock in the morning. We got there about eight or nine. The sun dance was going on. There was only about fifteen dancers and maybe ten women. But there was a lot of people watching. There was the most people I'd ever seen in Pine Ridge. I think they were there because of the powwow, but they got a chance to see the sun dance. Back in those days, everybody thinks that those two go together. Everybody thought that was the way to do things. I thought so, too! We thought that was part of the whole deal. So there's this big old sun dance tree in the middle. You can see it from far away. And those flags that were hanging from the tree, they reached all the way from the tree to the ground. They were just hanging, big long flags. They were more like a show.

They were filming it and taking pictures. All kinds of tourists were there taking pictures of the sun dance and the people that were dancing. That happened in 1970, in '71. That's the first time I ever met some of the AIM Indians. In 1971 they danced there. I think Russell Means was dancing and Dennis Banks, but they were just walking around the powwow in the afternoon. Everybody got undressed and went back to their camps to do whatever they want. Everybody thought that was the way. So I knew it was sacred, and I knew that someday I was gonna do it, but I didn't know when. I was just concentrating on my own world.

Around that time, being Indian was getting popular, especially when the media became involved. People started to grow their hair in the late sixties and the seventies. Prior to that, in the early sixties, many Indians, they had short hair. There was a law passed in the early 1900s that reservation Indians had to cut their hair, so a lot of people had short hair, especially when the boarding school days came around. A lot of them went to the military, too. So it was relatively rare to see another Indian wearing long hair. And right about that time, a group of Indians took over Alcatraz. It started there. The Trail of Broken Treaties. All kinds of different protests, fishing rights, and then the American Indian Movement. There was a lot of AIM activity. Everybody feared them, too. Everybody was scared of them. I knew a lot of them before they were AIM members. Russell Means and his brothers, they're originally from here, Wanblee and Porcupine. They were born here on the reservation and then moved to California and grew up over there and got their education, but they're from here. During the seventies, Russell moved back to Porcupine and Wanblee, so he lived here for a while. We kind of have a long history with those guys. They were all good people. At least I got along good with them anyway. But they were just regular Lakotas. But the power of the media is amazing. When they get in front of the cameras, everybody knows who they are as defenders of Indian rights.

I met John Trudell back in 1967. He was headed for college. I met him when he was just a regular Dakota Indian. He wasn't no leader or anything like that. He had just got out of the Navy and relocated to California. I think he might have had some relatives or parents or somebody that was part of the Relocation program. He's from Santee. Some of his relatives came around to visit, and that's where I met him. And then he went to college. I think he went to Berkeley. He was trying to become a media broadcaster, a radio disc jockey, something like that. He was part of a radio show in California. And then he took part in the takeover at Alcatraz. That's where he picked up his new journey. He can speak really well in the media world. He's a talented speaker. And he became known as the national spokesman of the American Indian Movement. I was a little kid when I first met him. Then in the early eighties, I started to see him more often. He sun danced out here behind my house. He even got married back there. We were at his bedside before he died. We had a ceremony for him. He wanted a ceremony, so we had a ceremony and all his friends were in the room. That's where I met Jackson Brown. After the ceremony, everybody ate and sat around, visited. They made a big bed for John in the living room, so he could visit with people. He went to sleep for a while, and then he woke up and said, "I caught my ride now." Everybody looked at him. And then he died.

I knew Floyd Westerman, too. He was a good singer. He hung around in California a lot. He used to come to the sun dance a lot. He really supports our sun dance. Every year he kept coming. He's originally from Sisseton. He's always coming every year to support our sun dance.

When AIM first came around the reservation, nobody wanted to talk to them, especially the traditional people, because they didn't know them. All they knew was that they came from the city. They were kind of looking for help and guidance. They went to the medicine people in Rosebud, but nobody would talk to them. So those medicine people referred them to Crow Dog, old man Crow Dog. They all went down there, and that's how they met him. That's how they got involved in AIM. Russell didn't join them until later, 1969 or '70. The rest is history. AIM started out of Minneapolis. It was a legitimate nonprofit. They were trying to promote housing and education, trying to do some good things for the Indians living in the cities. Nobody cared for a while, until some citizens stood up and started complaining. That's how they got started.

The rebirth of the sun dance started at Crow Dog's Paradise. After my first sun dance, I came back and stayed at my house for a while. The following year they were going to have one at Selo Black Crow's, and they asked me to help. One day some elders came by. They said they were gonna have a sun dance east of Wanblee and they wanted to do it the right way, because everybody saw how Pine Ridge ran it, and they all agreed that that's not a sun dance. They don't want to confront anybody. They just say it among themselves and stay away. The sun dancers ate at night and went home. Some got drunk and were hung over the next day dancing. So they all said, "That's really mocking our sun dance. They should have just put it away." Those old men were kind of like ahead of the messengers, saying, "Hey, be ready, they're gonna bring a pipe to you and they're gonna ask you something."

I was just a young man. I was only seventeen, eighteen years old. I was wondering what was gonna be my role, and sure enough, some people showed up. They brought a pipe and said, "We want you to help us with the sun dance." So I was up front. I've never been involved in a sun dance. I danced before, but that wasn't my choice. It was against my will. I got pushed into it. So I didn't really consider that a sun dance even though I did it for my mom. I didn't know anything about sun dancing. I just learned the verbal teachings from my father, and how it's supposed to be done and how to behave. And he always tells us, "If you can't do it, don't do it." The only thing that my grandpa said, and my dad said the same thing, when I told him that I was gonna sun dance—I was young then, I wanted to hang in there with those guys, I wanted to sun dance—was, "If you can't live up to it, don't do it." At first I thought he meant you have to be strong physically, you have to dance hard, dance four days without food and water. I thought that's what he was talking about. I barely made it through the sun dance. I fasted. I didn't drink water or eat food. By the end of the day, I was barely dragging myself. But that's not what he meant. What he meant was that you have to live that way of life. You have to change your way of life, live a good life, be a good person. That's what he meant. It's a way of life. What he meant was if you don't live that way, if you can't live that way, don't even do it. You'll make life harder for yourself. If you're a sun dancer, you're not supposed to be drinking or doing drugs. You're supposed to be an example of doing good. That's what he was talking about. Sun dancers are supposed to live a good life. Drug-free, alcohol-free. Try to be an example.

There were about seven dancers, so my job was to fill the pipes for the sun dancers. So I said, "Okay, I will." I'd be like a pipe chief, take care of the pipes. That was my job. And when they put up the sun dance tree and everybody went off their own ways to get ready, they brought their pipes to the tipi. I put sage in there and a pipe rack and made it look nice. And whoever brought their pipes there, I put it in order. I rolled up my sleeping bag in front of the tipi and went to bed. I was the only one there, just me and the fireman. All of a sudden, everyone was gone, probably eating a last meal or something. And I fell asleep, just snoring away. I woke up, and here the sun dancers were all back. Some of them were running from their camps and into the sweat lodge. They all got dressed. They all looked nice standing there. So I gave them their pipes. There's also a little girl there watching the Čhaŋnúŋpa (pipe). We were all ready to go.

But the sun dance chief wasn't there! Everybody's waiting for him. We all sat down in our chairs, waiting around. Finally, one of the guys said, "I'll go drive into town and see where he's at." He lived in Manderson, between Wanblee and Manderson. It's over an hour. He took off, but he must have found him because he turned around within an hour. Now he's walking toward us. He says, "I've got some bad news." Everybody looked over there. The sun dance chief, his name was Charlie. Uncle Charlie. He's passed out, drunker than hell, out of this world. Now what are we gonna do? The tree's up. The singers are out here. We're ready, but no leader. I didn't know what to think. I was just sitting by the fire. And I heard them talking and naming off names. Then they said, "Well, looks like we're going to have to go down to the bottom of the barrel, and ask Dickie." I'm at the bottom of the barrel. The guy was coming this way. I already knew what he was gonna say. I said, "I can't do it. I can't. I'm only watching these pipes. Look even more from the bottom of the barrel—you'll find somebody else."

So anyway, I ended up running it for them. But I went to consult with my father and some of the old people. Even Fools Crow was there. I said, "I'm going to need your help. I never ran a sun dance before." I danced, but that was different. The old man said, "The way you saw the structure at our sun dance"—he showed that to me, reminded me how that goes—"you line them up that way." And it took off. It went real good, the whole day. But the whole time I kept running back and forth to my father's camp, asking, "What next? How am I doing?" He says, "Yeah, go easy on them." So the day went down, and the second day came around, more and more I started getting more and more help, the old people, everyone took their turn telling me how to do it. And they were pretty good dancers. They didn't eat. They stayed at the camp and followed rules. We finished the whole four days. I didn't know how to pierce them, so I had to ask one of those old people to pierce them. That was how I got involved. It was done in an old-style way. And it grew. A lot of people were coming in, and some of their own relatives started dancing. I sort of like eased myself off, backed away a little bit. It belongs to them. It's a family sun dance.

*

I had an adopted brother. His name was Dennis Banks. He was one of the cofounders of the American Indian Movement. Well, he was involved in a riot that took place in Custer. He didn't incite it. He just went in there and talked to the prosecutor, and angry words got exchanged between the policemen and the Indians. Then a fight broke out, and they ended up burning down the courthouse. So the police took Banks to jail and charged him with inciting a riot. And they found him guilty in state court. He was supposed to go to prison, but he took off. He says, "I'm not going to go to prison in the state of South Dakota. I'll be dead." Somebody inside the prison told the Indians that if Dennis gets sent here, there's some other Indians that don't like him either, so they're going to kill him. So that's valid information. It wasn't made up. So he took off. There was a manhunt for him for a long time, about two years or so. During that time, he ended up in California. Jerry Brown, the governor of California, gave him asylum. He says, "Stay here in California while I'm in office." He kind of pardoned him, let him live free in California. So he got a job at a place called D-Q University, in Davis, west of Sacramento. The college gave him a position. They called him a chancellor. So he had a job, but he wanted to fulfill his commitment to the sun dance in Rosebud, where all the AIM leaders are dancing. He couldn't do it. So here my father and Matthew King and Ellis Chips and Fools Crow said, "Go over there and help him. Set one up and let him finish his dance." So I had an uncle living over there. So two of my uncles and some other people got together, and D-Q University let them use the campus. So they built a sun dance ground there and a sweat lodge. Dennis's followers had a good sun dance over there. I ran it the way I run it over here. It was really hard for them. They were really suffering. One hundred fifteen degrees in the shade every day. But they got through it. They danced like that for a number of years from the 1970s all the way to '85, I think, '84. But after Jerry Brown lost the election, a new governor got in there. He didn't like Dennis. He says, "The first thing I'm gonna do is get him on a plane and send him back to South Dakota." So Dennis took off. He drove all the way back to New York, and the Onondagas took him in. They have a little sovereign world over there. He ended up with them. It's a real small reservation. It's easy to get lonely.

So after he left, we brought the sun dance back to Wanblee, right here, where I live. Dennis came back from the Onondagas and stayed with us here. The feds were looking for him, but he was living here. There's a cabin right behind our house. And then in September 1984 he came back and turned himself in to the state authorities. He got on the phone from our house and said that he's going to turn himself in. He didn't tell them where he was at. He just said, "On such and such day, authorities can pick me up at the airport in Rapid City." So the federal marshals and policemen and militias, they were all gathered, the media, they were all gathered at the airport waiting for his arrival. Sure enough, when they checked the records, a Dennis Banks checked in at the airport in New York and was headed to South Dakota. So they kept track of that plane. It flew into Minneapolis and then to Rapid City. But he was over here the whole time.

So the day he was supposed to show up over there, we all caravanned over there and drove him in. He made arrangements with the Custer County Sheriff's Department. The guy's name was Glasgow. He's friendly to the Indian people, but he was a sheriff, so Dennis made sure that he was under Glasgow's custody. But the other chief police and all the Rapid City FBIs were in the Rapid City airport waiting for him to get off that plane. Sure enough when the plane landed, all of the cameramen were running that way. And sure enough, Dennis was getting off the plane but it wasn't Dennis! It was a guy named William Kunstler, his attorney. "Wait a minute, this isn't Dennis. Who is this guy?" He says, "I'm Dennis Banks's attorney. He has to have fair treatment here, so I flew from New York." And then somebody noticed that we pulled in the front of the airport, and they saw Dennis in Glasgow's custody already. He handcuffed him and put him in a police car. All the media and the police were running that way like a football team, but he was already in somebody else's custody.

The sun dance has been here ever since. We've kept it up. A lot of young people came through and really kept it going the way of the original teachings. People started to come over here and wanted to join it, but we have a reputation, so they're scared of that part where they have to fast and not eat and stuff like that. That scares a lot of people away. We teach the sun dancers to suffer, to fast, to focus on praying. We don't allow them to talk to their family members until it's over. That kind of puts people in the right mind. They feel like they really did something. Sun dance. It's good. So that's how we ended up with it. It was like in the memory of Dennis. It was because of him that the sun dance came over here. And the flags represent all the different nations coming together, praying together.

Wiping the Tears

With the teachings of the Grandfathers, the circle of life is a concept of manifesting and unmanifesting. It never dies. The Lakota people never really believed in death. We always go somewhere. And when Creator sees fit, we come back. We don't have any memories of our previous lives, but our spirits do come back from time to time. Maybe your spirit will come back as one of your grandchildren or great-grandchildren. Maybe you become another life form. People do believe that they'll come back someday. It's a privilege that only God grants. It depends on whether you did well. So there was no real definition of death. We only say that we manifested in the world and we unmanifested. The Lakota word for that is *oúŋčhaǧe*. A life. The transition of a life. The circle of life never really ends. It never really begins. It's just being and unbeing in Lakota thought. Our understanding is that the spirit moves on after death. Our bodies go back to the earth, where it will someday become dirt, or soil, grass, water, but it doesn't end. You're just constantly moving. Your spirit, your soul, will move on to another world.

So back in my grandfather's days, when somebody passes away, they'll say *iyáya*, "he left." He went on to the next dimension. People still mourn, but only for a number of days. If you grieve for a long time, it'll stay with you, it'll change your character, and it'll affect your life. So grieving is a dangerous stage of life. We call it *wašígla*. *Wašígla* is an unmeasurable amount of time. It's like a dimension that you wander into when you lose a loved one or your relative goes away. You mourn because that person is no longer going to be there. That's why there's sadness and sorrow. So mourning and grieving are a sacred journey, a sacred process. That's why we have the Wiping of the Tears ceremony. It takes you out of mourning and brings you back to normal but without that sadness. If you don't get rid of it, that sadness will move around in your body and rest in your soul. The ritual psychologically brings you back into your circle of life.

Wiping of the Tears is for people who mourn and grieve. It also resolves conflicts. When someone goes through a traumatic experience, they'll do a Wiping of the Tears for that person. I used to think that it only covered death, but the Wiping of the Tears also has to do with domestic relations like divorce. So we don't just use the Wiping of the Tears for death. We also use it to wipe the tears of people who have broken up, broken homes, broken marriages. We discovered that a Wiping of the Tears is necessary for families that have broken up because that's worse than somebody dying. Leaving a loved one can be worse than somebody passing away. And even worse, the children carry the burden, they inherit it. A family breaks up, but the children suffer even more, and they don't know how to express it. So they internalize it, and carry it. But they also act it out, so young people do alcohol and drugs and join different social groups to ease the pain. And then the next thing you know, they have a rough life. It's pretty sad it has to be that way. So now we use Wiping of the Tears for families that have broken up.

That's where the pipe comes in. Today many Lakota families have a generalized culture, but every family, or *thiwáhe*, has their own miniculture, too, something that they do, the little traditions. In our family, for many years, ever since my girls grew up, every Sunday is a family day. We always get together. No matter where our family's at, we get together on Sunday. We still do that. We started that when they were little. No matter where they're at, they've got to come back Sunday and check in with everybody. No special occasion, just a family day. We all just hang out and spend a day together, and then they all go back to their normal things. That's been going on for a long time. So that's a family culture, a miniculture. I guess if you don't have that, life can get difficult. You can easily fall into something like depression or confusion. There's some families that don't even know what family is. They just live together, but they have no idea. That's the real sad part. That's probably one of the reasons why young people are confused and turning to drugs and gangs and suicides, because what is missing is the love of that family. Sometimes families are there, but there's no connection, no relationship. That explains a lot of suicides in Indian Country. That has a lot to do with it. In our own country, Indian Country, our ceremonies and our culture became foreign to our younger people. They act like it's something new, but those were our real ways of life that they never even knew.

I remember back in the old days when my grandfather was young, they never had mental illness. Nobody had mental problems. Depression was unheard of. It wasn't until the 1950s that our people started having anxiety attacks and depression, mental illness. A lot of that's due to alcoholism. It took their mind. It made it weak. The energy of the mind became so weak that they experienced these different illnesses that they never knew existed. And now they're common. We've got people suffering from bipolar issues, anxieties, and depressions. It's normal now. But it was unheard of a long time ago. Now it's common. That's what causes them to commit suicide. They're hurt. Every suicide, something triggered them to make that decision. It has nothing to do with mental disability. It has something to do with the sensitivity of your soul. When that gets hurt, your world is shattered. Nothing else matters. At that moment, you might become very angry. And that's how suicides get carried out.

We're living in a modern world that's not suitable for us. So people kill themselves. I've told people that every one of those who died left a message behind for us. I don't think anybody got that message yet. We've got so many experts. They even have a suicide prevention program on Pine Ridge, but our people are still suffering. They should use the pipe to figure it out. When you use the pipe to solve a problem, and you want to help the people, you think about the love of God and love of the people. Then it'll get somewhere. It'll just take off on its own.

Wanblee used to have a more traditional life back in the 1900s before alcoholism became real strong in Indian Country. The suicides that happened in the early 1920s were not due to alcoholism. They were due to individuals' mental disorders. But then in the early 1970s, when they built the housing projects, at least three people committed suicide. They were older men, but they had a past of drinking. And there were no mental health clinics back in those days. People were ashamed or were not used to mental health help, because if you went to a mental health psychologist and anyone found out about it, they're gonna think you're nuts. They'll make fun of you. So people don't like to go to mental health people for help. The only place for mental health breakdowns was the state hospital with the psychiatric breakdowns or the psycho wards in eastern South Dakota, but people with mental health problems were punished rather than helped. They'd lock them up and they don't get out. And so we had a wrong history about mental illness. They think that if you have suffered from mental illness, they'll take you away and lock you up forever. So people were afraid to admit that they had problems. So when people had alcohol problems, they don't want to admit it because they could get sent off. It was a punishable illness. That's why a lot of Indians didn't want to go to treatment. It's only been recently that they started looking at alcoholism as a curable illness. You can manage your life around it. They didn't know that back then. The same way with mental health. I remember I had some uncles in the 1960s and '70s. You can tell they're drunk and that they've been drinking, but if you ask them, "Are you drinking?," they'll say, "No, I'm not drunk." They'll say that even though you know they're drinking, like staggering drunk, they'll say, "No, I'm not drinking."

The problem got worse in the 1950s, when alcohol became legalized. That's when Indians really started experiencing the side effects of alcoholism, like depression, loss of self-esteem, and broken spirits, battling that addiction in themselves. They want to quit that habit, but they can't. It just keeps drawing them back. And pretty soon the families, mom and dad, join in the addiction, and the kids grow up wrong. They lack family ties, family tradition. And they can't handle the oppression, and their whole outlook of the world starts to fall away. It doesn't make sense to them anymore, and death seems like the only way out. About 90 percent of the suicides on the reservation today are done under the influence. They didn't think about it when they were sober. It's when they're under the influence and emotional, and stuff from a long time ago comes out, that they carry it through. The problem is that Native people don't know how to handle that. How do you handle a suicide death differently from a normal-illness death? They don't know how to do that. There's no instructions. There's got to be a separate ritual that honors that person but at the same time discourages other people from doing it. They glorify the way people die because there's no other way to do it, so they end up having wakes and songs with everybody going there and weeping. The young people standing there might be having some trouble, too. Well, he's looking at that and says, "Oh yeah, that's gonna happen to me. They'll miss me when I'm gone." But the reality is nobody misses them when they're gone. They just forget about them unless somebody else puts on a memorial walk or something like that.

It all starts from the broken circle of life. The family's been broken. Every suicide that happened on the reservation, they left a message, but even the experts didn't get it. Until they get the message from the people who died of suicide, our troubles will continue. Nobody has read the messages that they left behind. That's the sad part. We have all the suicide experts across the reservation. Well, they didn't accomplish anything. Nobody really got the message. Change has to come to Indian Country. Enough is enough. They don't want to be here anymore, because there's no future for them here. There's no cure. There's no savior in their suffering. There's no jobs and there's no future. So it's got to change. They left a message behind. Every one of them. And the message is that the life that we are living is not the life that our ancestors had in mind for us. And we have to change. The message is that they want the people to change the way of life. It's got to change. We have to have a different way to make a living here.

When a person completes suicide, that person is at peace. Their troubles are over. Whatever decision that that person made with God, that's his problem now, not ours. He did it. Because obviously he's not happy here. He's suffering here. I don't care how he died, whether he hung himself or overdosed on pills or he let the cops kill him. However he did it, obviously he chose, he made a decision with God, and took his own life. I don't think it's good to punish that person or interpret where he's going to be at. Some leaders are saying that it's a wrongful thing. We all know it's wrong. We all know that we don't want that for our children. But we didn't do anything to prevent that. Nobody rolled up their sleeves and sat down and said, "Let's make a better life for our people to see that there's a life worth living in our country." So it's everybody's fault. Everybody's responsible for that.

We're driving around in an old 1925 school bus. It's so old it can only go ten miles before it breaks down. And everybody that rides the bus gets out and tells each other how they should fix it, and they get it to run for a little while, but it breaks down again and nothing ever changes. And other places change their buses every year, but the reservation is still riding an old bus. When they first built that bus in the 1920s, it was meant for a better life for our people. And that's the truth. But it never grew. They didn't build a life for our people. And that's part of the reason why we have a lot of broken souls on the reservation. People kill themselves. Because we're living in a world on the reservation that's taken us away from our own world. They are victims of colonialism. That's why people die that way. So I'm not mad at my nieces, and I'm not mad at my cousins for killing themselves. I just say, "You're right. You made a decision.

It was the wrong decision. But that's the only thing that you saw. And you made that decision. That's yours." If they had come to me, I would have said, "That's not the right way." There's other worlds. It doesn't just end at Pine Ridge or Kadoka. The little world that they carry in their minds got tunnel vision, and they didn't think they had any options, so they completed it.

The Christians say they want to discourage people from killing themselves, but they don't know how to do it. They threaten our people with hell if they do this, but it's like we're living in hell already. So when they get the drugs and they get the drink, why not? They'll do it. They'll kill themselves. I'm sad, but I won't glorify their burials. I will always remind people that, yes, somebody died because there was nothing here for them. Nobody was there to pick them up when they were reaching for help. Every one of those people who killed themselves, they were probably reaching out for help at one point. Nobody listened to them. So it's sad when my nieces and nephews kill themselves. I say, "I'm sorry. We were supposed to be there for you, hear your problems, and find a way. You jumped through our cracks somehow. We missed you somewhere. We missed each other." Either they didn't call us or we should have chased after them, but we didn't. It's the people's problem. When a young person is troubled, and they see their peers do that, then they'll say, "Wow, there's an option." The only thing we can do is make ourselves available. You just have to reach out to Creator and say, "Bless all of them."

Everybody's looking for love and happiness. But it didn't happen. That's the bottom line. All they want is somebody to love. All they want is to be happy. But the world got too complicated for them. It's sad. But even our relatives that committed suicide on the reservation, hundreds of them, it's not a waste. They didn't die in vain. They gave a message to us, and they went home. And it's gonna have a positive impact. They died sadly, but if you take a look at that picture again, because they died, the world will change. Change will happen on the reservation. It may take years, but because of the way they left a message and decided to leave early, to sacrifice their own life and cut off their opportunities to live in the world, they went home early. They shared a message and they went straight to God. And God probably took them back, washed them down, gave them love, restored them, and said, "Okay, I'll send you back someday when you're ready." Even in the Bible, Jesus spread the word, using himself as an example. And they got jealous of him and killed him, but it didn't end that way. He made a huge impact. And many people believe in his words. They don't go to church every day. They don't build shrines, but they live with his teaching in their hearts. His death had a positive impact on human life everywhere. The same way with Martin Luther King. He died early, but they didn't kill him. His words and his life lived on forever. Now everybody learns to respect him even though the battles continue. His legacy of teaching continues. The same with Mahatma Gandhi or Crazy Horse or Sitting Bull. The words never die. Their work continues. That's the positive impact. They didn't die at that moment. They spread like a wildfire. The goodness is stronger everywhere. So I think there'll be a time when reservation life will change.

More and more people are realizing that our life condition has to change. The people that died made that statement, and from there we will learn. And for every person who died by suicide, two or three more were born in this world. Life continued. So we have to learn from their teachings and change ourselves. So there's a goodness. They planted a seed, like the bird that gets up in the morning and digs a seed from the tree and hides it in the prairie and buries it, thinking he's going to come back to eat it later but never does. That seed turns into a tree. Years from now, you'll see a tree coming out. We're kind of like that. More children will be aware that suicide's not the way to go. Somehow they'll learn to speak out that they want change.

So that goodness is starting to come right here on Pine Ridge. There's a lot of death and a lot of agony and drugs and sad, broken homes. Whiteclay was selling beer there for years, and our relatives were all lying in the streets. That highway from Whiteclay to Pine

Ridge is full of death signs. We never thought there was going to be an end. But the struggles of those people marching up and down those roads had a huge impact, and now all the liquor stores are closed down and something good is happening there. People are building stores, and you don't see people staggering around in those places anymore. But it took a lot of sacrifice. Look at how many lives ended up on that road buying all that liquor. They had to make that sacrifice to bring something good. I think we're headed the right way. It's happening, but it's real slow.

*

Language is an issue in our country today. They want the Lakota language to come back, and they're teaching it like crazy everywhere. Everybody's teaching language, but it's still a struggle. Our language came from the sacred world. Our language is connected with the trees, with the birds, the buffalo, the animals. And we spoke it before I was born. Our people spoke it 100 percent. There was no English in there, but when I grew up, my generation, we kind of mixed it up with English. Most of the people my age and older were psychologically harmed and ashamed of their language. There used to be a lot of people embarrassed to speak the language, because back then, everybody tried to learn English. If you spoke broken English, they'll make fun of you, laugh at you. So you've really got to try to speak the proper language. But by concentrating on English, you forget your own language. So that barrier of internal oppression has a lot to do with our people losing connection with our culture and spirituality, the language. That generation of shame and oppression caused our people to lose their language. Our people were punished for speaking our language. Our people were encouraged, psychologically, to make fun of it as some kind of weird language, so people didn't want to speak it. People were embarrassed about it. Maybe their grandfather was punished or treated bad for speaking the language, so there's a history of resentment toward people who prevented him from speaking it. People may have some issues about the language that they can't address right away. So there's a psychological barrier there, and the embarrassment and shame are also mixed in with that.

Indians in the 1950s, '60s, and '70s were psychologically programmed. They learned the language, but they don't want to use it. They say that their ancestors had a hard time because they spoke the language. And that they don't want their children to suffer like that. They say, "My mother told me she doesn't want me to suffer like she did, so she didn't want me to speak the language, so I have to learn myself." I think that was probably true at one time, but not anymore. We need programs where they recognize families for speaking the language. If you learn to speak the language at home, then you're making progress, you're getting somewhere. My mom knew a guy named John Around Him. He was a language teacher at Little Wound High School for many years, since the eighties. So one day my mom asked him, "Where do you work at, nephew?" He said, "At the school, I teach the language, auntie." So, "How many years you been doing that?" So he said, "About twenty years." So my mom sat there for a while and said, "So how many of those students that you taught actually speak the language?" John Around Him sat there for a while and said, "None of them." John Around Him used to talk about that and laugh. He said, "I can't even name off any of them. They all learned it, but they don't use it."

What's the use of learning it if you don't use it? The education institutions miss the point. They need a program to help families actually use it. We're using up all our energy teaching the kids daily language and they get certificates, but it doesn't mean anything if that certificate is just sitting in a shoebox somewhere, not used. That goes with our culture and our ceremonies. We learn the language and ceremonies and songs and rituals, but our people don't use them. They just use it whenever they're in crisis or they use it in a Western model, so they think it's okay to go to church on Sunday and then forget about it the rest of the week. It doesn't work like that with our culture. You have to use it every day. You have to live it. I think the schools are just now allowing a Lakota curriculum. Our next step is applying those things to daily life. You've got to put it into practice. You've got to get up Monday morning and speak it. It doesn't matter if it's broken as long as you're speaking it. That's what's missing in our generation.

Now, in our generation, the younger people are really taking an interest in culture, the language, especially the ceremonies and spiritual practices. When our ceremonies went underground, a lot of the song keepers didn't teach them to us. They kind of disappeared. That's one of the things that we lost. So today people sing sun dance songs or prayer songs, but they might have no idea what they're singing. I met a couple of young Lakota singers who don't know anything about the language. They just learned the song. And the words that they use in the song are really beautiful. So after he finished he says, "Now what did I say? What song did I just sing?" They sang the words, but they had no idea what they just sang! That happens a lot today. All of the songs that I sing came from my grandfather. He had different songs for each ceremony, the Yuwípi, the tie-up, and the Five Stick. Nobody knows them anymore, just our family. When my father was young, he was trained to know these songs. It was part of my work as well.

*

What would be the change that needs to happen to make it better on the reservation? How do we make it so that the present and future generations will understand the difference between classism and racism? All it takes is one person—a handful of people—to change that around. I think the challenge is education. The common goal is to build a better relationship. When I was little, we used to enjoy Tom Mix and Roy Rogers. We used to cheer them on, because they were coming to rescue the stagecoach from being robbed by the Indians. When those heroes come in there, we always say, "Hey, all right!" That whole scenario really took our minds, whites and Indians. And we created society that way. All those fake movies taught us wrong.

The first thing the spirits told my grandpa Sam was, "You have to love everybody." That's a practice. It's not just a word. It's a practice. You have to get along with everybody. So that was what my grandpa Sam, Tȟahúŋska, and my father understood. They don't acknowledge color. They used to say, "Everybody's the same." You don't have to turn the other cheek, though. Jesus tells us to turn the other cheek when we get smacked, but we won't let that happen. I don't think any of my Indian people will turn the other way. But they will pray. They will pray that everybody gets along good. It comes down to Tȟuŋkášila and the pipe and our spiritual teachings. It comes down to the individual person, their soul, their spirit, and God. As long as you have those connections, and never break that connection, then all the things that happen in the world, it doesn't matter. It'll get better. We have to teach each other the reality of spirituality. And we have to practice that. The gentleness and the peacefulness. It doesn't just come. There's sacrifice in it. My grandpas were good at learning that.

There was a time here on this reservation when the white people and the Indians got along real well. They were like true neighbors around here. It's because they understood the spirituality and the culture. They were all in it together. The white people that went to ceremony, they got help just like the Indians. They got health, and some even saved their lives. They didn't understand what they were working with, but they knew it was real. And they tried like hell to learn. They learned it. "What was all that about?" "What are you guys doing in that dark room, sitting in there, singing?" "What's that?" They learned. They learned. And what they found out was that it wasn't just darkness. The darkness became light.

Epilogue

I went to a funeral yesterday where they buried my cousin. All my relatives, my first cousins, nephews, nieces, and aunts, they all showed up. I was sitting there listening. Nobody talked. Nobody gave a talk. I think everybody was still stunned about how she died. But then in reality they all knew too that it was gonna happen. Everybody just wanted to get the funeral over and move on with their lives. They didn't want to get stuck there. There's too much truth in that event. They're not ready to accept it. They don't want to talk about it, because the truth is something that we are all afraid of. But it's part of our life. We mentioned our grandpas' names a lot during that funeral, but it didn't matter. We forgot the teachings and the importance of our grandpas' names. We just tried to live in our own world. But it didn't work.

In 2015 a friend of mine from California came out here for *haŋbléčheya*. He wanted to know where Wóptuȟʼa and them guys are buried. So one morning we had coffee and breakfast, and we loaded up in the car, and I took him to Wóptuȟʼa's burial site. He offered tobacco. I don't know what he said. Then after that, he wanted to find out where Horn Chips is buried and Tȟahúŋska and Grandpa Sam. So we went to the Catholic church. We found Horn Chips's grave, but nobody took care of it. It's just neglected. A bunch of weeds. We barely found the headstone. It sunk in the ground, and just the top of it was peeking out like that. We almost lost it. Over the years, nobody watched it, so it just sunk right into the ground. So I said, "We have to dig around here." It was there, but it was not taken care of. That's how far we got as a people. We forgot our dead. Some white folks were hanging out at the Chips's after Godfrey died. Some people were still there. So we asked over there, "Hey, could you guys help us?" So they came over. "What do you want?" "I need some strong guys to dig this back up and cover it up with fresh dirt and set it on top so they remember him. We use his name a lot, but we forgot to take care of him. So over the years the headstone sunk into the ground." They were strong guys. They just kind of went to town and dug up around there. Those things are like five hundred pounds. One of them went away and came back with some gravel and poured underneath there, and leveled it off. He put it back on top of the ground. And then we said, "As long as we can, we'll keep that clean, we'll take care of it." That's their responsibility, the great-grandsons.

So that was that. And then we went to the top of the hill where Tȟahúŋska is buried and my grandpa Sam. But we almost never found their burial sites. There's only a little wooden cross that has "James" and "Moves Camp-Chips" on there. We found it, but it's all rotten away. So we raked it and just stood there, and he prayed. I guess he prayed to them over at the haŋbléčheya, so he wanted to see where they were buried. He went to my grandpa's grave. So we went home and we came back. He spent the next couple days here, and then he was gonna go back to California. But he's asking people where those headstones are made. So we went to Rapid City the day before he left, and we went to the headstone place. And he purchased brand-new headstones for Tȟahúŋska and Sam. They're not fancy, but at least they're there. They lay flat on the ground. He spent a lot of money on them. We marked where the burial ground is. They probably wanted to have a stone there so their grandkids could remember them.

Our relatives were in a very dark world where we lost that love for our people. We lost the love for our ancestors. It wasn't our fault. We were just caught up in the colonized world. The majority of people died of alcoholism. When they used alcohol, a lot of stuff left their minds. Their self-esteem and self-worth and the people's love sort of died out. That's what happened to my people. They forgot what was important to them. They didn't realize that we wouldn't be here if it wasn't for those ancestors. So we owe it to them. What we should have done is all of us brought our resources together, worked hard, and built a little shrine, a better place for them to be remembered, but we didn't do it. We got caught up in a different world.

I look back at our world, at Wóptuȟ'a, Tȟahúŋska, and Horn Chips, and how the next generation forgot who our ancestors were. We were dealing with a colonized world that really influenced my relatives' minds. We all got exposed to alcoholism. But they forgot where they came from. That's the only thing that I kind of regret, wishing I had brought this information to them. Maybe they would have thought about it. But they were lost at that time. But now it's turning around, and the seventh generation might have some idea where they came from.

That is why I developed a nonprofit organization called WKT. Wičháhpi Khoyáka Thióšpaye Foundation. Our mission is to reestablish the cultural teachings and offer it to all nations, not just to Indians but to everybody. We're using the universal language of English to reach all people and help them to understand the power of energy and how it works. Our goal and vision is to build a house, a healing center, on our land here that'll be like a hospital. So if you need help, you will be able to come there and it'll be a twenty-first-century building, with bathroom, showers, kitchen. The only difference is that nobody is going to be able to go in there except for you, the provider, and the helpers. That's why we started that foundation. Hopefully someday we'll get that going while I'm still here. So that's my goal, to establish a home for ceremony. I'll call it a hospital, a healing center. That's what we're doing. That's what WKT is all about.

In the world I came from, it's all about your connection to the other beings. We believe that everybody has power. Every individual has a certain amount of energy. That's why you're encouraged to pray, pray to the Creator. It'll come back. It'll come back to the people. It doesn't go away. It's been here after centuries and centuries. There are societies that did everything they could in their power to make sure it was gone forever, but it survived somehow.

So that brings hope. I'm always hopeful that it'll get better someday. It doesn't have to be the tie-up. It doesn't have to be all that. All they have to do is pick up the pipe, be truthful to themselves, go on the hill, and speak the truth only. That will make a perfect medicine person. Speak the truth only. And that's what we're trying to teach the young people. Don't fantasize. Be real with ceremony, with the pipe. Pray to the Creator. If he doesn't answer you, don't make up stuff and tell people. Just stay real with everybody. And pretty soon your following will get stronger and stronger. Then they'll know when the real ones come to talk to you. Then we'll all rejoice together.

The old people tell us, "The old days will come back." The days of *wathípi*, living in a *thípi*, will return. That doesn't mean that we're gonna live in *thípis* again, but the name and concept of the *thípi* still remains. So our modern home today is still called *thí*. It was called that hundreds of years ago. It's still the same name but in a different form now, a modern form. But the concept's still the same. The sacredness of what was a *thípi*, what was a nest, remains.

The important part is teaching our people how to pray. That's the key. People suffer a lot in a world that doesn't have that connection. That's my biggest worry. I want my children to still have access to those guys. Then after that it doesn't matter how they live their life. As long as they have that connection, they'll be good that way. That's always a part of the prayer. I don't know if there's any other people in this world that have that connection like my grandpa. I haven't met anybody yet. Not one person. That's the sad part. But the good part is that you have that sense of security. So that when it's needed, you can always refer back to them. They'll give you comfort, talk to you, show up. That's our sense of security. I don't care if I'm broke or I don't have anything in the world, but as long as I have them guys, and I can call them and they show up for a little while, I'm okay. Everything will be all right. That's the important part.

Appendix — The Wóptuȟ'a *Thióšpaye*, a Family History

Wóptuȟ'a married a woman from Lip's Camp. Her name was Hó Wakȟáŋ Wíŋ, Sacred Voice Woman. Wóptuȟ'a and Hó Wakȟáŋ Wíŋ had three sons and one daughter. Their sons' names were Jefferson, Geoffrey, and Paul. Their daughter's name was Mollie (chart 1).

Wóptuȟ'a's first son was named Jefferson, but his Lakota name was Ȟoká Khuté. A *ȟoká* is like a muskrat or a badger. "Shoots the Badger." That's his original name. After the government came and gave everybody English names, they named him Jefferson. Jefferson married three sisters, not at the same time but over the years. His first wife's name was Fannie Stranger Horse. Uŋčí, or Stranger Horse, they call her. They had one son. They named him James Joseph Chips (chart 2). Joe lived with an uncle from his mother's side named Fred Ashley. Fred Ashley had a son that looked exactly like Joe Chips. So for that reason, Fred Ashley adopted Joe Chips as his son. So they adopted him and gave him their last name, Ashley. That's how he ended up with the name Joe Ashley. But he was born Joe Chips. He was the oldest one of that family. Joe Ashley married Mary Larvie. They had one son. His name was Everette Ashley. Joe Ashley's second wife was named Victoria Red Elk. They had three children, Cleo, Gail, and Gerti Ashley. Gerti Ashley married Delane Yankton, and they had seven children, Randy, Royden, Rhonda, Reva, Raqual, Rella, and Randene Yankton.

After Joe was born, Jefferson left his first marriage and married a second sister. Her name was Lucy Stranger Horse. They had two sons (Andrew and Dallas) and three daughters (chart 3). The first daughter's name was Angeline (Emma) Chips. Angeline married Joe Bull Man, and they had two sons, Silvester Bull Man and Melvin Bull Man. The second daughter's name was Ethel Chips. She married Morris Has No Horse. Ethel and Morris had a number of children, including Morris II, Arthur, Ramona, Althea, Rosaland, and Charity. The third daughter's name was Winnie Chips. Winnie married Willie Blue Arm. They had two sons, Bredell Blue Arm and Yuwores Blue Arm, and one daughter, whose name is unknown.

Jefferson then married the third sister. Her Lakota name was Uŋčí Yuma (charts 4 and 5). They had four sons and one daughter. Their sons' names were Andrew, Philip, Dallas, and Joe Čík'ala. Their daughter's name was Winnie Chips.

Their son Andrew Chips married a woman named Conquering Bear Woman, and they had two daughters, Martha and Isabelle Chips. Andrew and Conquering Bear both died at the same time at a very young age. So Martha and Isabelle were orphans. They were raised by Tȟahúŋska. Martha married a man named Isaac White Bull. They had a number of children, including Melvin, Isaac II, George, Boyd, Sylvia, Isabelle, Mae, Rose, and Faye. Isabelle Chips married Burgess Red Kettle, and they had a number of children, including Norma, Johnny, Lorraine, Ophelia, Bernadine, Mable, Ambrose, and Nonaba.

Jefferson and Uŋčí Yupa's second son, Philip Chips, married Mary Bull Tail, and they had a daughter named Alice Horn Chips. Their third son, Dallas, died as a young man. Their fourth son, James Joe Chips was also known as Joe Čík'ala. He became a medicine man. He had the ability to doctor children. They called him "Little Joe," because he's a small guy, a short guy: "Joe Čík'ala." But he died relatively young, when he was about seventy-one years old. Joe Čík'ala married a woman from Rosebud, Albert White Hat's sister, Rose White Hat. They had two children, Dallas and Vivian. Vivian's children are still alive. They live in Wanblee. Dallas had no children, but Vivian married Steven Red Elk. Steven and Vivian had five sons and three daughters, Rodger, Earnest, Calvin, Howard, Harlon, Lydia, Marlene, and Roseland. Joe Čík'ala's second marriage was to Louise Bourdeaux. They had one son, Gillard Chips.

Wóptuȟ'a's second son's name was Waȟpé Ǧí, Golden Leaf, Golden Leaf Boy. His English name was Geoffrey (chart 6). He attended Carlisle Indian School at a young age, but he managed to come back. Geoffrey married a woman, but her name is unknown. They had a daughter named Alice Chips (Jack) and a son named Oliver (Abbe) Chips. They had a third son, but he died when he was young. Abbe married Corrine Broken Rope and had a daughter and a son, Bernice Chips and Lawrence Chips. Alice Chips (Jack) married Oliver Reddest Jack, and the couple had two children, Isadore Jack and Margarette Jack Maldonado. Isadore Jack married Edith Red Willow and had six children, Lester, Allen, Seymour, Patrick, Ted, and Twila. Margarette Jack married Manuel Maldonado, and they had one daughter, Irma Maldonado.

Wóptuȟ'a's third son's name was Paul. Paul, Tȟašúŋkezí. His Lakota name was Buckskin Horse. He chose the name Paul, but he died young. He didn't have any children.

Wóptuȟ'a's daughter, Mollie, got married to a man named Yellow Eyes from Allen. After their divorce she married somebody else, and their children were named Yellow Hawk.

Wóptuȟ'a's second wife's name was Feels Around the Pipe. Her English name was Gap. She was from the Rosebud area. They had two sons, James and Charles, and a daughter named Nellie.

Tȟahúŋska (1869–1949)

Wóptuȟ'a and Gap's oldest son was James: James Tȟahúŋska Chips (charts 7–12). He later earned the name Moves Camp. He married a woman from Rosebud. Her name was Helen Kills (daughter of Chief Lone Elk). They had four children: two sons, two daughters.

James and Helen's first son was my grandpa Samuel Chips Moves Camp. Their second son was Benjamin Chips Moves Camp. Benjamin married Cora Bad Wound, but he died at a young age. James and Helen's first daughter was Bessie Chips Moves Camp. She married John Coyote Belly and had one daughter, Eva Coyote Belly. Eva married Frank Good Voice Elk, and they had Frank II, Evans, Elisabeth, Doris, and Mae. James and Helen's second daughter was named Belle Chips Moves Camp. She married Edward Yellow Eyes, and the couple had one daughter, named Edna Yellow Eyes, who died at a young age (chart 8). Belle then married Philip Zack Poor Bear and had Raymond, Waldon, Edith, and Delia. Belle divorced Philip and then married a man named Little Chief. They had one daughter, named Nora, who married Felix Standing Soldier and had two sons and one daughter, Anthony, Kenneth, and Lucille.

Sam married Winnie Iron Rope. They had three sons and four daughters (chart 9): Bernard Chips Moves Camp, Rose Chips Moves Camp, Mary Chips Moves Camp, Richard Chips Moves Camp, Marion Chips Moves Camp, James Chips Moves Camp II, and Dorothy Chips Moves Camp.

Sam's first son, Bernard Chips Moves Camp, married Florence Elk Looks Back, a woman from Rosebud (chart 10). They had two daughters, Evelyn Sylvia and Elsie Torres. Bernard's second marriage was to Esther Standing Elk. They had one son, Bernard Richard Chips Moves Camp II. He married Arvella Little Bald Eagle. They have six children: Tina, Dawn, Sylvia, Faith, Loretta, and Bernard Moves Camp III.

Sam's second son, Richard Chips Moves Camp, never married or had any children. He died in 1951. Sam's third son, James Chips Moves Camp II, married Ellen Winters, and they had five sons and one daughter: Samuel II, Louie, Vernon, James Dean, Michael, and Germaine. James's second marriage was to a woman named Inger White Feather, and they had two daughters, Mona and Bernadette.

Sam's first daughter, Rose Chips Moves Camp, married Thomas Bad Cob (chart 11). They had a number of children: Thomas Rede Bad Cob II, Ione Bad Cob, Renabelle Bad Cob, Betty Bad Cob, and Seth Bad Cob. Sam's second daughter, Mary Chips Moves Camp, married Paul Between Lodges. They had Wilbur, Ramona, Matilda, Lavinia, Wayne, and Darlene. Sam's third daughter, Marion Chips Moves Camp, married Norman Janis, and the couple had one daughter, Pearl Janis. Pearl had a son named Norman Dominic Janis. Pearl married Guy Dull Knife II and had one son and three daughters: Terrie, Tonya, Tonette, and Guy III. Marion had a second marriage with William Whistler and later divorced, but they had a daughter named Evelyn Moves Camp, who married Fred Sitting Up and had three children: Corrine, Carrie, and Fred II. Marion then married a man named Leonard Yellow Elk, and they had Linda, Joyce, Cora, Glenda, Sue Ann, Renee, Lenee, and Leonard II (chart 12). Sam's fourth daughter, Dorothy Chips Moves Camp, married Paul Bear Shield, and they had no children.

Charles Horn Chips (1873–1946)

Wóptuȟ'a and Gap's second son was Horn Chips, Charles Horn Chips. Charles was the youngest of all of Wóptuȟ'a's sons. Horn Chips married a woman from Allen (chart 13). They had a male child, who died. Horn Chips also had a daughter from his wife's sister. The child's name was Suzie Horn Chips. She married Paul Iron Rope, and they had two children, John and Lima Iron Rope.

Charles Horn Chips divorced his first wife and married Maggie Thunder Horse. They had one son who died young. They had another son, named Ellis, Ellis Chipps, Martin Ellis Chipps. Maggie already had children from a previous marriage, so Ellis had a lot of stepbrothers and stepsisters from that marriage. Charles Horn Chips's stepchildren with Maggie Thunder Horse were Jessie Standing Buffalo, Charlette Standing Buffalo, and Isabelle Bull Bear.

Ellis married Alice Hawk Wing, and they had two children, Vincent Horn Chipps and Bessie Horn Chipps. Ellis's second marriage, to Agnes Jones, produced three children, but two of them died as infants. Their third child was named Arthur Chipps. Ellis's third marriage was to Mari Lou Swan. They had one son, who died as a child. Ellis's fourth marriage was to Cora Lip. Ellis's fifth marriage was to Victoria Bear Lodge Skin. They had three sons, Charles, Philip, and Godfrey Chipps.

Horn Chips's third wife was Maude Jack, from Rosebud. She already had children from a previous marriage, Eugene Jack, Viola, Francis Jack, and another daughter, Victoria. Those were Horn Chips's stepkids.

James Moves Camp and Charles Horn Chips also had a sister named Nellie (see chart 7). She was born around 1895. She married a man from Lip's Camp named Robert Two Elk, and they had numerous children, two of whom were William (Billy) Two Elk and Aaron Two Elk. Some of the Two Elks are closely related to the Chipses in Wanblee. Before 1934, Robert Two Elk was one of the headmen of the Indian council in Wanblee.

*

After Wóptuȟ'a's father, Iron Whistle, passed away, Wóptuȟ'a's mother remarried, and she and her new husband had two children (chart 14). So Wóptuȟ'a had two half brothers. He grew up with them later on. They both lived and died in Wanblee. One of his half brothers was named White Squirrel. Tȟašnáheča Ská. Later on he took the English name Albert. He married Zičá Hó Wašté Wíŋ, a woman from Oglála country. They had three daughters and one son. Their second daughter was named Waŋyéča Wakȟáŋ Wíŋ, Sacred Lightning Bug. Her English name was Sarah Red Horse. She married Anthony Randall from Hisle, and their children were named Frank, Todd, Elisabeth, Jenny, Jessie, and Stella. Todd became a self-made rancher. He did it without borrowing money from the bank. So he was known as the first debt-free Indian rancher. He was very well known on the reservation.

Later, White Squirrel married another woman. Her name was Nellie, Nellie Larrabee. She was the widow of Crazy Horse. From that marriage, they had a son named Richard (Dick) Crazy Horse. Their daughter was named Julia Crazy Horse. Julia married Robert Holy Elk, and they had three children, Roy, Alice, and Nancy. Since White Squirrel was now married to Crazy Horse's widow, he changed his name to Crazy Horse because it was a renowned name. Today that causes a lot of confusion, because a lot of people claim that they come from Crazy Horse's *thióšpaye*, but the real Crazy Horse never had any children who grew to maturity. He only had one daughter, who died when she was a baby. So there are no direct descendants of Crazy Horse. He had siblings and he came from a *thióšpaye*, but there are no direct descendants of the man himself.

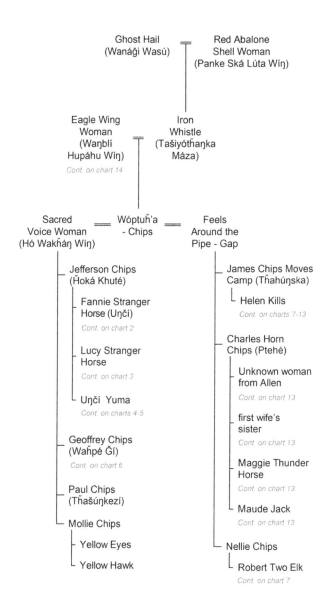

Chart 1. Wóptuȟ'a-Chips's children

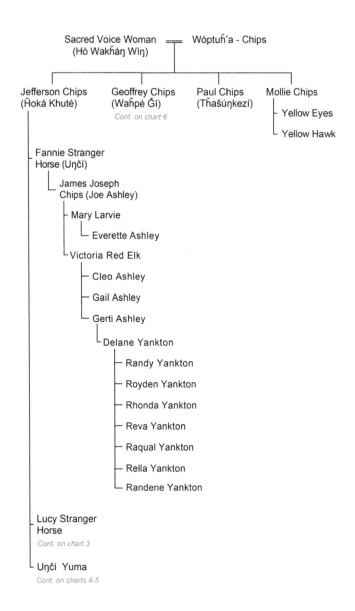

Sacred Voice Woman   ==   Wóptuȟ'a - Chips
(Hó Wakȟáŋ Wíŋ)

Jefferson Chips   Geoffrey Chips   Paul Chips   Mollie Chips
(Ȟoká Khuté)   (Waȟpé Ǧí)   (Tȟašúŋkezí)
   Cont. on chart 6   ├ Yellow Eyes
                                           └ Yellow Hawk

Fannie Stranger
Horse (Uŋčí)

   James Joseph
   Chips (Joe Ashley)

     ├ Mary Larvie

        └ Everette Ashley

     └ Victoria Red Elk

       ├ Cleo Ashley

       ├ Gail Ashley

       └ Gerti Ashley

         └ Delane Yankton

          ├ Randy Yankton

          ├ Royden Yankton

          ├ Rhonda Yankton

          ├ Reva Yankton

          ├ Raqual Yankton

          ├ Rella Yankton

          └ Randene Yankton

Lucy Stranger
Horse
Cont. on chart 3

Uŋčí Yuma
Cont. on charts 4-5

Chart 2. Jefferson Chips and Fannie Stranger Horse's extended family

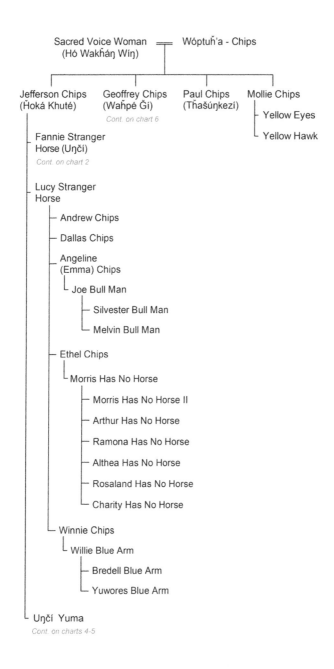

Sacred Voice Woman === Wóptuȟ'a - Chips
(Hó Wakȟáŋ Wíŋ)

Jefferson Chips   Geoffrey Chips   Paul Chips   Mollie Chips
(Ȟoká Khuté)   (Waȟpé Ǧí)   (Tȟašúŋkezí)
                     Cont. on chart 6   Yellow Eyes

                                                         Yellow Hawk

Fannie Stranger
Horse (Uŋčí)
Cont. on chart 2

Lucy Stranger
Horse

    Andrew Chips

    Dallas Chips

    Angeline
    (Emma) Chips

        Joe Bull Man

            Silvester Bull Man

            Melvin Bull Man

    Ethel Chips

        Morris Has No Horse

            Morris Has No Horse II

            Arthur Has No Horse

            Ramona Has No Horse

            Althea Has No Horse

            Rosaland Has No Horse

            Charity Has No Horse

    Winnie Chips

        Willie Blue Arm

            Bredell Blue Arm

            Yuwores Blue Arm

Uŋčí Yuma
Cont. on charts 4-5

Chart 3. Jefferson Chips and Lucy Stranger Horse's extended family

Sacred Voice Woman === Wóptuȟ'a - Chips
(Hó Wakȟáŋ Wíŋ)

Jefferson Chips
(Ȟoká Khuté)

Geoffrey Chips
(Waȟpé Ǧí)
Cont. on chart 6

Paul Chips
(Tȟašúŋkezí)

Mollie Chips
├ Yellow Eyes
└ Yellow Hawk

├ Fannie Stranger
Horse (Uŋčí)
Cont. on chart 2

├ Lucy Stranger
Horse
Cont. on chart 3

└ Uŋčí Yuma

Andrew Chips
├ Conquering
Bear Woman

Philip Chips
└ Mary Bull Tail
Cont. on chart 5

Dallas Chips

James Joe
Čík'ala (Little Joe)
├ Rose White Hat
└ Louise Bourdeaux
Cont. on chart 5

Winnie Chips

├ Martha Chips
└ Isaac White Bull
├ Melvin White Bull
├ Isaac White Bull II
├ George White Bull
├ Boyd White Bull
├ Sylvia White Bull
├ Isabelle White Bull
├ Mae White Bull
├ Rose White Bull
└ Faye White Bull

└ Isabelle Chips
└ Burgess Red Kettle
├ Norma Red Kettle
├ Johnny Red Kettle
├ Lorraine Red Kettle
├ Ophelia Red Kettle
├ Bernadine Red Kettle
├ Mable Red Kettle
├ Ambrose Red Kettle
└ Nonaba Red Kettle

Chart 4. Extended family of Andrew Chips (son of Jefferson Chips and Uŋčí Yuma)

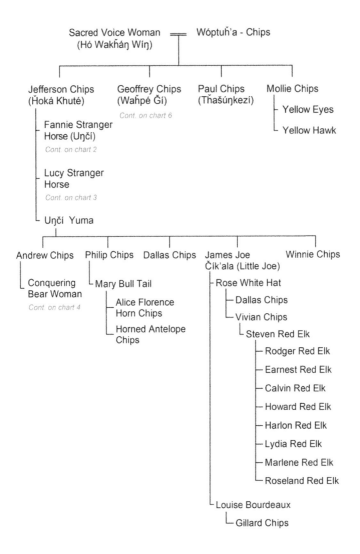

Chart 5. Extended families of Philip Chips and James Joe Číkʼala (sons of Jefferson Chips and Uŋčí Yuma)

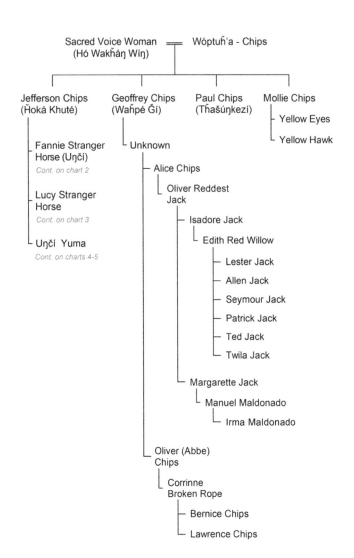

Chart 6. Geoffrey Chips's extended family

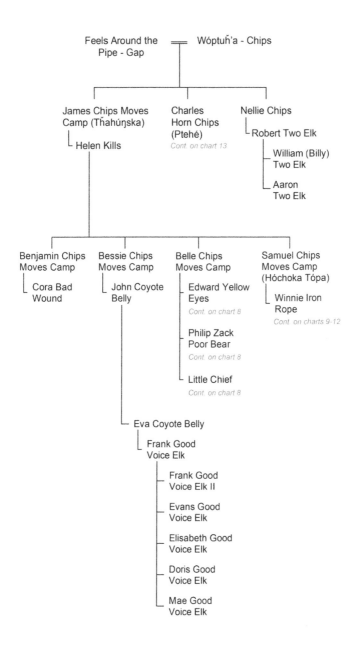

Chart 7. Bessie Chips Moves Camp's extended family

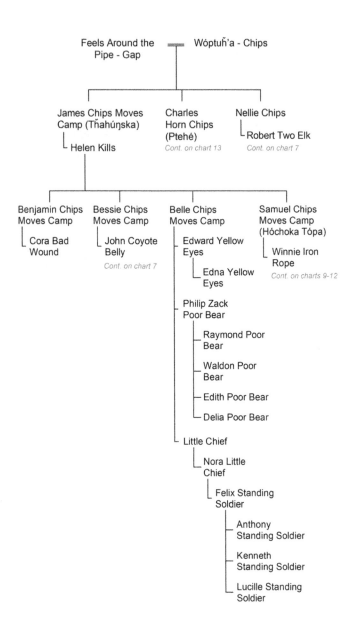

Chart 8. Extended family of Belle Chips Moves Camp

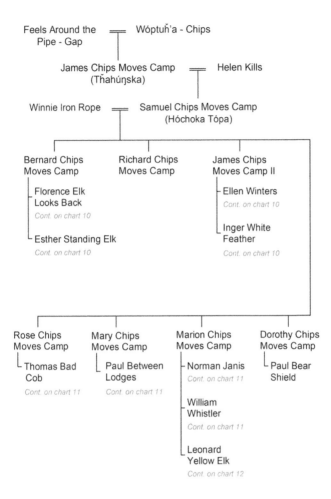

Feels Around the Pipe - Gap ══ Wóptuȟ'a - Chips

James Chips Moves Camp (Tȟahúŋska) ══ Helen Kills

Winnie Iron Rope ══ Samuel Chips Moves Camp (Hóchoka Tópa)

Bernard Chips Moves Camp
- Florence Elk Looks Back
  Cont. on chart 10
- Esther Standing Elk
  Cont. on chart 10

Richard Chips Moves Camp

James Chips Moves Camp II
- Ellen Winters
  Cont. on chart 10
- Inger White Feather
  Cont. on chart 10

Rose Chips Moves Camp
- Thomas Bad Cob
  Cont. on chart 11

Mary Chips Moves Camp
- Paul Between Lodges
  Cont. on chart 11

Marion Chips Moves Camp
- Norman Janis
  Cont. on chart 11
- William Whistler
  Cont. on chart 11
- Leonard Yellow Elk
  Cont. on chart 12

Dorothy Chips Moves Camp
- Paul Bear Shield

Chart 9. Family of Winnie Iron Rope and Samuel Chips Moves Camp

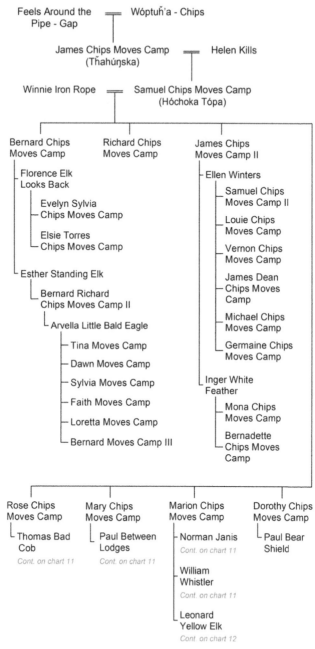

Chart 10. Extended families of Bernard Chips Moves Camp and James Chips Moves Camp II

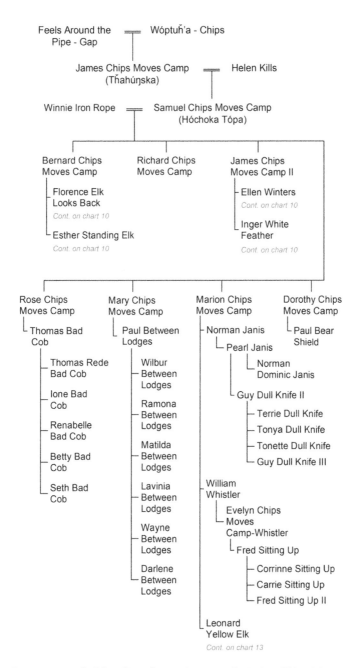

Chart 11. Extended families of Rose, Mary, and Marion Chips Moves Camp

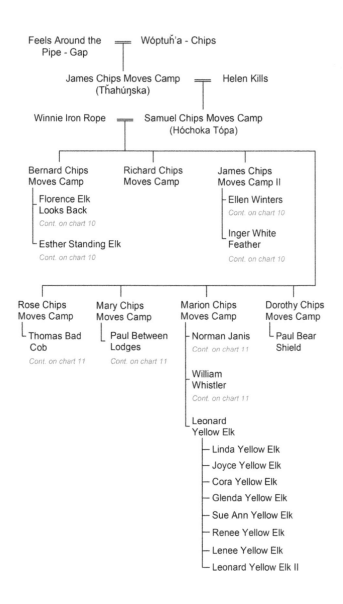

Chart 12. Family of Marion Chips Moves Camp and Leonard Yellow Elk

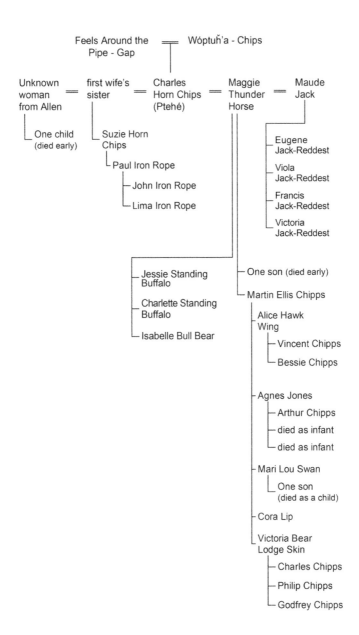

Chart 13. Extended family of Charles Horn Chips

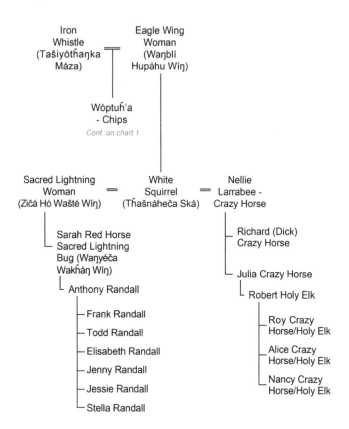

Iron
Whistle
(Tašiyótȟaŋka
Máza) ══ Eagle Wing
Woman
(Waŋblí
Hupáhu Wíŋ)

Wóptuȟ'a
- Chips
Cont. on chart 1

Sacred Lightning
Woman
(Zičá Hó Wašté Wíŋ) ══ White
Squirrel
(Tȟašnáheča Ská) ══ Nellie
Larrabee -
Crazy Horse

└ Sarah Red Horse
Sacred Lightning
Bug (Waŋyéča
Wakȟáŋ Wíŋ)

└ Anthony Randall

├ Frank Randall

├ Todd Randall

├ Elisabeth Randall

├ Jenny Randall

├ Jessie Randall

└ Stella Randall

├ Richard (Dick)
Crazy Horse

└ Julia Crazy Horse

└ Robert Holy Elk

└ Roy Crazy
Horse/Holy Elk

└ Alice Crazy
Horse/Holy Elk

└ Nancy Crazy
Horse/Holy Elk

Chart 14. Extended family of White Squirrel

Glossary

anáǧoptaŋ. to listen
áŋpétu. day
čhaŋnúŋpa wakȟáŋ. sacred pipe
číkʼala. little
haŋbléčheya. crying for a dream, vision quest
hiyá za. without emotion
hó. voice
hóchoka. center, altar
hoȟpa khuže. "coughing illness," tuberculosis
hokšíla. child
hokšíla tahó. child's voice
huŋká. adopted person
Húŋkpapha. a Lakota band
huŋská. leggings
íčhimani. journey
Inípi. sweat-lodge ceremony
íŋyaŋ waphíye. doctoring with stones
išnáthi alówaŋpi. a woman stays alone ceremony
ištá pakhíŋta. Wiping of the Tears
kabúbu. skillet
kaká. grandfather
kȟolá. friend
kih. team
Lówáŋpi. ceremony (lit., singing)
maheta wówašake. premium power
misúŋ. brother
mni píǧa. beer (lit., boiling water)
mni šá. wine (lit., red beverage)
mni wakȟáŋ. whiskey (lit., sacred beverage)
naǧóya. record

Nažútala. Neck, founder of the Sun Dance
Oglála. a Lakota band
olówaŋ. song
Olówaŋ Wičháša. early reservation "code" for medicine man
ománi. "we travel"
opáǧi. to fill or offer a pipe
oúŋčhaǧe. form, likeness
oyáte. people
pápa. beef jerky
p̄ehíŋ sáŋ. Gray Hair (People)
Phuté. Lip
pté. buffalo cow
Ptehé. Horn
Ptehíŋčala Čhaŋŋúŋpa. Buffalo Calf Pipe
Pté Sáŋ Wíŋ(yaŋ). White Buffalo Woman
Sičháŋǧu. Lakota band on the Rosebud reservation
Siŋté Gleška. Spotted Tail
šúŋka. dog
šúŋka itéha. hackamore
tamahoon-wóčhekiye. praying inside your body
Tašiyótȟaŋka Máza. Iron Whistle
Tȟahúŋska. Depends On Him
tȟakóža. grandson
Tȟašúŋke Witkó. Crazy Horse
tȟatȟáŋka. buffalo (male)
tȟawáčhiŋ oúŋ. mindful living
thíŋpsiŋla. wild turnips
thióšpaye. extended family
thípi. house, dwelling
thí ská. white house
tȟiwáhe. family
thuŋkáŋ. stone
thuŋkáŋ oyáte. lit., stone-people nation
Tȟuŋkášila. Grandfather, alt: spirits
Tókȟa hwo? (colloquial) "What's up?"
uŋčí. grandmother
uŋčí makȟá. Grandmother Earth
Waglúla. Worm

waȟmúŋǧa. to cast a spell
wahoȟpí. nest
wakȟáŋ. mysterious, sacred, holy
Wakȟáŋ Tȟáŋka. Great Mystery, God
wákúŋza. to curse
Wanáǧi. ghost
Wanáǧi ób máni. Walks with Ghost
Wanáǧi Wačhípi. Ghost Dance
Wanáǧi Wasú. Ghost Hail
waŋblí. eagle
Waŋblí Hohpí Pahá. Eagle Nest Butte
Waŋblí Hupáhu Wíŋ. Eagle Wing Woman
Waŋhíŋkpe Wakȟáŋ. Holy Arrow
waphíya. to cure or doctor
wašíču. (colloquial) white person, messenger
wašígla. to mourn
wasná. chokecherry and dried (pounded) meat
wáta. boat
wičháhó. human voice
Wičháhpi. star
wičháša wakȟáŋ. sacred person (man)
wičhóuŋčhaǧe. a generation of life
wičhúŋte. death
wíŋyaŋ. woman
Wiwáŋyaŋg Wačhípi. sun dance
wiwíla. water spirit(s)
wóčhekiye. prayer
wóȟeyaka. a gift of honor
wólakȟota. peace
wóphila. thanksgiving
Wóptuȟ'a (alt: **Wóptuǧa**). Chips
wótȟawe. war medicine
wówačhaŋtognaka. patience
wówakȟáŋ. sacred power
wówakȟáŋ pazó. a display of sacred power
wówašake. energy, power
wóžapi. pudding
Yuwípi. a Lakota ceremony (lit., they tie [him] up)

Notes

Editor's Note

1. Two documented interviews with Wóptuȟ'a are known to exist:
One, from February 14, 1907, is in the Ricker Papers, tablet 18,
Nebraska State Historical Society. I thank Andrea Faling for her
assistance in obtaining digital scans of the Ricker interview. The
original manuscript of the other interview, from July 11, 1910, is held
in the Walter Mason Camp Papers, manuscript 57, box 4, Nineteenth
Century Western and Mormon Manuscripts, L. Tom Perry Special
Collections, Harold B. Lee Library, Brigham Young University,
Provo, Utah. I thank Rachel Maxwell at the reference desk for her
assistance in obtaining a digital copy of this interview. See also *Pute
Tiyośpaye: Lip's Camp; The History and Culture of a Sioux Indian
Village* (Wanblee SD: Crazy Horse School, 1978).

2. Simon J. Joseph, "Yuwipi: A Postcolonial Approach to Lakota Ritual
Specialization and Religious Revitalization," *JAAR* 86, no. 2 (2018):
364–93. Yuwípi is a Lakota ceremony in which a "Yuwípi man" is
wrapped in a blanket and bound with cords while the medicine man
calls his spirit "friends" (*kȟolápi*) for assistance in healing, finding
lost objects, predicting the future, or solving community problems.

3. On Lakota religion, see David C. Posthumus, "Transmitting Sacred
Knowledge: Aspects of Historical and Contemporary Oglala Lakota
Belief and Ritual" (PhD diss., Indiana University, 2015); Sandra
Garner, *To Come to a Better Understanding: Medicine Men and Clergy
Meetings on the Rosebud Reservation, 1973–1978* (Lincoln: University
of Nebraska Press, 2016). For older studies, see William K. Pow-
ers, *Oglala Religion* (Lincoln: University of Nebraska Press, 1977);
William Stolzman, *The Pipe and Christ: A Christian-Sioux Dialogue*,
6th ed. (Chamberlain SD: Tipi Press, [1986] 1998); James R. Walker,
Lakota Belief and Ritual, ed. R. J. DeMallie and E. A. Jahner (Lincoln: University of Nebraska Press, 1980); Joseph Epes Brown,

The Sacred Pipe: Black Elk's Account of the Seven Rites of the Oglala Sioux (Norman: University of Oklahoma Press, [1953] 1971); Paul B. Steinmetz, *Pipe, Bible, and Peyote among the Oglala Lakota: A Study in Religious Identity* (Syracuse NY: Syracuse University Press, [1980] 1998); Paul B. Steinmetz, *The Sacred Pipe: An Archetypal Theology* (Syracuse NY: Syracuse University Press, 1998); Raymond A. Bucko, *The Lakota Ritual of the Sweat Lodge: History and Contemporary Practice* (Lincoln: University of Nebraska Press, 1998); and Raymond J. DeMallie, *The Sixth Grandfather: Black Elk's Teachings Given to John G. Neihardt* (Lincoln: University of Nebraska Press, 1984).

4. Francis Prucha, *Documents of United States Indian Policy* (Lincoln: University of Nebraska Press, 1990), 187–88: "Any Indian who shall engage in the practices of so-called medicine men, or who shall resort to any artifice or device to keep the Indians of the reservation from adopting and following civilized habits and pursuits, or shall use any arts of conjurer to prevent Indians from abandoning their barbarous rites and customs, shall be deemed guilty of an offense, and upon conviction thereof, for the first offense shall be imprisoned for not less than ten days." The official sanctions prohibiting traditional religious practices were lifted in 1934. A 1934 Circular on Indian Religious Freedom and Indian Culture, authorized by U.S. Commissioner of Indian Affairs John Collier, states that "no interference with Indian religious life or ceremonial expression will hereafter be tolerated." It was not until 1978, with the Native American Freedom of Religion Act, that many Native religious practices were officially legalized. On the 1978 American Indian Religious Freedom Act, see Lee Irwin, "Freedom, Law, and Prophecy: A Brief History of Native American Religious Resistance," *AIQ* 21, no. 1 (1997), 35–55.

5. During our conversation, Richard disclosed that Wóptuȟ'a never practiced Yuwípi. Rather, it was Richard's great-grandfather James Moves Camp, Ťȟahúŋska, who received the ceremony through a *huŋká* (adoptive) relationship he had made with another holy man named Holy Arrow. Ťȟahúŋska then shared this knowledge with his brother, Charles Horn Chips. These two brothers, working together, played a pivotal role in revitalizing Lakota religion during the most difficult years of reservation life early in the twentieth century.

6. Joseph, "Yuwipi," 387n18, 373.

7. These meetings took place between February and May 2021.

8. On non-Native "reexpression," see Mary Austin, *The American Rhythm: Studies and Reexpressions of Amerindian Songs* (New York: Harcourt, 1923).

9. Devon Abbott Mihesuah, *So You Want to Write about American Indians? A Guide for Writers, Students, and Scholars* (Lincoln: University of Nebraska Press, 2005), 21, holds that only Natives should be allowed to write about "private cultural information," and claims that "scholars . . . who publish sensitive information not intended for textualization, cause tribes to be suspicious of anyone who wants to write about them" (10), adding that "serious consequences can befall transgressors, both non-Indians who use sensitive data and Indian informants who are expected by their tribes not to divulge tribal religious and cultural information." Moreover, many topics are "taboo," such as "ceremonies, clan relations, and familial histories" (34). Mihesuah suggests that those writing about such taboo topics earn a "reputation for having no concern for the people" one writes about and that those "familiar" with a tribe's religion "already know" not to "discuss it." Nonetheless, Mihesuah herself wrote a "familial history" of her own father-in-law (Henry Mihesuah, *First to Fight*, ed. Devon Abbott Mihesuah [Lincoln: University of Nebraska Press, 2002]). Similarly, Angela Cavender Wilson, "Reclaiming Our Humanity: Decolonization and the Recovery of Indigenous Knowledge," in *Indigenizing the Academy: Transforming Scholarship and Empowering Communities* (Lincoln: University of Nebraska Press, 2004), 69–87, 73, suggests that "anything . . . dealing with the sacred, such as ceremonial life, should not be shared with those outside our communities or studied" (73–74). Nonetheless, Wilson embraces esoteric disclosures of Dakota ceremonial belief in seeking to "recover" Indigenous knowledge as part of an ongoing "decolonization" project (see Waziyatawin Angela Wilson [with translations from the Dakota text by Wahpetunwin Carolynn Schommer], *Remember This! Dakota Decolonization and the Eli Taylor Narratives* [Lincoln: University of Nebraska Press, 2005]). For her part, Paula Gunn Allen, "Special Problems Teaching Leslie Marmon Silko's *Ceremony*," in Devon A. Mihesuah, ed., *Natives and Academics: Researching and Writing about American Indians*, 55–64, 62, suggests that "telling the old stories, revealing the old ways, can only lead to disaster. . . . [To use] the oral tradition directly is to run afoul of native ethics,"

both politically and metaphysically (55–56), insinuating that Native religion is "forbidden territory" and that "ethical violations" and "security leaks" may lead to metaphysical retribution (63, 61, 57–58), yet Allen fails to differentiate between the "special problems" she is familiar with in her own Laguna Pueblo oral tradition and the diverse practices of other sovereign nations (56).

10. Rodney Simard, "American Indian Literatures, Authenticity, and the Canon," *World Literature Today* 66, no. 2 (1992), 243–48, 245, refers to "circularity, polyvocalism, ambiguity, an ecosystemic view, tribalism, inherent mysticism and spirituality, strong place identification."

11. Nicholas Black Elk's collaboration with John Neihardt represents a complex process of composition. Black Elk shared his life story in Lakota with Neihardt, but since Neihardt did not understand Lakota, Black Elk's speech was translated into English by his son, Ben Black Elk. Neihardt then rephrased Ben Black Elk's translations so they could be written down in shorthand by his daughter, Enid Neihardt, acting as stenographer. This multifaceted process of transmission— from Lakota oral tradition to English translation to shorthand to Neihardt's final literary composition—has created "controversy among scholars" regarding its authenticity.

12. For a somewhat similar approach, see Wallace Black Elk and William S. Lyon, *Black Elk: The Sacred Ways of a Lakota* (San Francisco: Harper and Row, 1990), xvi–xvii. Lyon describes his process as "an attempt at translation" insofar as "all of the material used . . . was taken from tape-recorded sessions during which Wallace spoke in English." This material was then "transcribed," using "only the material that in some way related to Black Elk's practice of shamanism" so that the text contains only material you could "also hear Black Elk saying at some point on one of these recorded tapes." Lyon's approach to the "Black Elk" tapes required two "major alterations in the material as recorded on tape" (xvii). First, he "edit[ed] together into one single account disparate parts of the same story." Second, he "altered" the "shaman's" language and "grammar to conform, for the most part, to our standards," in order to make for "smoother reading." According to Lyon, this text "contains about as true and accurate a picture of his [Black Elk's] views as one could possibly present in English and without extensive additions" (xviii). For criticism of Lyon's approach, see Harvey Markowitz, review of

Black Elk, Ethnohistory 39, no. 3 (1992), 360–63, 362, noting that this text was "apparently produced" for a "New Age audience" and that Black Elk's views are "highly idiosyncratic" and do not "represent how contemporary Lakotas experience and partake in their religious traditions." Elizabeth Cook-Lynn, "Life and Death in the Mainstream of American Indian Biography," *Wicazo Sa Review* 11, no. 2 (1995), 90–93, identifies this text as an "'as told to,'" "built for the purposes of 'pedestal raising'" (90–91), "always written by white writers . . . who offer their services because, one supposes, Indians whose lives need to be told and held up to acclaim are unable to acquire the necessary literary skills to do the writing themselves" (91). For Cook-Lynn, *Black Elk* purports to "translate" the "esoteric knowledge of native shamans," rendering it more of a "'how-to'" than a "genuine biography" (93). Cook-Lynn does not say that such "collaborations are corrupt," nor does she seek to limit "the possibility of academic freedom so necessary to the growth of intellectual curiosity and speculation" (93), but she nonetheless declares "a war for the future of Indian intentions" and objects to "the Indian story written by whites in America with so-called Indian informants and collaborators" because this pattern is "*not in the hands of the subject*" (emphasis in original; 93).

13. The "as-told-to" (auto)biographical genre is a literary tradition that may be marketed as a first-person account but is all too often the product of editorial overwriting, with the "Indian" sounding like a "white man" "talking over" the "Native" voice packaged for commercial consumption. For criticism, see Elizabeth Cook-Lynn, "American Indian Intellectualism and the New Indian Story," in Mihesuah, *Natives and Academics*, 111–38, 119–24. Cook-Lynn suggests that the Indian biography or "life story" can be traced back to the "quick rise of the discipline of anthropology" and "the model claimed by ethnographers." This genre is "dominated by the university presses," and its works represent "offshoots of biography, a traditional art form in European literature." Consequently, this kind of "ethnographic biography is not an Indian story at all and does not have significant ties to the interesting bodies of Native literary canons produced culturally and historically" (119). They follow a predictable pattern of "informant-based" Indian story (122) and are "by and large, fantasies of Indians" (123), "the result more of the dominance and patriarchy

most noted in American society than of tribalness" (128). See also Edward Valandra, "The As-Told-To [Auto]biography: Whose Voice Is Speaking?," *Wicazo Sa Review* 20, no. 2 (2005), 103–19. While one could easily object to the idea of a "formula[ic]" process in which a "non-Native writer" necessarily brings "all of his or her cultural and racist baggage" (109), which includes "cultural bias and an embedded white agenda" (113), Valandra correctly notes that non-Natives "must justify" their presence in Indian country and usually do so by being "validated" (i.e., called or summoned) by a "medicine man" (109), that many of these works reproduce a "predictable storyline" of "tragedy" and "triumph" (à la hagiographical literature) (111), and that they often traffic in stereotypical assumptions about the nonliterary nature of Native oral communication. Arnold Krupat, "The Indian Autobiography: Origins, Type, and Function," in Brian Swann, ed., *Smoothing the Ground: Essays on Native American Oral Literature* (Berkeley: University of California Press, 1983), 261–82, 262, describes this as a work of literature "jointly produced by some white who translates, transcribes, compiles, edits, interprets, polishes, and ultimately determines the 'form' of the text in writing." For a notable exception, see Gerald Mohatt and Joseph Eagle Elk, *The Price of a Gift: A Lakota Healer's Story* (Lincoln: University of Nebraska Press, 2000). For a first-person memoir, see Joseph Iron Eye Dudley, *Choteau Creek: A Sioux Reminiscence* (Lincoln: University of Nebraska Press, 1992). On Native American autobiographical forms, see Hertha Dawn Wong, *Sending My Heart Back across the Years: Tradition and Innovation in Native American Autobiography* (New York: Oxford University Press, 1992). Wong seeks to expand the definition of "autobiography" to include nonwritten forms of personal narrative, non-Western concepts of self, and traditional tribal modes of self-narration, charting the transition from orality to literacy. For discussion, see Emily Levine's introduction to Susan Bordeaux Bettelyoun and Josephine Waggoner, *With My Own Eyes: A Lakota Woman Tells Her People's History*, ed. Emily Levine (Lincoln: University of Nebraska Press, 1999), xv–xxxviii, xxx: "Editorial attitudes are changing with regard to historical works by native peoples. Editors are now interested in allowing the voice of the Indian to be heard and in maintaining the oral quality of that voice. Undermining, intrusive footnoting and excessive rewriting are absent in most recent scholar-edited narratives. Explanations, when needed, are now placed at the beginning or end of the text." Cf. Kathleen Mullen Sands, "American Indian Autobiography," in *Studies in American Indian Literature: Critical Essays and Course Designs*, ed. Paula Gunn Allen (New York: MLA), 59: "The editor's principal duty is to establish an accurate text and to preserve the integrity of the narrative within the bounds of publication requirements. This requires not only a thorough knowledge of the narrator's culture but also a sensitivity to Indian perceptions of language, landscape, time, reality, and the nature of the cosmos." For similar approaches, see Nancy O. Lurie, ed., *Mountain Wolf Woman, Sister of Crashing Thunder: The Autobiography of a Winnebago Indian* (Ann Arbor: University of Michigan Press, 1961); Margaret B. Blackman, ed., *During My Time: Florence Edenshaw Davidson, a Haida Woman* (Seattle: University of Washington Press, 1982); Kathleen M. Weist, ed., *Belle Highwalking: The Narrative of a Northern Cheyenne Woman* (Billings: Montana Council for Indian Education, 1979); Brian Swann and Arnold Krupat, eds., *I Tell You Now: Autobiographical Essays by Native American Writers* (Lincoln: University of Nebraska Press, 1987); Anna Lee Walters, *Talking Indian: Reflections on Survival and Writing* (New York: Firebrand Books, 1992); Greg Sarris, *Mabel McKay: Weaving the Dream* (Berkeley: University of California Press, 1994); Arnold Krupat, ed., *Native American Autobiography* (Madison: University of Wisconsin Press, 1994); Luke Eric Lassiter, "Authoritative Texts, Collaborative Ethnography, and Native American Studies," *American Indian Quarterly* 24, no. 4 (2000), 601–14.

In the American Indian Lives series

I Stand in the Center of the Good:
Interviews with Contemporary
Native American Artists
Edited by Lawrence Abbott

Authentic Alaska: Voices
of Its Native Writers
Edited by Susan B. Andrews
and John Creed

Searching for My Destiny
By George Blue Spruce Jr.
As told to Deanne Durrett

Dreaming the Dawn: Conversations
with Native Artists and Activists
By E. K. Caldwell
Introduction by Elizabeth Woody

Chief: The Life History of Eugene
Delorme, Imprisoned Santee Sioux
Edited by Inéz Cardozo-Freeman

Chevato: The Story of the
Apache Warrior Who Captured
Herman Lehmann
By William Chebahtah and
Nancy McGown Minor

Winged Words: American
Indian Writers Speak
Edited by Laura Coltelli

In Defense of Loose
Translations: An Indian Life
in an Academic World
By Elizabeth Cook-Lynn

Life, Letters, and Speeches
By George Copway
(Kahgegagahbowh)
Edited by A. LaVonne Brown
Ruoff and Donald B. Smith

Life Lived Like a Story: Life Stories
of Three Yukon Native Elders
By Julie Cruikshank in
collaboration with Angela Sidney,
Kitty Smith, and Annie Ned

Too Strong to Be Broken: The
Life of Edward J. Driving Hawk
By Edward J. Driving Hawk and
Virginia Driving Hawk Sneve

Bitterroot: A Salish Memoir
of Transracial Adoption
By Susan Devan Harness

LaDonna Harris: A Comanche Life
By LaDonna Harris
Edited by H. Henrietta Stockel

Rock, Ghost, Willow, Deer:
A Story of Survival
By Allison Adelle Hedge Coke

Rights Remembered: A Salish
Grandmother Speaks on American
Indian History and the Future
By Pauline R. Hillaire
Edited by Gregory P. Fields

Essie's Story: The Life and
Legacy of a Shoshone Teacher
By Esther Burnett Horne
and Sally McBeth

Song of Rita Joe: Autobiography of a Mi'kmaq Poet
By Rita Joe

My Side of the River: An Alaska Native Story
By Elias Kelly

Viet Cong at Wounded Knee: The Trail of a Blackfeet Activist
By Woody Kipp

Catch Colt
By Sidner J. Larson

Alanis Obomsawin: The Vision of a Native Filmmaker
By Randolph Lewis

Alex Posey: Creek Poet, Journalist, and Humorist
By Daniel F. Littlefield Jr.

The Turtle's Beating Heart: One Family's Story of Lenape Survival
By Denise Low

First to Fight
By Henry Mihesuah
Edited by Devon Abbott Mihesuah

Mourning Dove: A Salishan Autobiography
Edited by Jay Miller

My Grandfather's Altar: Five Generations of Lakota Holy Men
By Richard Moves Camp
Edited by Simon J. Joseph

I'll Go and Do More: Annie Dodge Wauneka, Navajo Leader and Activist
By Carolyn Niethammer

Tales of the Old Indian Territory and Essays on the Indian Condition
By John Milton Oskison
Edited by Lionel Larré

Elias Cornelius Boudinot: A Life on the Cherokee Border
By James W. Parins

John Rollin Ridge: His Life and Works
By James W. Parins

Singing an Indian Song: A Biography of D'Arcy McNickle
By Dorothy R. Parker

Crashing Thunder: The Autobiography of an American Indian
Edited by Paul Radin

Turtle Lung Woman's Granddaughter
By Delphine Red Shirt and Lone Woman

Telling a Good One: The Process of a Native American Collaborative Biography
By Theodore Rios and Kathleen Mullen Sands

Out of the Crazywoods
By Cheryl Savageau

Printed and bound by CPI Group (UK) Ltd, Croydon, CR0 4YY

13/04/2025

14656557-0001